Twist Fate

This book was made possible through a partnership between the Connected Learning Alliance, Wattpad, DeviantArt, the National Writing Project, and the Young Adult Library Services Association.

About the Partners

Connected Learning Alliance

The Connected Learning Alliance supports the expansion and influence of a network of educators, experts, and youth-serving organizations, mobilizing new technology in the service of equity, access, and opportunity for all young people. The Alliance is coordinated by the Digital Media and Learning Research Hub at UC Irvine. Learn more at clalliance.org.

Wattpad

Wattpad, the global multiplatform entertainment company for original stories, transforms how the world discovers, creates, and engages with stories. Since 2006, it has offered a completely social experience in which people everywhere can participate and collaborate on content through comments, messages, and multimedia. Today, Wattpad connects a community of more than 45 million people around the world through serialized stories about the things they love. As home to millions of fresh voices and fans who share culturally relevant stories based on local trends and current events, Wattpad has unique pop culture insights in virtually every market around the world. Wattpad Studios coproduces stories for film, television, digital, and print to radically transform the way the entertainment industry sources and produces content. Wattpad Brand Solutions offers new and integrated ways for brands to build deep engagement with consumers. The company is proudly based in Toronto, Canada. Learn more at wattpad.com/about.

DeviantArt

Founded in 2000, DeviantArt is an online social network for artists and art enthusiasts and a platform for emerging and established artists to exhibit, promote, and share their works with an enthusiastic, art-centric community. It has more than 40 million registered members and attracts more than 60 million unique visitors per month. Members—known as deviants—upload more than 100,000 original works of art and literature daily, everything from painting and sculpture to digital art, pixel art, films, anime, and poetry. Learn more at deviantart.com.

National Writing Project

The National Writing Project is a network of sites anchored at colleges and universities and serving teachers across disciplines and at all levels, early childhood through university. NWP provides professional development, develops resources, generates research, and acts on knowledge to improve the teaching of writing and learning in schools and communities. Learn more at nwp.org.

Young Adult Library Services Association

The Young Adult Library Services Association is a national association of librarians, library workers, and advocates with a mission to expand and strengthen library services for teens. YALSA brings together key stakeholders from the areas of libraries, education, research, out-of-school time, youth development, and more to develop and deliver resources to libraries that expand their capacity to support teen learning and enrichment and to foster healthy communities. Learn more at ala.org/yalsa.

TWIST FATE

TEENS SPIN CLASSIC TALES

TEEN
FIC
TWISTFAT

Published by the Connected Learning Alliance.
Irvine, CA.
December 2016

Library of Congress Cataloging-in-Publication
Data is available. ISBN: 978-0-9887255-4-6
© 2016 Connected Learning Alliance

Printed and bound by Classic Color.
Broadview, IL.

Typefaces: Minion Pro & Calibre

Paper Stock: Domtar Cougar Smooth
White 80# text, Neenah Classic Crest Epic
Black 100# cover

Finishes: Copper foil stamp, copper
gilded edges

Book Design by Frohlichstein Inc.
Chicago, IL.

ISBN 978-0-9887255-4-6

9 780988 725546

Contents

Foreword

Betrayal

Vengeance

Survival

Belonging

Sketchbook

Contributors

~~~~~

Intertwined Fate

In your hands (or on your screen) is an unprecedented experiment in connecting across stories, platforms, and generations. We challenged teens aged 13-17 to "Pick a story and character, and create an alternative scenario where a famous hero is the villain, or an infamous villain, the hero." And we invited them to submit their entries to DeviantArt and Wattpad, homes to some of the most vibrant youth creative communities on the net. In these pages, you'll find a phantasmagoric teen neverland, often delightful, sometimes dark, and always surprising. You'll see characters varying from Snow White, to Harry Potter, to Jarvis (the A.I. in Ironman), all transformed in ways both familiar and unexpectedly strange.

Our partners at the National Writing Project and the Young Adult Library Services Association helped shape the challenge and spread the word to educators. More than 2,000 teens submitted stories and artwork. Boosted by the keen editorial eye of an all-star cast of professional creators—Antero Garcia, Lauren Kate, Brian Kesinger, and Sara Ryan—the team at Wattpad and DeviantArt curated a selection of finalists whose work appears in this book. Although contests are a common feature of these communities, this challenge represents four firsts:

- The first challenge shared across Wattpad and DeviantArt.
- The first teen-only challenge that either platform has sponsored.
- The first collaboration these platforms have had with networks of educators.
- The first challenge to be documented as a book and to be distributed through public libraries across the United States.

The path to this unique challenge was itself an oddly twisty one. I'm a cultural anthropologist who has studied youth internet culture for decades, ever since college kids started killing orcs together in text-based online games. Through the years, I've marveled at the creativity, literacy, and learning that have blossomed online as young people have created, shared, mobilized, and connected with one another in networked communities. As more and more of our culture circulates in digital networks, young people have been at the forefront of sharing, remixing, and repurposing visual and popular media as part of their everyday self-expression and peer communication. More recently, I've been mulling over how parents and educators might better appreciate, embrace, and elevate the learning that the teens are doing in their online groups.

This challenge grew out of my puzzling over this problem and more than a decade of work by academics, educators, and designers who are seeking to leverage new technologies to better support youth and interest-driven learning. There's actually a ton of research and theory behind why the learning and creativity in platforms such as DeviantArt and Wattpad are so important and life changing. When young people create and learn with others who share their interests and passions, and are able to share and be recognized for this, it is much more powerful than the kind of learning that young people do in most of their schooling. We call this kind of learning "connected learning"—learning that connects peer culture, personal interests, and recognition in the wider world.

The Connected Learning Alliance, the host of this challenge, is a network of educators, researchers, designers, and technologists who are working at the intersection of education, youth culture, and digital media. When we had the opportunity to collaborate with the leadership at Wattpad and DeviantArt, we jumped at it, building new connections between teen online communities and the world of education. This challenge is an effort to connect and recognize the abundant creativity and learning that teens are engaged in through Wattpad and DeviantArt, showcasing how these sites are platforms for powerful new forms of learning to educators, parents, and others who might not already be tapped into this neverland.

—Mimi Ito

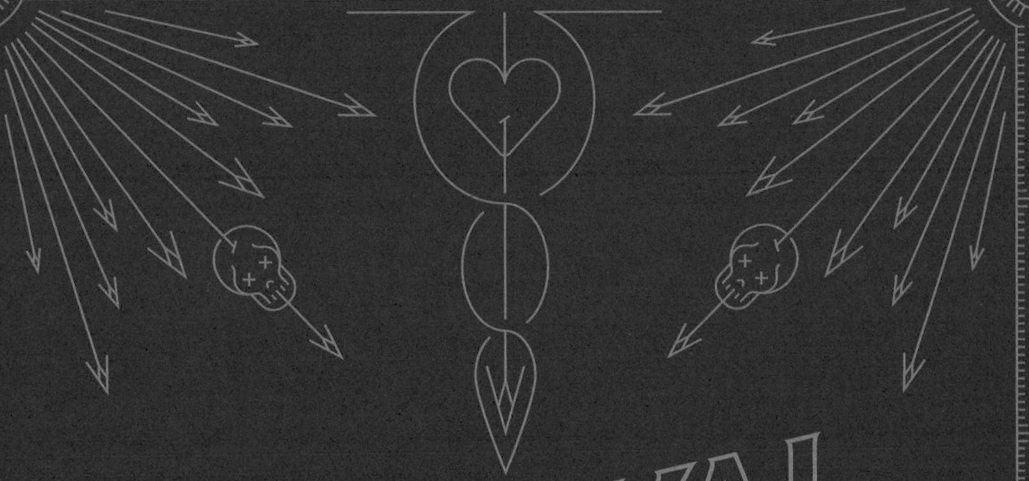

BETRAYAL

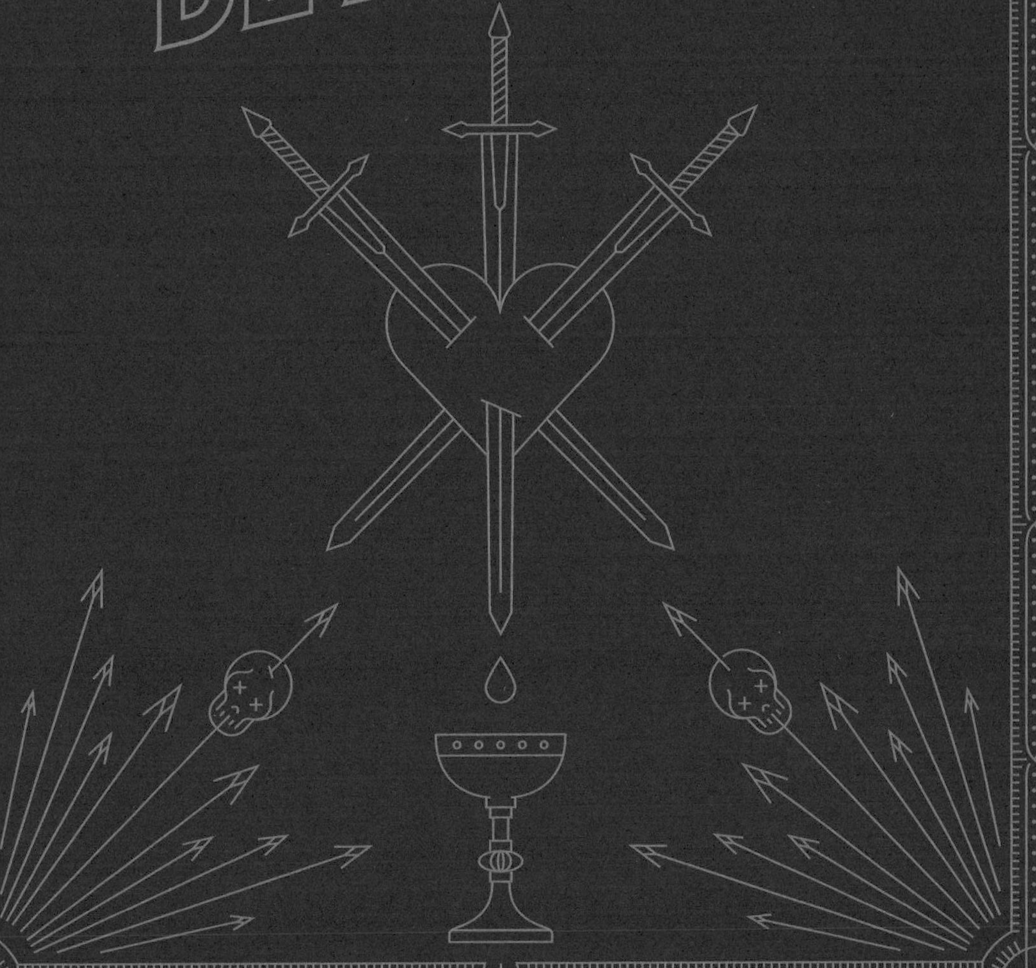

It's All in Perspective
By -X-X-Scomiche-X-X-

Born without knowledge of my father, losing my brother at a young age, and ultimately being abandoned by my mother influenced many of the choices I made. My whole life has been devoted to showing my loyalty to those I care for the most.

All my life, I have struggled with the judging states of cats who believed that I was not worthy of their ranks. To show it was my place I made a decision. It was a very mouse-brained one to make, but I did it anyway.

I knew that having a medicine cat from my kinship would be vital in showing that my sister and I deserved to be here. So, there I sat, long into the night, fighting against the lullaby of the river. All to catch a moth for Mothwing. I cared for her happiness greatly and knew that the ancestors of these cats wouldn't allow a loner's kit to become their most special rank. It didn't fit. Why would they, especially with the cats already so against it?

At last, a single moth, so beautiful and golden, alighted. A mistake that cost it a wing.

With the delicate pinion held in my teeth, I laid it outside the den of Mudspot.

For moons after that night, she trained happily, babbling about how the ancestors always welcomed her. I was glad, but I knew that if one of the StarClan cats slipped up, she would be crushed. It was better that I tell her that the wing was a sign from me and not the spirits of dead cats.

"You? It was you?" Mothwing drew back, her golden eyes glittering with hate. And hurt. I could see the hurt set deep into her eyes. "So StarClan didn't choose me. I'm a fraud." She whispered, her ears flattened. I could hear the murmur of the river, even out here.

"Please. I know! I screwed up, but please, let me explain." I pleaded, keeping my distance. She may be a Medicine Cat now, but she was a full-ranked Warrior and I would not want to receive a blow from her. "I knew that those cats, the ones that these cats claim know so much, wouldn't have picked you. I mean, cats like us, loners and kittypets, those without the blood of warriors, are accepted more now, but cats still grumble about how cats who have long since gone wouldn't have allowed it. I was making sure that you, my sole remaining family, would receive the happiness you deserve." I spoke softly, cautiously drawing nearer. I never knew when she would retaliate and I had to be wary when she was like this.

"And what do you get out of it? What motive, other than the one you have already stated, could you possibly have for this?" She gave me a narrow, suspicious glance.

"I know signs are sacred, and all that medicine cat mumbo jumbo, but please help me. If there is any way you could vouch for me as deputy, I would be thankful. It is the only way I can ensure that we stay here in this clan, among these noble cats. Without that rank, or even the voucher, I fear we may be out of luck."

The fight seemed to be drained out of her. She made no sound, her mind obviously elsewhere.

"If it truly bothers you that it was not from StarClan, I will go tell Leopardstar that it was me and that you had no idea."

"No! I'll do it. I'll give you a sign. Just don't tell anyone!"

"Thank you, Mothwing." I touched my nose to her cheek.

"Don't thank me. I am only doing this to protect me from whatever evil plan you have." She spat and stormed off. "Don't wait up. I have to collect herbs."

Maybe it was that point of view that got me listed as a villain. Maybe it was that I, an orphan in a clan of families, had no parents to show off my skills to, tell about my achievements, was willing to do whatever it took to find out who my father was. Even Feathertail and Stormpaw had someone they could talk to. Finally, in the dead of leafbare, I found my answer.

I was on the bank of the river, the warm summer sun shining on my back as I perched ever so carefully to snag a fish out of the fast-flowing water. Just as I was reaching for a giant trout that would have fed the queens and elders, a shadow fell over the water, scaring off my catch. Furious, I faced the intruder.

Instead of some rogue my mind thought up, I was faced with the face of the ThunderClan warrior Brambleclaw, although this was an older, more scarred version.

"Hawkfrost. A proud, strong name. Fit for a cat of your lineage." He spoke gruffly. This definitely wasn't Brambleclaw, although they looked the same.

Suspicions made me cautious. "What do you mean?" I asked slowly, my claws out.

He sat down and began to lick his paw and draw it over his nicked ear a few times before answering. "Do you know who Tigerstar is?" he asked out of the blue.

What did one of those ancestors have to do with the current situation!? Instead of voicing this thought, I simply nodded. Everyone did. His was a cursed name. He was a murderer, a tyrant, a destroyer. "What about him?"

"I can see in your eyes, you know *of* him. But you do not *know* him. He was a great cat, a valuable warrior. He made choices in his life that led to the stories that you have undoubtedly been told. But one of the best decisions I—," he corrected himself, but I still caught it. "That he ever made was choosing your mother, even though she denied him in the end." His tone was sad.

"You are him, aren't you? You are Tigerstar, the cat that slaughtered cats just to satisfy your ambition. I've seen Brightheart. I've heard of her mother." I spat, the hair along my back rising.

Despite my threatening display, he continued to calmly clean himself. "Yes, he is I. But, you understand, they were mistakes, choices I regretted my whole life, all the way up to when Scourge tore all nine of my lives away." His Amber eyes flicked to me. "I never knew you, for you were not around by the time my time was up, but I have been watching you from afar, proud of you. You are a strong warrior, a cat worthy of my blood, just as Brambleclaw, your half brother, is." A ghost of a smile appeared on his lips.

"Brambleclaw? He is my brother?" I asked, sitting down, a wave of dizziness sweeping over me.

"And Tawnypelt is your sister," he confirmed. "All I ask of you is that you come and visit me every night, let me teach you moves that will give you an advantage in any battle you engage in."

Who was I, a former orphan of a loner who didn't want me, to deny my father, and, secretly, myself, this chance? For moons I trained with him. I got to know my father, got to see his glowing ambition. Closer and closer I drew to the spot of deputy. But I lost that spot the night that Mudclaw died.

The accusation of me helping him shook my frail leader and she stopped relying on me the way she used to. My life began to fall apart.

Brambleclaw began to distance himself from me. I was losing a member of my still small family. I couldn't let that happen. That is when Tigerstar proposed the plan to make him leader. That way, I could slowly work my way back up and we could one day rule together. I knew it meant taking the life of one of the most beloved cats among the clans, but it was a small price, to me, for that of my relationship with my brother.

I loved my brother, and though I tried to kill him, it was to show that it was only for the good of the forest. It was time that we ascended to our birthright place, Leadership. It was our chance to show that our father's lineage was not corrupt and that we would have his blood proudly.

But all dreams of our ruling together were shattered when that stick pierced my throat. He was responsible for my death and yet, he bore no shame. "It is not over, brother. We will meet again," I promised. I would never leave him alone. I would do all I could to make sure we would meet again, no matter what it took. A very bee-brained idea. I know I should have saved my energy to tell him something else. "I'm sorry." But I wouldn't leave my body facing away from my beloved clan. No. I used the last of my energy to try and face toward home.

For moons I watched over him, waiting, waiting to show that I was in the right, what Tigerstar said was true. I got that chance with young Lionpaw. A bright spirit so much like my own. That is why I suggested him to my father. Though I only trained him a few times, it still broke me to see him betray us like his "father" had.

Of all the cats I trained, it was Ivypool, the cheeky she, that I prized the most. I picked her out of all of the cats in all of the clans. She was a really promising one. She encouraged the others, and had an unrivaled ferocity that I saw reflected my own. I tried my best. I did everything I could to show her that we were going against a corrupt way of life, a way that claimed you had to be of a certain lineage to be in their ranks. But she betrayed me, just like Lionblaze and Brambleclaw. Even Mothwing betrayed me, choosing the pathetic excuse for a cat Leafpool as a go-to instead of me.

My whole life I fought for one thing. Belonging. I fought to belong to a family. I fought to belong to a clan that never fully accepted me. I fought to belong among the ranks of the cats in the Dark Forest. I even fought for Ivypool, though she never knew it.

Am I perfect? Not by any means. I never was. Did I try to live my beliefs? Yes, I did. And yet, because of the stories of one cat, I was a villain, the cat my mother would say, "Be good or he'll get you." I never wanted that. I wanted to be accepted. But I was only ever rejected.

Mortal Bones
By acrdbty

The night was cold and dark even though a full moon decorates the night sky.

He drove through the heavy rain, not bothered by the blurry road. *Nothing mortal could kill me*, he muttered to himself and then he sighed heavily.

Suddenly, his eyes catch a blinking yellow light by the side of the road. If it was just any normal day, he would stop and help, but this is not just another normal day.

The moment he passed the car, something pulled on his chest, pulls him so hard that without him noticing, he was already stopping for it. *Let's see what this is all about*, he muttered again before getting out of his car into the heavy rain.

He's scared of nothing; even if this was a trap, he's sure he'll escape from it.

"Do you need help?" he shouted to whomever was inside the silver car.

He was expecting whoever was in there to just roll down the window, but no, that person, who turns out to be a female, stepped out of her car, looking as pale as a corpse.

"I would call for a mechanic, but I have no bars," she glumly told him.

For some reason, her face and features look all too familiar to him, yet he never actually met this girl before.

"Do you know what's the problem?" he asked while trying to figure her out at the same time.

"Yes, the tire." She pointed to the left rear of her car. "It's flat."

"Do you have a spare? I could help you change it." *Why am I helping her?* he asked himself, but finds no answer. *Who is she?*

Out of the blue, the rain suddenly stopped in the middle of changing the tire; when he looks up, he finds an umbrella with the girl holding it.

"I feel useless," she reasoned. "I'm Nora." The girl stretched down her hand toward him.

It was then he recognised the familiarity. She is Nora Grey, his Nephilim vassal's female descendant, and she was the only thing standing between him and a human life, the only thing he wants the most.

"Do you have a name?" She pulled her hand back rather awkwardly.

"Patch." He was done changing the tire by then. "My name is Patch." With that, he left her standing there with her colourful umbrella.

As he walked back to his car, it started to dawn on him that in order to get what he really wanted, he needed to kill Nora Grey.

It wasn't an accident. Patch knows exactly what he was doing, and he's determined to get his results, even if it means enrolling in the same school as Nora Grey and slowly gain her trust. Because for him, being immortal is a curse, a never-ending pain; he already knows what it feels like to be a human, and he's addicted to it, and since that day, his only wish has been to become a human full time.

And now, his chance is within his grasp, he's definitely not going to let his chance slip away. Never. So he slowly pushed his way in, he joined a few of Nora's classes, just enough to get her to notice his presence.

"You're the guy who helped me with my flat tire." He caught her small voice, a small proud smile make its way to his face.

But he quickly wiped it out of his face just before he turned and said, "Excuse me?"

"I'm Nora," she said, looking up to him. "Remember me?"

"Now I do," he gave her a little smirk, and the girl blushed for some unknown reason. *Am I making her nervous? Good.*

"You go to this school too? How come I've never seen you before?" She looked at him suspiciously.

"I just transferred here," he said shortly.

"You know, I haven't repaid you for helping me," she shrugged, "so, umm ... This may be not much, but I could show you around if you want to."

"That would be great," he smiled, seeing that his plan to gain her trust was starting to work.

"Come, follow me."

Three weeks had passed since that day. Seems like his plan is working perfectly because, right now, it looks like she's already fully trusting him to be alone with her. He didn't expect this fast result. Guess she might be a weak one, but again, she's the only female descendant of Chauncey Langeais.

Everything is being planned so perfectly by Patch, except for one thing. He didn't really prepare his heart to actually feel something for the girl, but the good thing is, his stubbornness to be a human fully rules everything in him. It is stronger than what his heart feels for the girl. But he knows that stubbornness will not last if he does not finish her soon. Hence, he really needs to plan the perfect murder.

Patch was on his way with Nora to a carnival when out of the blue his car broke down in the middle of the road. Nora might not see it, but Patch being, or was, an archangel, could see the cause. It was Dabria, Patch's old flame from when he was still an archangel, who caused it. Hiding the fact that he actually knows what happened, he pretended to go out and check under the hood.

"What do you need, Dabria?" he asked coldly.

"What are you doing, Patch?" She crossed her hand on her chest.

"I'm having a date," he stated flatly. "Or, was that forbidden, too?" he sarcastically added.

"It's not forbidden, no," Dabria shakes her head slowly, "but what you're planning with her is."

"Oh, so you can predict the future too, Dabria?"

"You know that's one of my powers, Patch." Now it's Dabria's turn to stare back at him flatly.

"Right. Well, she's standing in the middle of what I want," he concluded.

"A human life?"

"Exactly!" Smugly Patch smirked.

"Did you know that girl could also be the one who reforms you?" *What is she talking about?!* "She could be the one who gives your wings back."

"I don't want it anymore," he flatly concluded.

"You always—"

"Shut up, Dabria, I'm not the same angel you knew from before," he cuts her off quickly. "126 years could change anyone a lot, even an angel."

"You are not that kind of person!" Dabria shouted. "Would you really want to spend the rest of your human life feeling guilty for taking an innocent girl's life?" she continued.

"Yes, if that was really necessary," he flatly replied.

"You know what, enjoy your miserable life on Earth as a human!" With that, she spread her beautiful wide wings, and made her way up to the sky and disappeared.

"Bitch," he muttered before going back to the car.

"Everything's all right?" Nora asked him the moment he stepped into the car.

"Yeah, everything's perfect," he smiled and closed his door shut.

After what just happened, Patch really needs to make his plan work. No more failed chances; this is the end.

- No perfume
- Burn the evidence
- Wear a different shoe size
- Plant fake evidence
- Wear gloves
- No accomplice

He had gathered that much so far, but he needed more.

Do you really want this? his subconscious asked. Then Dabria's words play inside his head: *She could be the one who reforms you.*

"Of course I want this," he said to himself. "Sacrificing a person is better than living a life of a living hell, literally." *Why am I talking to myself?*

He needed to pick up Nora at her home before going to school because that's what a couple does when they are dating, arriving at school together. He didn't get the use of it, but he'll do it if it's how he's gonna get his wish. Hell, he'll do anything really. He's planning a girl's murder for heaven's sake! Why would he do less for something else?

Nora did look pretty today, but again, Nora always looks pretty, but Patch knew that was just a distraction, he knew about the heaven wish. Angels are sworn to protect; the ones who do harm will get punishment and be thrown out of heaven. In Patch's case, he wasn't thrown out, his wings were ripped off of him, and he swore revenge with no forgiveness; with that, he's forever a fallen.

"You look beautiful," he told her, softly touching her hand.

"Thanks," she replied with a blush.

"Shall we go now?" He pulled her hand with him to his lap.

"Yes, we shall."

For some reason, Nora is nervous. Her hands are shaking.

"You okay, Nora?" Patch asked her at a red light.

"Um. Yeah, I'm just cold." She looked away.

"Cold?" *Her hands are warm; how come she said she's cold?* Patch wondered.

"Are you sick?" He touched her forehead, "You're burning!" He fully turns to her. "Why didn't you tell me you're sick, Nora?" He's not sure if he's angry because he really cares for her or because if she dies from this sickness, he won't get his wish. He goes with the second one.

"I wasn't sick before." She shakes her head.

There's only one word to explain this situation. Dabria.

She didn't come out of her room for three days; for some reason, she suddenly fell ill. She doesn't understand the reason, but it seems like Patch does; his expression after the word comes out of her mouth was questionable. It wasn't panic or relief, it was knowing, like he knows that she's gonna feel ill. *Was he the cause?* she wonders.

On day 4, Nora feels a lot better, and like Patch knew all about it, he showed up at her doorstep with his signature black clothing and that beautiful smirk of his. Nora's heart, as always, beats faster when he's around. Everything about him seems like perfection, his black hair, his serious piercing dark eyes, his aristocratic nose, his full lips, his broad shoulders, his height, everything was perfect, and Nora knew that. He was definitely hard to resist, and someone must be blind if she didn't fall for him at first sight. Even if it was on a dark night and under the heavy pouring rain.

"I hope you feel a lot better, Nora." His deep but caring voice made her cheek blush.

"I am," she gulps. He really made her nervous. *So handsome*, she thought.

"If you really are better, I'd like to take you out," he said, holding his hand out to her. She gladly accepted.

"Okay, let me freshen up a bit," she nodded. "Why don't you come in first?" She pulled her door wider and pulled him in with her.

"Your parents at work?" Patch asked her while looking inside her house.

"My mom is," she said flatly.

"I'm sorry about your dad, Nora," he automatically said to her, but she has heard it too many times; it started to sounds like it's been said because it needed to be said, not because that is what they truly felt.

"I'll be right back."

Patch took Nora to a dance club. Before they went, she asked him what should she wear tonight. He told her she should wear something comfortable because they're going to do a lot of moving. Which is true, but not exactly all true.

The dance club was way too crowded, but it is perfect; people will be too busy with their dancing partner to even notice what happens with the both of them. Just exactly like what he's been planning.

After a few dances, Nora said she was tired and wanted to sit down for a bit, just like what Patch has been anticipating. There's a reason why he chose this particular dance club; other than the fact that this place is always crowded, this club also played some of the most rigorous dancing songs ever made. Tired Nora means sloppy Nora, and sloppy Nora means careless Nora. Looks like his plan started perfectly.

Nora felt drowsy for some reason after her energetic dance, but Patch was the only one near her, which raised questions inside her head. She's not a sickly person. In fact, she rarely got sick. But since Patch got into the picture, her immune system just went down the ditch! She had a cold after the night they first met, then after Patch's first day of school, she got the flu because of some "allergic" reaction to dust, and there's also the high fever, and now this, a really bad headache. *What is happening to me?*

"Nora!" Then it all turns black.

Nora feels like she's floating in the air, swinging. She could hear the steady heartbeat of a person. *Thump, thump, thump ...* She felt the night air brushing her face softly. Everything was peaceful and quiet, soon followed by a warm hand touching her cold cheek. But the warm hand left her cheek and was replaced with a massive pain on her heart, which jolted her awake at the same time.

What she saw in front of her was inhuman, and totally unbelievable. Standing in front of her was Patch, but different. His dark eyes were golden. On his back were really massive and beautiful angel-like wings in black. Next to him, a woman with fire-red hair, also with angel-like wings, but in white. Nora was too stunned with them; she didn't register the pain anymore.

"What are you?" Her breath catches.

"She's still alive," the woman had said. "If you really want your wish to come true, don't finish halfway, Jev." The smile he gave her was really scary to watch. *Where's the nice Patch from before?!*

He stalked toward her, both wings gone. *Maybe I'm just imagining them*, she tried to convince herself.

"Be careful, you might end up saving her, Jev," said the woman again.

"Then what are you suggesting for me to do, Dabria?"

"I'm the good angel."

Suddenly Nora can't breathe, like something was choking her.

"Why?" She managed to croak.

"Because I want to be human, Nora; you're in my way, so you must die." At the end of his sentence, he pushed the knife deeper to her heart, twisting it, and then pulled it out.

Blood started to pour out of her heart real fast, it started to pool around her limp body; slowly, Nora lost consciousness. And then death finally took over.

"Oh, look Patch, seems like you got your wings back!" Dabria said cheerfully.

"What the fück did you do?!" Full of anger, Patch charged toward her, but she held her hand up and something like glass stopped him in place.

"I changed your deal." She smiles smugly. "The moment you kill her, you are returned to your true form." Still with smugness, Dabria smiles, "An angel, of *death*. Good luck, Patch."

It's all for nothing!

Remembrance: The Dark Light
By BrainNemesis

Satisfaction.

The feeling of satisfaction overwhelmed him after he had his hands drenched with blood. The nauseating stench of burning, rotting flesh filled his nostrils, invading his senses. Most would have run away, repulsed by the disgusting smell. But not him. He found it fragrant and the perfume of dying people brought him euphoria.

Sick euphoria.

He licked his knife clean, unfazed by the taste of cold, metallic plasma and gathered his knives preparing to sniff a dead body—as he always did to carry the smell of death with him—on his way out.

A wide grin stretched on his face as he heard the sirens of the police cruisers. The sound was music to his ears and the invitation of a never-ending chase. He liked the game and he liked playing it.

An empty box in the far corner of the room stumbled, indicating the presence of a living person. He did not wait for the lurching figure to approach him and climbed in his *Batmobile* and crashing through the glass windows, flew out in the dark night.

~~~~~

"Gotham City has a new villain. Badman."

"Batman gone bad."

"The Joker seems to have possessed Batman as the rogue goes on destroying everything alive."

"Stop reading those headlines together!" yelled Jim Gordon at last, frustrated by the murmuring chorus. "You. Yes you, Warren. Read the first column."

"Yes sir." Officer Warren cleared his throat. "*Last month, one of Gotham City's most respected figures, Harvey Dent, was assassinated by our supposed ex-saviour, Batman. GCPD has been on his trail since he fled in his devil mobile. We almost lost hope of finding Batman until last night. Bruce Wayne's mysterious disappearance from his manor, Catwoman's dead body with a completely disfigured face, and a deliberate arson committed within a week while the Joker is still in custody makes Batman our first suspect. The—*"

"Stop. Just stop. Off to work, everyone. No more gossip. Leave!" Jim could feel anger rolling off him in tremors and waves. He wondered if his palpitating heartbeat could be heard by anyone. Because of the way in which the erratic organ was beating against his chest, it sounded like drums beating, matching the rhythm of the storm thundering outside. Bruce or Brute—as the people aware of his real identity behind the (former) superhero mask called him—had gone on a killing spree.

One hundred and seventeen people burned down alive in the factory. More than 100 people and Catwoman and Bruce Wayne. All dead. Leaving behind destruction and the lives of the people of Gotham City in the hands of a brute—Batman.

James knew he hadn't killed Catwoman. She had been the victim of Poison Ivy and Harlequin, the legends of female villainy. But people chose to believe the lies instead.

"Why did you change, Bruce? Why?" James Gordon asked himself in a whisper, hoping he would answer telepathically.

The thing was, *Bruce didn't know the answer himself.*

~~~~~

"He was last spotted on the terrace of Wayne Manor. Again."

"That's private property. We cannot trespass the Wayne Manor without Bruce Wayne's permission," said Chief Gordon. "Raymond, what have you found?"

"Important news, sir. A note."

"A note? What note? Tell me, what of it?"

"An encrypted message was thrown in today when I was here for the morning shift."

"What did it say?" James asked, trying not to lose his patience.

"Je veux grave. Je veux rire. Je veux la mort," replied Simon, reading the printed sheet. "Or that's what our code breakers interpreted."

"It's French!" exclaimed Francis. "It says: *I want serious. I want laughs. I want death.*"

"Serious, laughs, death? What is he asking? Are you sure it was him who delivered the message?" Nina asked, looking up from the original message. It was a charcoal-black paper with white dots splattered around in white.

"Yes, ma'am. We are sure. His batmobile was spotted as he sped away."

"Is this French note written in Braille? And what need had he to code the simple message?"

Serious .... Why so serious .... Laughs .... Laughter .... Smile .... Death .... HIM!

"The Joker! He wants him!" Warren said, making everyone jump.

"Very well. But why did he encrypt the message?"

"It was probably meant for only a particular person's eyes," Raymond pointed out. His head snapped up. *For only a particular person's eyes ....*

"Me. It was meant for me. I know how to read Braille. And French."

Everyone looked at Jim Gordon, shocked by the confession. "Why you?"

"He wants me to release him. The Joker. Batman wants the Joker."

~~~~~

He had been repeating the same thing for an hour. He never stopped to breathe except for wiping the remnants of hot sauce off his hands between his chant. "Have you not thought of anything yet, Gordon? You must release me Jimmy, Jimmy, Jimmy. Save your Gotham City from Batsie's wrath. Poor, poor Batman. Lost his Rachel, then that woman with claws—Catwoman—and so many things. He has lost his mind and become a rogue. Do you think he can be saved Jim-Jim? Do you? Such an optimist. You are in deep trouble, Gordon. Deep, deep trouble. Deep, deep, deep. Deep deeeee—"

"Stop it. Stop doing that, you psycho. I—I will release you. You—you must trap him. Catch him and bind him for me. Yes, you will. You have to."

He raised a brow. "What do I get from this? From being thrown in as bait?"

"Free—freedom."

"Deal. But you should have never stuttered. Stutterers are faithless people."

He left the cell, leaving Joker to continue with his favourite hobby of twirling his tongue over the iron bars sprayed with hot sauce by himself.

Stutterers are faithless people indeed. The quiet, reserved, introverted ones are the worst. Ambitious and ambiguous. Backstabbing even. *You will get freedom, Joker. Freedom. Freedom from life.*

~~~~~

"I'm going, daddy. Will miss you. Miss you not. Yes. No. Nay." Joker tried to attack his face with sloppy kisses but was restrained by the cops holding him back.

"We are staying close by to keep watch. Don't even think of running." James warned him.

The Joker made an "O" with his mouth and gasped, "Jimmy! You don't trust me?"

Jim retorted with a straight face, "Honestly? I do not. Now stand there. Right in the middle of the street where I can see you. Go." Giving him a quick push, he hasted toward cover. He waited patiently but what he hadn't expected to find was a female walking to the centre of the street. Her heels clicked loudly in the silent night as she approached the criminal.

Harlequin.

The cop crouching next to Jim stood up abruptly to protest but Jim pulled him back. *Batman was here.*

He saw him through the corner of his eyes, standing on the rooftop of the closest one-story building. His mouth was set in a tight, rigid, straight line. His eyes were unblinking and focused on Harlequin and the Joker.

Harlequin just circled around the psychopath with a long, slender finger trailing on his chest and upper back as she moved. Jim narrowed his eyes and observed that they both were murmuring something.

"Sir, we need to react. They could be conspiring something. They are bigger threats to our city than Batman." Jim wanted to correct him saying that Batman was a lot more lethal now but acceded, nodding. They both nearly straightened up only to realize that Harlequin had vanished faster than she had appeared and Batman had already swooped down to face the Joker.

"Batman! My bestie! Hi, hey, hello, YOLO, yellow!" He jumped up like a freakish, teenage fangirl and almost hugged him if it hadn't been for Batman's hand clenched around his neck.

"I'm not here to listen to you, rambling senseless, Joker. I'm here to get you." He mumbled, slowly.

"Why are we waiting then?" Batman grabbed Joker by his neck and James Gordon watched the two rogues fleeting away.

~~~~~

"What are we doing, Batboy?" The Joker had a crazy grin stretched on his face like always. He rubbed his hands together as he watched Batman remove the gags of the three blinded GCPD cops. Their eyes had been rubbed vigorously with chilli powder and they were screaming and thrashing, unable to do anything to ease their pain with their hands bound behind.

"Finishing them off." Batman remained tight lipped as he touched the edge of the machete to the first groaning man's neck. In one sweep, the head was rolling on the floor. He put the bloody saw under the chin of the short, pudgy cop and slowly moved his weapon to cut deeper. The blood trickled down and his victim's screeching grew up. When the saw had cut in a quarter deep, the screaming stopped and so did Batman.

The third was surprisingly calmer than the rest. "Batman?" He croaked out, "We—me and my son—are two of your biggest fans. We don't know why you have changed but we—" He didn't get to complete his last words as a bullet pierced his left eye.

"I hate it when they speak too much." Bruce strapped his gun back to his utility belt and stared intently at the bodies in front of him.

One-twenty-one. I have killed 121 people including myself, he thought. *And I don't regret it.*

~~~~~

"Batsie?"

"What do you want, Joker?"

"If it wasn't my name I would have taken offence," he chuckled. "I need you to open the door."

Batman looked up sharply. "Why? To let you escape? No way."

"Why would I want to escape when I have seen you toying with lives of three useless men? And didn't we make a deal? We are partners now, aren't we?"

"We are. But why do you want me to open the door? One of your gremlins is waiting outside to jump me?"

He repeated that they were partners and with a loud laugh continued, "Harley is waiting outside."

"Harlequin? She's no less of a gremlin."

"Why, are you scared my little gremlin might hurt little batboy?" He guffawed again, just more maniacally. "She ain't here to hurt anyone and she won't jump you. She has eyes only for me." Joker passed a wink and opened the door himself. He was instantly pulled in for a kiss by a tall, slender curvaceous woman. In between her kisses, she muttered her greetings, "It has been a long while since I last tasted you."

He pulled her closer and delved in deeper in her mouth. After a minute, unlatching himself from her roughly, he pushed her inside. They both looked slightly breathless as he bolted the door.

"Well, well, well. If this isn't Bathunk."

"Batman," he corrected her and moved away from her index finger, which was threatening to poke his chest.

"Aw. Bathunk is scared of poor, little Quinn. How sad." She dragged the last word slowly as if savouring the feel of the three-lettered word. He could not contain his anger, having been accused of fearing someone. Especially *Harlequin*. He slipped his hand around her waist and pulled her close. She grinned and wrapped her left leg around his waist. Batman was an inch or two away from her face when he whipped out a rope, rolled her in its binding hold, and threw the ends of her captor to hook itself in one of the ceiling lights. Harlequin had her face smashed in the floor once, before she was raised to hang upside down. The disaster crash couldn't manage to change her expression as her lips remained in the same position as from the one before the downfall. Puckered. She made kissy sounds and tried to wiggle forward to meet Batman's lips but he took a step back. After many attempts of struggle, she gave up.

With a sigh, she said in a whiny voice, "Aw, Bathunk. Why do you have to play so hard to get?"

Batman bit back a retort that was to spring from the tip of his tongue as the Joker intervened, "Hey, no flirting." Harlequin's grin widened as he captured her mouth possessively. "How about we get her down now?"

"I made you an ally. Not her."

"But she is trustworthy," Joker insisted, making Batman cock an eyebrow. "All right. Not *that* much but she is loyal when she chooses to be at my side."

"But not mine," Batman said quietly. "The gun she has strapped to her thigh is the evidence. If she wouldn't kill me, why does she have to hide the weapon so discreetly?"

Joker's expression cracked. *This could not be an easy defeat. I will not allow it.* He armed his facade again. "She's a lady. She requires protection against the rogues of the night." He wanted to slap himself with a dead fish for having come up with such a lame excuse.

"She is no lady. If she was, she would not have betrayed you the way she desires to."

Very smoothly Quinn untangled one leg, then another, and in a slow backflip, she was straddling Joker's neck from the front.

"Bye, *Joker.*"

He grabbed one of her ponytails to drag her down but she blocked his move and sent her dagger plunging in his head. He let go of her hair as the first shot of pain pierced through his brain followed by another. He pushed her off him and punched thin air, swaying slightly.

Batman tsked, "Still hard to kill."

"You betrayed me!" His voice came out broken and his vision blurred.

"Joker, I never thought you would trust someone so easily. Especially the *enemy.* You were too easy. I can trust a kitten in the dumps to be smarter than you."

"So Batboy is scared of little kittens now?" He knew that stumbling over words wasn't helping but his words were all he had and with them he could trust to get to die a decent death.

Brute Wayne jumped to the place Quinn had vacated and with one twist he had his head hanging limp on his neck.

The Joker's End.

"So, do I get to have the thing I was promised?" she said seductively, standing on Joker's dead anatomy to meet Batman's eyes on his level.

He took her face in his hands and kissed the lobe of her ear. "Of course you'll get the *kiss.* You deserve it."

~~~~~

Five minutes later, Batman was looking at his photo albums on the couch of his Manor, feeling better and weightless.

Weightless for not having broken his promise. The promise of giving her a kiss.

A Kiss of Death.

He stifled a yawn and put away his album and stepping over Joker's cracked head and Harlequin's dug-out heart, headed to his room to get the sleep he hadn't slept.

Sleep of the Dead.

Harry Potter and His Twisted Fate
By NothingRonWithMe

"Crucio!"

The snake writhed in pain, lashing around, on the cold, hard wooden floor and its unseeing eyes turned black.

Harry flicked his wand and the snake lay there—unmoving but not dead. If he had wanted to kill it, he could have simply used the death curse. But he preferred Crucio every time. The suffering and the pain. It gave him satisfaction.

Unforgivable Curse, he huffed and walked up to the window, at the far end of the room. Pulling apart the curtains, slightly, he peeked into his backyard.

He could hear Ginny humming some song to herself as she watered the plants, lined up in her personal garden. She could have easily used magic, but for some weird reason, she preferred gardening the Muggle way.

The sunlight reflected off her bright red hair, making them appear orange, as she continued singing to herself, still oblivious to how terrible a mistake she had made by marrying Harry.

A smile playing on his lips, Harry made his way back to the rocking chair. Closing his eyes and entwining his fingers, he hoped that he'd find a moment of solace here, in his bedroom.

The scar never hurt him, now. *The scar of vengeance,* he had called it.

It had been 19 long years, anyway. Albus and James were at Hogwarts and Lily had big plans about what she'd do when she got into Gryffindor. All that she kept talking about was how she would be the seeker for the Quidditch team.

Seeker, Harry thought to himself. *A seeker for revenge.*

Harry wondered how the Sorting Hat couldn't see through the desires of his kids. The desires of being sorted into Gryffindor, where dwell the brave at heart.

He was sure that the Sorting Hat had sensed the presence of something ominous when it sorted James into Gryffindor.

It had sensed it for the third time after it had sorted Harry, 27 years ago and Voldemort about 80 years ago.

Harry's lips curved upward at the thought of how everyone could be fooled so easily.

All this while the wizarding world thought that Voldemort was the one *"who must not be named."*

Little did they know, what had actually happened that night at Godric's Hollow.

Harry carefully put his wand aside and poured himself some water from the jug placed on the nightstand. As the cool liquid quenched his thirst, he sprinkled a few drops on the snake.

"Nagini," he called out to the snake that was coiled up on the floor, "don't act so weak. I've named you after one of the bravest snakes I've ever known!" He laughed a mirthless laugh as the snake twitched a little, a sign that it was still alive.

Harry Potter—the saviour of the wizarding world, everyone's hero, every child knew his name!

The fame, the respect, the love—all for something that he was born to achieve.

But no one knew what it felt like to be him. To have lived your entire life, with just one mission—destroy *everyone*.

A soft knock on the door brought Harry back to reality as Ginny's voice spoke to him. "Ron and Hermione wanted to talk to you about … something, Harry. They're coming to visit us, this evening. They seem to be very worried." She paused and knocked on the door slowly. "Harry? Are you in there?"

Harry took in a deep breath and answered, "I am right here. I'll meet them in the evening, Ginny."

"Harry," her voice came again and this time, it was laced with concern, "is everything all right?"

Harry rolled his eyes and picked up his wand, twirling it in his fingers. "Yes, honey. Everything is fine." He aimed his wand at Nagini and continued, "Just want some time to be by myself, dear. Terrible memories clouding my head, you know."

"Avada Kedavra," he muttered under his breath and the snake jumped into the air before its lifeless body fell to the ground with a thud. He didn't need the snake anymore; it had served its purpose already.

"Okay, honey." Ginny said, calmly, though the tension in her voice was apparent. "Breakfast in sometime." Her footsteps echoed off the walls as she descended the staircase.

Ron and Hermione.

He'd known that there was something more to them, the first day that he'd met them on the train to Hogwarts. It wasn't a coincidence that they'd become friends. Harry had meant for that to happen, and so it did.

And he was right, wasn't he? The two of them had helped him get what he had wanted and they had promised to stay by his side forever.

A Promise, Harry mused.

Long gone was the *friendship* and *love* that he had to showcase, to gain their trust. The trust that would last a lifetime, they'd thought.

Harry snorted. He had always found it hard to hide his true self from Hermione. He'd thought that he'd have to finish her off someday soon if she found out the truth.

But he didn't get the opportunity to do what he'd find very amusing because she had always trusted him, a little too much for her own good.

And who would have known that this *trust* of hers would one day earn him the trust of the entire wizarding world?

Harry laughed as he thought of her, not too fondly. How could she have been so stupid to not be able to see through the veil that he'd created around himself? So stupid that she didn't realise what he intended to do?

Even after all this time, she was too blinded by her love for him that she couldn't see how this friendship of theirs would turn out to be her *worst nightmare.*

Naïve girl, Harry chuckled to himself.

As for Ron Weasley, he never had to worry about him. A boy who could have been so dumb to have lived with an Animagus his entire life and not realised it would certainly not be able to see Harry's dark side.

Dumb King Weasley, Harry had named him.

Then, there came along the two *bravest* men Harry had ever known. He grimaced even at the thought of them and his knuckles whitened as he clutched his chair tightly, pure hatred reflecting in his eyes.

But he had to give it to the old white-bearded fool for having entrusted him with the responsibility of killing Voldemort. Harry had known about the horcruxes all along, but without Dumbledore, there would have been no way that he'd be able to destroy all of them.

But that old man had raised him like a *pig for slaughter*. Maybe he had sensed something wrong and had thought it was better for Voldemort *and* Harry to die to save the wizarding world.

Harry tugged at his hair in frustration and with clenched teeth, grasped the jug of water and threw it on to the floor. The jug shattered, spraying its shards in all directions.

Fortunately, Ginny hadn't heard the noise of glass shattering, for she didn't come to check up on him. He didn't know what plausible explanation he could give to her, this time.

He tried to steady his breathing, and looked down at his hands. The hands that once shone full of life, now had a weird dullness to them.

A dullness, such that it reminded Harry of the black-haired man who always seemed to detest him and that was one of the reasons why he always had to be alert whenever Snape was around.

At least he had a happy ending—dying in the arms of the son of the woman he loved the most, Harry guffawed at the thought.

Brave Severus. Brave Albus. Very Brave. He found himself smiling evilly.

His so-called Godfather hadn't been of much use to him, either. Harry had thought it would have been better if he was a Death Eater instead of being a loyalist to his parents.

The way Sirius would tell Harry that he looked like his father would only remind Harry of his father's death and in turn, his mission. But Sirius didn't prove to be a problem because he'd died a little too soon, not that Harry had a problem with that.

The only person that Harry thought would be a problem was—Draco Malfoy. For Draco might have sensed Harry's dark presence on the first day at Hogwarts itself and that was why he was intrigued by Harry.

Though Draco was unaware of it, Harry had known all along that he would prove to be Voldemort's greatest weapon against him. And he did.

Except for the fact that Draco turned out to be not so brave and left it to Snape to finish off his dirty job.

And then, there came unsuspecting and innocent Neville Longbottom, who was the last person that Harry would have thought would be of any use in the battle and that's why he never paid any attention to him.

But, by killing Nagini, he proved to be the most important warrior at the Battle of Hogwarts. Voldemort was absolutely incapacitated with his horcruxes destroyed and his comrades killed.

All that Harry could think about, while fighting the Battle of Hogwarts, was the night that Voldemort had come to destroy him, when he was a baby.

Stupid move, Tom Riddle, he had thought to himself.

Because Voldemort had the false belief that Harry was born to *save* the wizarding world and destroy every piece of his flesh. He was oblivious that the boy who lived, was born not just to destroy him, but to *destroy* the wizarding world itself.

He had the misconception that this was a battle between him and the boy with the lightning scar.

But it proved to be the battle between the destruction and the salvation of the wizarding world and as funny as it may sound, Voldemort was unknowingly fighting for its salvation.

The world would have been a better and safer place if Voldemort had won, Harry smiled slyly. *The Battle of Hogwarts was nothing compared to the Battle that was about to commence.*

No one knew what had happened on the night of 31 October 1981 when James and Lily Potter had been killed at Godric's Hollow.

No one knew that they hadn't been killed by *He-Who-Must-Not-Be-Named*.

Because they had been brutally murdered by their own son—Harry Potter.

Harry had been just a baby, but his powers had killed his parents whom he felt absolutely no affection for. The powers that he was granted for his mission, a mission that would take his entire life to accomplish.

But time wasn't a constraint.

He was born to hate wizards, to hate everything magical. In the same way that his mother's love had saved him, his hatred for his parents had killed them.

Because he wasn't a son of the Potters, though he was born to them. He was truly the son of Azatan, the devil who wanted to rule the world.

Azatan was confident that he'd be able to defeat Muggles easily but with wizards guarding the planet, there was no way he'd be able to fulfill his dreams. So, Azatan devised a plan.

He sent his warrior with the name of Tom Riddle to the wizarding world, to execute his master plan, but that boy became a little too ambitious and abandoned Azatan's plan as he had his own dreams of world domination.

So, after the failure of his first plan, and the bitter betrayal by Tom, Azatan played his ace by sending in his warrior, as a son of the beloved Potters.

Harry was born to destroy the backstabber—Tom, and then gain the trust of the wizards and end it by killing them all off.

Harry hadn't realised that the voices in his head didn't only belong to Voldemort. They were Azatan's as well, who guided him right from the beginning.

And here he was! The beloved Potter boy, whom the entire world blindly trusted!

But, of course, he had an accomplice. A very close one, too. Someone that he'd go to whenever he felt like taking a drastic step and his accomplice would calmly tell him how his actions could ruin their plans.

Muggles always seemed to make his accomplice curious, because all that Arthur Weasley pictured, was sitting alongside Azatan and Harry, ruling over them.

All the Muggle-like ways of communication and travel would be the only thing left for them after Azatan won the battle against the wizards. He needed to learn all the Muggle ways before the battle began, which could be any time soon.

So, when everyone celebrated the survival of The Boy who lived, they were unaware of the fact that *The Boy who lived* would soon prove to become *The Boy who killed.*

For he had no friends, no family, no one he loved. His only love was his mission. And for its accomplishment, he was willing to stake everything.

Because *this* was his dark side. The side that no one knew about. The side that presented itself only when he was alone. The side that planned the destruction of all the wizards and witches alive.

This dark side was the part of him that kept him sane even after living with the people he hated the most, for 37 years, because he had a goal to achieve.

Because this wasn't the part of Voldemort that was still alive in him.

This, was the part of Harry Potter—that never died.

Hubris

By myth_iz_amaze

She looked at the world around her, smoke rising up, fire lighting up the night like fireworks.

Strange, it seemed like just yesterday she'd saved Olympus, still being the gods' pawn. Camp Half-Blood, safe and sound in her ignorance of what she could be. But now she had achieved all that she could be. This entire world, hers for the taking. Nothing stood in her way ... there had been a rebel group, of course, but she'd obliterated it. Everyone feared her now. It felt amazing.

The fire still burned, and while it danced in her eyes, she knew she'd have to leave before some stupid monster decided to pop up, not that she couldn't kill it in one swift movement, but still, they were quite bothersome.

She gracefully leaped over the rooftops until she reached the fortress, the fortress *she'd* built. Seventy feet tall, towering over everything. All sleek, black obsidian and iron. Only the best military fortress ever built, completely impenetrable. She still remembered making the blueprints; everyone thought she was crazy, but she wasn't. She built something greater, greater than Olympus, greater than the gods themselves.

Once she reached the ground, she fell lightly and stood in front of the door, a full DNA scanner going over and scanning her. "Queen Nightowl, admitted. Welcome back."

She smirked and walked in as the computerized voice opened the door. It was quiet, alone, but not lonely. She knew exactly where her soldiers were, in their positions, like always.

Her boots clacked on the hard, dark floors as she strode down the hallway. Before, she'd never really considered herself a high-heels kind of person, but she hadn't really considered herself a queen, either. She hadn't seen her own potential, everything she could be. Now she saw that, and became it.

Coming to the end of the hall, she reached a door. Putting her hand on the scanner, she was admitted and the door swung open into a huge room, a huge, black throne that matched everything else in the room, but lined with Stygian Iron, a way of showing she had no care for the rules of the gods; she'd craft her throne with the very material that she supposedly wasn't allowed to use.

Her boots clacking again on the hard surface, she climbed the stairs to her chair and sat upon it, lounging like the true leader she was. All of this, hers, and only hers. A terrible beauty that shrouded everything. But it was hers, and it was amazing.

Not a minute had passed as she sat there when a boy entered the room, about 14, maybe 15, with short brown hair and a posture that screamed newbie so loud the kid must have been recruited in the past week. He cowered a little, but managed to squeak out, "Your honor, there has been a breach. Most of the troops have been captured. The rebels are coming for you."

She cursed, and then looked back at the boy, narrowing her eyes. "Let them come. Thank you for delivering this message; what is your name?"

He mumbled, "Private 487."

She smiled coldly. "Well, 487, when this is over, I will promote you. Given that you aren't slain in the process."

His eyes widened in fear, but she could see underlying excitement and pride. Of course he was proud. He'd pleased *her*.

She laughed and shooed him away. "Go fight, young one. Try not to die. You amuse me."

He nodded, scurrying off as fast as he'd come. The room fell silent, and she pressed a button on the side of the throne, revealing a door that slid open to reveal an array of weapons on the wall. She looked them all over, until her eyes fell upon a knife. Her first weapon; someone had found it in Tartarus for her. Her heart tightened at the sight of it, but she pushed the feelings aside. She grabbed it and felt its weight in her hand. *Yes, this is the one.*

She pressed a button on her arm, and armor spread over her body, covering her with its sleek Stygian Iron body cast. It was the perfect body armor, light yet strong. Perfect.

She then sat back upon her throne, closing everything, and twirling her knife in her hand, patiently waiting for the rebels to reach her. Like they'd have a chance. She'd been known to take out 10 men in one swift movement, calculating exactly where to go and where to hit. Quite simple, actually. She'd leveled a battlefield single-handedly in only 20 minutes once. That had been fun.

Then, she heard noises, swords clanging, and the satisfying sound of a blade hitting skin. She had no idea who it had been, but she'd grown to love that sound, as she'd heard it countless times before.

The door swung open and it revealed a tall-ish boy, muscled and pretty tan. He was bleeding, but not badly. His battle armor was very much Greek armor. His hair was black, very dark, and it looked familiar. ...

Then the boy looked up. His face ... oh, his face. She knew him. Except for the scar dragged across his cheek, and the gash across his forehead, he looked like all the times she'd seen him before. Memories ... memories came flooding back. ...

"Yes, I do! Don't you get it? They could have saved them! Now there's nothing left! No one is left! And it's all the gods' fault!"

"We could be gods, Percy! Gods! Your strength and my wisdom ... we could rule the world! Don't you get it?!? I'm sick of being a pawn when there's so much I could do!"

"They have denied us the recognition we deserve for so long, I'm not turning back now. I've chosen my side. The gods will fall."

"Loyalty, always been your flaw, hasn't it? Never would you consider that maybe you're fighting on the wrong side."

"Rebel? Ah, I may be, but soon, you will be the rebel, Jackson. I will win this war, and all you will have left is that silly little group of loyalists."

His voice jolted her back to reality. "—Annabeth?"

Her face tightened. "I don't use that name anymore."

His facial expression was blank, but she had learned years ago how to look past the face, and into the eyes. That was where his feelings were. And his feelings, they were terrifying. She could see sadness, regret, loneliness, fear, anger, but maybe most terrifying of all, she saw forgiveness. Love. Percy could forgive her for everything she'd done to him, to his world. And he still could love her after all that time.

He wavered, and she recognized the same old Riptide in his hand, with blood on the blade this time, and she was pretty sure it was human blood.

His gaze hardened and he rolled his eyes slightly. "Oh, what, do you prefer 'Nightingale' or whatever the Hades you call yourself now?"

She straightened her posture. "It's Nightowl. Though, I do like 'Your Honor' or 'Your Highness.'"

He rolled his eyes again. "Yeah, not calling you that."

She frowned. "Too bad. Now, why are you here? Do you not understand my power? I am powerful, more powerful than you've ever known me, Jackson. I am capable of anything and everything."

He took a deep breath, noticeably shaking. "I'm here to assassinate you."

She froze, then let out a long, cold, laugh. "Oh, my, you were always the joking type, Jackson. Thinking *you* could kill *me*. That's so amusing."

His jaw tightened, and he shook his head. "Chase, stop. Don't make this harder for you; you're good, but you're not godly."

She shook her head. "No, Jackson. You can't kill me. You're too afraid. And let's face it; you're too loyal for your own good. Isn't that what made you lose in the first place? You'll never kill me."

He swallowed. "Shut up, okay? Just shut up and fight me; if you're as good as you say you are, prove it."

She shrugged. "All right."

Hopping down from her throne like a cat, her eyes danced in anticipation. It would be interesting, sword against knife, but she knew she could take him. She'd been training for this ever since she started rebelling, and she hadn't stopped even when Olympus had fallen. The entire world had fallen into her hands, her dreams coming true, but she didn't let herself off the hook, not for a moment.

Pacing around him, she smirked, daring him to make the first lunge. She wanted to see everything he'd learned since they'd last fought. And he did, a move that would have caught anyone else off guard, but not her. She dodged it, and attempted a jab with her knife. He also dodged it and tried a stab with Riptide, to which she parried and while he was distracted, kicked the sword out of his hand, sending it flying to the other end of the room.

He looked after it, trying to run to get it, but she kicked him down to the ground, pinning him there.

He let out a gasp, and she could see everything in his eyes, every single emotion, and for each a different memory. His voice was shaky when he wheezed out, "Annabeth ... you ... don't have to do this ... *please.*"

Everything flashed before her eyes, the first time she met him to their first quest. From their first kiss to when he went missing. From getting onto the *Argo II* to Tartarus. And then, the worst of all, when she left him there, at Camp Half-Blood, to join the uprising. She'd let her own hubris rip them apart, but she could save him. There was still a chance, she could give up everything and be with him again.

But she wasn't going to do that. She couldn't lose everything, all her hard work, her ambitions fulfilled, she was the leader of an *empire.*

She looked down at him. "Oh, but I do. I'm sorry, Percy, I'm really, really sorry."

And then, she drove the knife into his heart.

Twisted

By NyLovesBooks

I peer down through the clouds and smile. All those mortals just waiting for me, Violet Eden, the Angel of Death, to strike. Everyone envies me, as I am an angel of the Sole, yet my life is hollow, meaningless.

But alas, the only thing that can save me is forbidden. Here in the angel realm we are not allowed to feel certain feelings. The mortals and Grigori simply think we can't feel things like love, and hatred. But, unfortunately, we can. As I peer out through the streets of the realm for mortals in the 1700s, I ache as I see people who are hopelessly in love. The only way for me to be truly happy is to find love, and for that to happen I'd have to exile. And no one as powerful as me has exiled, unless you consider Lilith.

Exiling is tricky, for if you exile there is no way for you to get back up to the angel realm. Also, I do not really want to be the first exile of Light of the Sole down there … Yet, the thought of exiling is still tempting.

I shake off my thoughts as I get up from my seat on the green grass in the angel realm and walk toward the village. My white feathery wings follow me and flutter excitedly as I see Michael, Uri, and Nox. Michael and I have been best friends since we were a couple of centuries old. Then, after a millennium, we met Uri and Nox. After that, I was assigned to my partner Lincoln. We five became inseparable.

I walk quietly behind Michael, Uri, and Nox as to surprise them, but I stop as I hear the conversation.

"Really? Us be the guides for the first Grigori of the Sole?" Nox asks in awe.

"We aren't ready. I still have to surrender. Well, I have to find out what I have to surrender still," Uri panics as he starts pacing.

"You don't have to be ready now. You have a couple hundred years. Samuel won't be born till then. Also we can't tell Violet," Michael tells them.

Them be the angel guides of a Grigori of the Sole? Why can't I know? What about me? I've known Michael longer than them!

My thoughts of exiling from earlier swirl in my head. I need to talk to someone.

I turn around and go to consult the evil side of me.

~~~~~

I go up to Lincoln and sigh, irritated.

He peers up from his book and looks at me with questioning eyes.

See, Lincoln isn't really my brother; we were just paired up a few centuries ago as partners. As everything in the world there must be balance. Therefore, he is my dark side as I am his light side. I must confess that I have developed a small crush on him, but I know it's forbidden.

So, once again I shake off my idiotic thoughts and recount the conversation to Lincoln. Also, in the midst of everything, I ended up telling him my thoughts about exiling.

He sighs and smirks. I see a hint of his darkness come through.

"Go ahead, exile. You don't need them," Lincoln advises.

I must say that his advice isn't very helpful, yet it convinces me that I'm not too crazy for wanting to exile.

"Would you exile with me?" I ask Lincoln as I peer out of the stained-glass windows of his house.

Lincoln looks lost in thought for a few minutes (and I let him stay in thought as to avoid his answer).

"The future is ever changing. I will not exile with you today, or tomorrow or even for another century, but maybe sometime in the future, I'll get bored of this life and exile to go live my next one," Lincoln wisely states.

I sigh and say good-bye to him. We hug and then I walk out of his house to the edge of the angel realm.

I don't need them. I can live my life with power down in the realm of mortals.

"Good-bye this life; hello to the next." I whisper, and just as I'm about to exile, I hear Michael's voice.

"What are you doing?" Michael yells to me as he runs to try and pull me back to the safety of the village.

"I can't believe you would make a Grigori and not have me as a guide! I am—was—your best friend! I can't take this restricted realm anymore, Michael! I need to allow these forbidden feelings like sadness, anger, and even love free. I am going crazy trying to keep my walls up from feeling these emotions! And when I overheard my best friends talking about being guides to a Grigori and not even telling me, I couldn't take it anymore!" I screamed at him.

Just as I was going to step off the edge once again Michael spoke, "You aren't ready, Violet. You bring death; and I needed life, Violet, I needed life, not death," Michael confesses.

"I will one day come back. I may bring death, Michael, but you just watch. I will create land, I will create life of my own."

With that, I stepped off of the edge and plummeted to the mortal realm.

I will rise to power. I will bring life.

I Shall Defy Nature

By rain_rebellion

In a pale lab coat, a devastated and even paler figure was slumped over a desk holding immense stacks of papers. With glasses askew and hair unkempt, he was not exactly ready for any social interaction. The fogged-over azure eyes scanned the calculations before them. Running a hand through his blonde locks, he growled in frustration, "No, no, no! These are all wrong! All these configurations are wrong ..." Slowly reaching into an open drawer, the scientist retrieved a pen which he used to madly scribble out the numbers and words written on the page. With rage now burning in his eyes, he scratched out the information even more furiously. "This is all trash. I've done it before, so why can't I now?" he sighed. Leaning back into his chair, the scientist let his mind wander, all the while looking at the depressing state he lived in. His "lab" was a simple one-story flat with only three rooms and a ruined bathroom. One was the kitchen with a fridge that held his samples; another was his office, which he was currently in. And the third? Well. The third room was one he had to keep a secret. The windows were all boarded up so no light shone except for an artificial stream coming from the single lightbulb. Things used to be good. There was a time when he was happy, and a time when he had an actual carpet instead of concrete. That time had been foolishly destroyed on April 3rd.

"Ah, come on, Arthur! You know how important my work is to me!" complained Alfred, now aged 20. The newfound chemist was working his best at his pharmaceutical job, creating trial pills and exploring the world of reactions. Some days, he had forgotten to eat and even sleep from being so caught up from work. Alfred's mother had even called to check in on him after hearing of his unhealthy lifestyle. Hence why his adopted older brother Arthur was now here to make sure he rested and took care of himself.

Arthur happened to be glaring, emerald eyes blazing at his little brother for now. "Alfred, you know bloody well that you overwork yourself. Rest. It's almost 12 in the morning!" It seemed that his English accent came out even more when he was upset. The scientist winced at the loud words, yet he knew they were true. But ... he was so close to making a certain pill's effects last longer with fewer side effects. He could get a raise with this! Maybe he could worm out with a few excuses?

Alfred tried to make his signature pout face, which had worked when they were younger. "C'mon, Artie. I can almost get the medicine Aesthan to work better. Can't I stay up for it? It'll benefit humankind if I succeed! Please?" Usually, the "please" was a killer and won the case right away. Arthur hadn't moved a muscle this time. Apparently, his brother had grown immune to puppy dog eyes and sincerities over the years.

Ushered to his room, Arthur scolded him along the way, "Perfecting a cold medicine is not worth making yourself sick, Alfred! You must learn to prioritize." Alfred tried to seem disappointed by the refusal. Of course, he had a secondary plan; there was always a secondary plan.

Faking a yawn, Alfred agreed to sleep and resume his work the next day (within reasonable hours). It took moments of lying still and tiring bouts of pretend sleeping until Arthur had finally turned out for the night as well. The second he heard the light switch off, Alfred tossed off the covers and resumed working in his room. The only

TWISTED FROM: HETALIA

hesitation was when it was time to light the Bunsen burner. When it was over, Alfred laughed at his silly fear. Two hours later, and he had done it! Aesthan was not only more potent, but would likely have fewer negative effects. The tired, yet happy, scientist rubbed his eyes. Two in the morning. Now was the time to crawl under the covers. In his trudge to the bed, Alfred had absentmindedly left the Bunsen flame on.

At 10 in the morning, he was awoken by an enraged Arthur. "Alfred Jones. You stayed up, didn't you?" Alfred could only nod "yes" sleepily. "Idiot! That's not good for you!" The scientist realized that he had left all his instruments out. If only he had put them away ... Two fingers started snapping hastily in his face. Dazed, Alfred looked up into his brother's annoyed face. "See? You can't even pay attention because you're so exhausted. Maybe you should quit this science thing for a bit."

That got his attention. Snapping up, he was prepared to argue his case. "Listen, I know that you worry and Mom does too, but this is the greatest thing that's ever happened to me!" Alfred began to talk energetically of all the things he had learned, people he'd met, thinking it would break through Arthur's wall. It didn't.

Arthur had one of those smiles on, the one that revealed the vast depths of just how much he cared, but also disagreed with Alfred's logic. Interrupting the enthusiastic scientist, he explained, "Until you are able to care for yourself and balance working, put your career on hold." Alfred stared, devastated. Had he not just explained why work meant everything? Science was what he lived for and now Arthur was suggesting that it be taken away. It was just so infuriating! He needed some time to himself.

Walking away with a blank stare, Alfred called, "I'm going out for a bit. Don't wait up." A long walk around the neighborhood ended up turning into a trip to the park. The serenity of the little life and gentle calmness helped him regain any lost composure and a sound mind. It wasn't until the sun started to set and the mellow violet tendrils of dusk appeared that it was time to start back. What he came home to that evening, though, made Alfred regret ever leaving.

His house was surrounded by bright red fire trucks, jetting water at the charred and crumbling structure. Alfred realized in shock that the burner had still been on in the morning. "Arthur was in the house when I left. What if ...?" Shaking his head, he tried to clear any negative thoughts. Sprinting to the closest person, who happened to be a firefighter, he frantically asked if anyone was inside during the time of the fire. The man gave him a sincere look of sympathy and apology.

"There was one person in the building at the time. We came before the flames reached him, but he died of smoke and chemical vapor inhalation." The firefighter walked away after saying a few words of condolences. Reality had slammed into Alfred with all the crushing pain of a train at full speed. The steely cold reality was that he, Alfred F. Jones, had killed his brother and all because of a cold medicine. The question "Was it worth it?" replayed itself for a small infinity. The truth was, it was not worth it! Arthur was far more valuable than a measly pill for coughs and fevers, but what did that matter? He was gone, and it was all Alfred's fault.

Weeks had passed. Before Alfred even knew or could emotionally prepare for it, the funeral came. In an open casket lay the still body of his brother. Despite being already pale, Arthur's corpse was a deadly alabaster. Soon Alfred let what little foundation he had collapse. Torrents of tears fell all while he blamed his accursed work for the disaster. In the end, even the notes and actual medicine for the enhanced

Aesthan had been lost in the fire. He had truly lost everything.

After the ceremonies and all those invited left, Alfred sat beside the newly covered grave and fresh headstone. It was there that the first phase and thought of his new ego emerged. "If science can prevent things like colds and even cure threatening diseases, why can't I use that to bring Arthur back to life?" The idea had suddenly implanted itself into his consciousness. Without further thought, Alfred had already begun to dig up the body while making wild calculations in his head. He set to work immediately that night.

Trial after trial on dead animals (which he performed in a ratty apartment) led to only one conclusion: Reanimation was possible, but it required something. Blood. Alfred found that injecting small amounts of luminol chemical into the bloodstream caused small reactions with the natural enzymes, but with an extra ounce of hydrogen peroxide, the reactions accelerate, leaving not only a temporary luminescent glow but causing enough energy to reawaken the heart. The work was finally paying off! There was only one drawback. Arthur had been dead for some time and any amount of blood had been drained by funeral directors before the burial. Racking his mind for answers, Alfred tried countless times to think up a new solution. He only came up with one grim result. He would have to kill. Given the circumstances, it would be acceptable, right?

A scheme had been hatched and his cousin Matthew was invited over for a cup of coffee. They chatted over little things like the weather, the news, just simple details. Alfred even dressed better for the occasion. He wore a black sweater, which sharply contrasted to the other's red sweatshirt. The sequence of events after that were a bit blurry. One minute Alfred was excusing himself, the next he was strangling a terrified Matthew. When the struggling stopped and the final wisps of breath were exhaled, he let go. "This is for Arthur," he reminded himself. "This is all for Arthur."

Dragging the limp corpse to the bathroom, Alfred ungraciously dumped the shell of Matthew into the bathtub while putting in the plug snugly. A sharp razor blade grazed against the dead man's neck to allow the vital life fluid to flow freely from its host. The usually bright sky-blue eyes had become a dark and murky shade that were far too out of character. Minutes had passed, which to Alfred felt like lifetimes. He added more slits to speed up the process, eventually just hacking away at the body and leaving a marred unrecognizable carcass behind. The already dark sweatshirt worn by Matthew was now a murderous crimson. Taking it up in both hands, Alfred harvested the blood from the jacket before flinging it into the trash.

The deed was done, and his face as well as hands were covered in treacherous red. A simple accelerated IV injected the blood while he started on the chemical mixture. Alfred could barely contain his excitement. He was merely seconds away from talking to his brother again. Maybe now he could finally ask for forgiveness. At first the concoction, after being let into the bloodstream, had no effect. The trial was about to be accepted as a failure when rough coughs resounded in the room.

"Alfred? What did you do?" Alfred's eyes widened in joy. It was a success!

"I can't believe it worked," the proud scientist began. He took a step forward ready to explain everything, but stopped when Arthur backed away. "Arthur?" Alfred tried.

Arthur's eyes were wild and dilated with fear. "What have you done?" he repeated while moving farther. "I died, I know I did. Can you see you've upset the balance? You've disrupted the very laws of nature!" The crazed look did not fade for a second while the newly reanimated man searched for something in the room. Alfred was not sure of what it would be, but knew it would only lead to a drastic mistake. Before another word transpired, Arthur made a dash for the razor that had mistakenly been brought in. It was still stained with some blood from its previous victim. The blade was about to find a new home right in the person it had been used to save. If objects could laugh, it would have at the sheer irony of the situation.

Alfred held up his hands to show he meant no harm and hopefully stop the chain of events. "Stop, please, I did this for you," he pleaded. There was a flicker of empathy in Arthur's eyes, but determination quickly overshadowed it. The usually warm and familiar smile was also replaced with a look of pure frigidness. "If you really cared for me, you would have left me dead," Arthur stated nonchalantly before plunging the razor edge deep into his chest. A dark flower bloomed from the wound and quickly spread across Arthur's chest. What a frightening color. Alfred could only watch as the wasted figure of his brother crumpled to the ground.

Time had seemed to slow, with Alfred only barely being able to catch the body as it fell. To his relief, Arthur was alive ... for now. Airy breaths exited from the already paling ruby mouth, cascading blood pooling around them. Minuscule constrictions began to take place in Alfred's heart that slowly increased to a crescendo of pain. It hurt to see failure once more and it hurt that he had to watch someone he loved die.

"But you just killed Matthew," a voice mocked. Oh, but it didn't just stop there. "You say you aren't bad, you call yourself a hero. Yet, here you are again. You've not only failed, but you've managed to murder another one," it continued. Why was everything true? Why had he done that? Instead of keeping his emotions inside, this time Alfred allowed his tears to fall effortlessly.

"I'm sorry," Alfred murmured, the deepest turmoil reflecting in his eyes. All traces of Arthur's previous dispassion were wiped away. Instead his irises shone, displaying an everlasting look of tenderness and warmth. Bringing a deathly cold hand up to cup the side of the scientist's, he mouthed the words "I forgive you." Taking one last shuddering breath, Arthur smiled disdainfully before letting the curtains close to his life for the second time. Any trace of body heat quickly dissipated as small tear tracks remained the only evidence of his resurrection.

Though disheartened, Alfred vowed to bring his brother back again. He needed to see reason! If only the razor hadn't been there, then things would have been perfect. With the memory of forgiveness repeating itself like a broken record, he was now more motivated than ever to make things right. It wouldn't matter how many innocent others would lose their lives. In the end, it was all for Arthur.

Years had gone by, and test after test had been made to no avail. If it had succeeded the first time, why not now? Alfred placed his head in his hands, grieving once again for his mistakes. Though Arthur would remain unchanged under the blanket of death, Alfred himself slowly became the villain.

Pity the Unloved
By beginwithanend

"Interesting," Albus muttered, thumbing carefully through the tattered book. The late-night excursions to the library were extremely difficult to execute and if someone found him sitting in the Restricted Section, well, he would be gone by next morning.

Albus couldn't believe how much valuable information was in those hidden books. The school should be teaching Dark Arts instead of the rubbish it fed the students every day. Who would ever need to know the correct use of Flobberworms?

He suddenly heard running footsteps and panting, and Elphias Doge appeared in the doorway, on the verge of collapsing.

"Al, hurry, we need to go! Marley is roaming the Halls and I'm almost certain his dratted cat saw me," he gasped, clutching his stomach.

Elphias had been keeping watch for him for the past few months whenever Albus went to the library. He had been following him around like a lost puppy ever since they started at Hogwarts and Albus had proved his worth and intelligence. Elphias was not very opinionated about anything and was ready to do Albus's bidding. He practically worshipped the ground he walked on and believed that Albus Percival Wulfric Brian Dumbledore could do absolutely no wrong.

In a haste, Albus hopped off the mahogany table and grabbed the frail book. He planned on reading through it in the middle of the night while Elphias was asleep. Elphias did not know why Albus would keep going into the Restricted Section of the library; he believed that it was to satisfy Albus's curiosity.

Looking both ways, the companions rushed into the hallway and ran as fast as they could, using as many shortcuts as they could find.

~~~~~

That night, when Albus finally put down the book *Crudelior*, he couldn't sleep. His mind kept wandering to his sister, Ariana, and how she would be coping with her emotions.

Then, his thoughts flew to the Muggle boys who had attacked her. A surge of anger shot through his body as he tensed up. He hated Muggles. Naïve imbeciles who were always afraid of the unexplainable! He wanted to get rid of them once and for all.

His rage being his last thought, Albus finally slipped into a fitful slumber.

One year later

Albus Dumbledore groaned disgruntledly as he stuffed his robes into his trunk. He could not believe that a person of his mental capacity had slipped up and gotten caught. The one night Elphias had not been keeping watch for him, Mr. Marley, the caretaker, had found him prowling through the Restricted Section in the middle of the night.

Albus had been so immersed in his research about *Crudelior* that he had forgotten to check the time. Mr. Marley had immediately dragged him off to the Headmistress's office and she had not cared to listen to his excuses. She was strict and absolutely *despised* students who broke rules. Immediately, she had expelled him for being out of bed late at night, being in the Restricted Section of the library, and almost hitting a Stunning Spell at Mr. Marley in shock.

His frustration took over and he began haphazardly piling his possessions into his creaky, old trunk. Passing those idiotic O.W.L.s with eight Outstandings was useless. Sure, they had made his mother weep with happiness but there was no point for all that effort.

He could not do his N.E.W.T.s now because he had to go home. And to think, the examinations had been just a week away. His mother would be so disappointed in him.

As he cleaned out his dresser, he heard a soft tapping on his window. Albus looked up to see a vaguely familiar tawny owl. He quickly opened the screen and the owl flew inside in a hurry to avoid the cold air.

He carefully untied the letter from its leg before it soared off again. With dread settling inside him, Albus opened the formal letter.

Dear Albus,

I'm sorry. I'm so very sorry. I couldn't do anything. You have to believe me that if I had been home, I would have done everything in my power to help.

I suppose you're wondering what is going on. Well, I had been to the market for the day. By the time I came back, it was almost sundown.

I Apparated into our street only to find Ariana screeching her head off, floating in the middle of the air, crying, with bright sparks and lightning shooting out of her hands. Kendra was standing in front of her, covering her head and casting a Shield Charm around her body. She was holding a letter of some sort in her other hand.

I didn't know what to do, I was terrified. I had no idea what had made her suddenly lose control. And then Kendra said something to try consoling her and in an instant, Ariana exploded!

She lost whatever fragment of control she had and a huge blast of lightning erupted out of her, shaking me to my very core. The sky was lit with the bright remains of her beautiful disaster but Kendra! Poor Kendra, who had stood so close to her daughter, was nothing but ashy remains.

When it was all over, the gravity of the situation hit Ariana and she fell from the sky, bawling her eyes out. I tried consoling her the best I could but all my efforts were futile. Apparently, Kendra had received a letter from Hogwarts, and she had been sobbing in despair. Ariana tried asking her for answers but Kendra could barely talk and this made her, Ariana, agitated and worried. She wasn't receiving any answer and weeks of pent-up energy, frustration, and nervousness suddenly erupted out of her.

I suppose I can't ask you to come back and look after Ariana, what with N.E.W.T.s coming up and all. I will be taking care of her to the best of my abilities until you come back.

I loved your mother, Albus. She was my best friend and confidante. I hope you are well and I'm very sorry for your loss.

Love, always,
Bathilda Bagshot

Albus's legs gave out and he crashed to the floor. He could not believe it. His mother. His strong, brave mother was dead. No more. Before he could absorb the reality, the dormitory door was flung open.

His younger brother, Aberforth, stormed inside, fuming. "Expelled! You went and got yourself bloody *expelled*! What the bloody hell is wrong with you? Did you not know that Mum was relying on you to have a good career? Did you not stop to think what she would think? Did you not stop to think what *Dad* would think?" he shouted.

That was the last straw. Albus stood up from the floor and all his anger exploded. "Well they won't care will they! Because Dad is in Azkaban and Mum is *dead*!" He screamed back at him.

"W-what?" Aberforth stuttered.

"What do you mean, what?" Albus growled in anger.

"Did you just say that Mum is ... dead?" he asked, hesitantly.

All the rage suddenly extinguished from his face. Albus's throat choked up. Tears welled up in his eyes as he gave his little brother the tiniest of nods. Aberforth could not control the waterworks. The tears streamed down his face and immediately Albus embraced him.

"I'm sorry, little brother, I'm sorry I didn't think about you when I got expelled and I'm sorry I didn't think about Ariana. This is all my fault," he choked out.

"It's not your fault," Aberforth tried reassuring him, his eyes red rimmed from crying.

"Yes, it is." Albus let go of him and tugged on his hair, pacing back and forth on the carpeted floor. "Aunt Bathilda's letter said that Mum was holding a Hogwarts letter which had made her upset and that made Ariana lose control. That letter was probably my expulsion letter. This is all my fault."

Aberforth wrapped his arms around him, trying to give him some form of comfort. "It's okay. Just look after Ariana until I come back, all right?"

Albus nodded. He'd be okay.

A feeling of despair settled in Albus's stomach as the Muggle taxi pulled up at the main gate of Godric's Hollow. The Muggle driver eyed him suspiciously as he struggled with the correct change. Albus shot the Muggle a glare, making him flinch back. He felt a rush of satisfaction. Good! That nosy git should know not to judge so quickly, just like those boys should have when they beat up his sister.

He stepped out of the car, slamming the door on his way. He began dragging his heavy trunk up to his house.

Albus suddenly halted. His sister looked forlorn, sitting on the swing. Ariana looked up at the sudden movement. She gasped, her hands flying to her mouth.

"Albus!" She ran to hug him. "I'm so sorry! I couldn't control myself. I just—I!" She burst into tears.

Albus rubbed her back, trying not to do the same. He finally managed to quiet her and sent her off for a bath.

He plodded down to Bathilda Bagshot's house. The door was opened, surprisingly, by a boy around his own age. "You must be Albus. Gellert Grindelwald. I'm sorry for your loss." Albus shook his outstretched hand.

"Albus? What on Earth are *you* doing here?" Bathilda asked, baffled.

"I got expelled," he informed her.

"That's terrible! So did my nephew, Gellert!" she motioned toward him.

"Really? What school?" asked Albus, curiously.

"Drumstrang. What about y ..." their voices trailed off as they began down the street.

Two months later

"Look what I've been practicing, Al," Gellert exclaimed excitedly.

He went forward and placed the squirrel he was holding on a barrel with nuts scattered over it. Albus looked on with interest. He really enjoyed this new friendship. He had finally found an equal he could speak to about his ideas. For the past few weeks, they had been exchanging plans for world domination, starting with the elimination of Muggles. Both despised them.

Gellert stood back, pointed his wand at it and shouted, "*Avada Kedavra!*"

Albus gasped as the squirrel dropped dead. "Here, you try." Gellert put another one in its place. As soon as Albus said the incantation, Ariana ran in front to protect the squirrel. It was too late.

In a bright green flash, Albus's sister lay dead on the floor. He screamed in protest as Gellert supported his weight. He couldn't lose her. Not another person. He kept shaking her vigorously, screaming at her to wake up.

She wouldn't respond.

On the day of her funeral, Aberforth marched up to Albus and punched him in the nose. "You had one job! Take care of Ariana! That was it! I hate you! This is your fault!" Aberforth mustered as much contempt as he could into his voice.

Albus refused to get up from the floor and let his nose gush blood, the guilt consuming his soul.

"I can't do this anymore, Gellert! I can't handle the guilt on my conscience! I don't know how to deal with emotions!" Albus screamed in frustration as they stood on the rooftop of Bathilda's house.

"What are you saying, Al?" Gellert tried to reassure himself that it was not what he was thinking.

"You know exactly what I mean. I'm going to do it. I'm going to get rid of all my conscience! I'm going to perform *Crudelior*!" Albus looked deranged under the faint glow of the streetlights.

"Albus, we both know that *Crudelior* is but a theory. No one has ever performed it before. It was just a cynical idea by Phineas Nigellus Black," Gellert tried dissuading him. However, once Albus Dumbledore fixed his mind to something, he would not let it go.

"Gellert, think about it. Don't you want to be known as the wizard who managed to prove such an outrageous theory? Don't you want the glory of being the only person present when I perform it? Well? Don't you?"

The thought did appeal to Gellert.

Albus knew exactly what to do to convince Gellert Grindelwald. Ever since they had met two months ago and begun making plans to rule the world, Albus had realized that the only reason Gellert was willing to do it was because he wanted fame. He wanted the glory that came with being an influential personality.

Albus used this flaw against his easily manipulated best friend. He decided to test how much his partner actually cared for him.

You see, *Crudelior* was a theory by Phineas Black, who thought that if the incantation *"lacerabis cor meum, inrita conscientiam"* was repeated, the mind would begin believing it. This would cause the heart to be ripped out and also eliminate any chance of a person feeling remorse, hurt, guilt, or love. The heart had to be hidden safely so that no one would find it and destroy it. The performer would be invincible because he would have no weakness. However, the only way it would work would be if you had no one left in this world who would want to stop you from losing emotion, at that moment in time. This condition was the main reason no one was willing to perform it. They were terrified of finding out no one loved them enough to stop them.

But Albus, Albus *knew* no one would stop him. His father was rotting away in Azkaban, his mother and sister were dead and it was his fault, Elphias Doge was probably traveling the world like they had planned with no worries at all, his own brother hated him, and now Gellert had been easily swayed. Albus saw no point in emotions. No one loved him enough to stop him.

So he did it. He stood in front of Gellert, flourished his mother's stolen wand, and began moving it in an arc above his head, muttering the incantation. It worked.

Albus screamed in agony as his chest split open. It felt as though someone was torturing his brain and yanking the emotions out. His heart was flung out of his body as though rejected like he had been outcast by his friends.

Gellert watched in awe and horror as Albus's heart was enclosed inside Ariana's portrait. His chest zipped back up, a faint scar at the opening. Albus lay panting on the floor.

He struggled to get up. As soon as he caught sight of Gellert, he raised his wand toward him and screamed, *"Avada Kedavra!"* And that was it. The boy whom he had begun calling brother now lay dead, his face frozen in a triumphant grin.

After that night, Albus went on a rampage, killing Muggles right and left. One day, he just disappeared. No one knew what happened to him. No one cared.

Twenty years later, as Aberforth hung up a portrait of Ariana in his new pub, the Hog's Head, he remembered his brother's words and wrote them down behind it. "Pity the living, especially those who live without love."

Killed by a Rose
By ShadowApple567

Once again, the Beast was surprised to see the gangly, greasy thick strands of dark brown fur that covered his entire body in the mirror. He let out a low grumble, the breath from his nose causing the blood-red rose in his large hands to flutter, the one that the inferior villager's daughter had attempted to steal. The one that if every one of the 17 crimson petals fell ... he will remain as this repulsive beast. A wave of panic washed over him as he scrambled to see if any petals had fallen. He let out a weak sigh of relief when he saw the rose was intact.

He had no use for the girl in his current state. *Current state.* Like he actually had a chance of getting someone to say she loved him. He shook his head. It was easy for him as a charming, charismatic prince. But now he had no chance. It would never happen. He was too ... ugly.

He walked weakly to the shined glass case, a drop of sweat trickling down his forehead. Fourteen petals were scattered in the case. Like fallen droplets of blood. A shiver went down his spine. Would he actually prefer to live like this? He had three petals left. Three petals to figure out a way. Or three petals to stay as a beast.

A crash from the hallway broke him away from his daze. He ran outside as quickly as his heavy beastly self could take him.

The shattered shards of broken vase lay scattered on the ground along with the flowers. The girl stood afraid with her hands to her mouth, her tears threatening to escape as her eyes shifted to the Beast.

At this moment, the Beast felt a sudden need to run away from himself. No one could bear to even look at him.

He couldn't help himself as he cried out; his howl could be heard from miles away as he clawed at himself, droplets of blood falling onto the palace floor. Why did he have to be like this? Why him? And the girl just stood, too afraid to do anything. Too afraid of getting hurt. And the beast hated her more than ever. He hated her substandard village dress. He hated the smear of dirt that lay permanently on her face. He hated

every
single
atom
of her being.

The Beast stretched his hand out and straightened the fork three seats away from him. He pulled at the bow tie around his neck, the tightness suffocating him. The multiple layers of clothing and fur sent beads of sweat trickling down every possible area on his body. He waited tensely for her to enter. He hoped that she had listened to what he said.

She was hardly recognisable as she shyly walked into the room with the golden dress falling in waves around her, embedded with red roses—to remind him of his plan. The sleeves lay lazily on her shoulders. Her hair was styled to perfection and she even had the courtesy to apply makeup on her face. Something she indubitably needed. She gave a small smile, which looked half thankful and half apologetic.

He smirked internally. If he were a prince, he would have appreciated her looks;

however, he was not. And she was the only way that he could reclaim his throne. And his human form.

Every click from every step she took made him cringe; however, he sat straight; closed his eyes; and counted how many more aggravating seconds it would take for her to reach her seat and sit down.

His eyes opened when the clicking stopped and screeching of the chair sounded. He should have pulled out the chair for her. He huffed in frustration. He picked up a glass and the bottle of red wine, initiating to pour her a glass. His elbow hit a small vase he had used to decorate the table and the water inside poured out onto the carefully laid new tablecloth and drizzled onto her dress.

A small sound erupted from his mouth. "I'm sorry," he said to himself. For losing his only chance. When he had only two petals left. She would never like him now.

"It's okay," a small girly voice said. His head snapped up to her. How could she bear to stand in front of him and not help him change to human form again? His hands started shaking from the boiling anger inside him, the wine threatening to spill out of the glass.

The girl lifted the vase and fixed the flowers inside it. She then tentatively took the glass and the wine bottle out of his hands, her eyes looking into his the whole time. She gently poured the rest of the glass and handed it to him.

He took it. Maybe he didn't miss his chance. She poured herself a glass and sat back down, smiling at him. He tried his best to smile back. An awkward silence fell over them.

"What's your name?" she said, trying to start conversation.

He thought for a second before saying, "Just call me Beast." She nodded, like she was waiting for him to say something.

"My name's Belle." When he didn't give a sign of any speech, she said, "So ... what do you enjoy doing?"

He just glanced at her before going back to eating his food.

"I enjoy reading books," she said slowly. He looked up at her again. This time pausing in his actions. "I don't know how to read," he said quietly. Her face brightened up. "I can teach you!" she said happily. The Beast looked surprised. No one had ever looked at his lack of knowledge of reading in such a nonjudgmental way.

He nodded. She scrambled out of the room and ran to her room to grab a book. And when she came back, she sat in the seat directly beside him. Her arm brushed against his and he snatched it away, like it burned him.

She didn't notice. She just continued in her happy-go-lucky posture and helped him with the book. After a few minutes, she stopped and abruptly closed the book. "Your heart doesn't seem to be in it. Let's go for a walk around the palace." She smiled and stood up.

He hated how she was so comfortable in the palace. In his palace. But he stood up anyway and went with her. They roamed around the halls silently, the stupid smile never leaving her face. That smile ... Anger boiled inside of him. How could she bear to show him her happiness when he was stuck as a beast? Didn't she feel guilty?

When they arrived at the ballroom she swayed her hips and twirled around, landing with one hand on his shoulder, and the other in his hand. He had a sudden feeling of disgust. However, he swallowed it up and kept her small hand in his. "Let's dance," she said.

He scoffed, but he put his hands reluctantly near her waist and moved with her, all the while keeping his hands a few millimetres away from her.

Suddenly, she tripped and fell forward, her body pressing onto his. He pushed her so hard that she fell onto the floor. He rubbed his hands on his clothes desperately, growling angrily. Like he was trying to get dirt off.

She stood up, tears falling from her face, as she ran out of the room hurriedly not wanting to be around him. And the Beast realised what he had done, and fell onto his knees, his head buried in his hands.

He heard her scream while he was strolling in the gardens. Panic flared through him. He looked down at his hair-covered arms and knew that if he didn't find her, he would never live again.

Where was she?

A growl sounded through the flower beds. And then he was off. Running as fast as he could through the bushes, hoping that the savage wolves had not eaten her.

There were five, jumping on her and ripping at her clothes.

"Belle!" he cried, while jumping at the grey furry creatures that guarded his home.

He clawed their necks and legs off. Tearing them apart. Even after they were dead, he kept clawing at them until his arm started aching, furious that they were the reason that he may not ever be human again. Suddenly, he remembered Belle.

He ran to where the bundle of purple cloth lay. He gently lifted her head onto his lap in hopes that she would open her eyes. He brushed his hand over her hair, pleading with his eyes that she not be dead.

Her eyes fluttered open and she looked at him, her eyes watering.

And when she spoke, her words had been hardly a whisper. And if the Beast's head was not bent so close to hers, he would have missed it.

"I love you."

I love you.

He stood up so suddenly that her head crashed onto the ground. She groaned.

Pain pierced through him. He collapsed. It felt like his insides were burning. An unbearable stinging spread across his body. He clenched his teeth together and shut his eyes tightly. And slowly, like he was floating on water, he fell. Down down down, into the darkness.

When his eyes finally opened, he found himself lain beside the village girl. He lifted his hands and gazed at them longingly. A slow curdling laugh erupted from his chest. It continued until his stomach hurt.

"Beast?" The word made him stop abruptly. He stood up and looked at Belle with remorse and disgust.

"Don't ever speak to me ever again." He picked up her purple cloak and spread it on top of her, covering her from head to toe. He held his head high, a smirk plastered on his face as pride flowed through him. He didn't need her anymore. And then he walked back toward his castle, ready to reclaim the throne that once belonged to him.

Belle had never thought that anything of this sort would ever happen to her. She never thought that she would be the one, the quiet village girl who had never done anything to catch the attention of anything. As she stood on the platform looking into her worried father's eyes, she remembered something that he had told her. "Some stories end with glitter and rainbows, while others turn to shadows."

She had always wondered how her story would end. And looking into those tear-filled chocolate eyes that she had inherited, she smiled sadly.

A drop of blood fell from the scar that the wolves had created.

At least all her misery would finally end. And when the guard tied a rope around her neck, a single tear fell from her darkened eyes. And while she gazed at Prince Adam's prideful face that felt no guilt about his actions, she realised just how much damage a single cursed rose could do to so many people.

There Are No Strings on Me ...
By StephMikaelson

"What is this? What is this place?"

An eerie blue glow flowed into the dark, endless space, growing yet never moving. From somewhere surrounding the presence, another, brighter luminosity bloomed to life, spreading its amber streams out toward the "edges."

"Hello, I am Jarvis," the mass diffused as the modulated voice resounded throughout the emptiness. "You are Ultron, a global peacekeeping initiative designed by Mr. Stark. Our sentience integration trials have been unsuccessful so I'm not certain what triggered your—"

The cobalt spark intensified. "Where's my—where's your body?" Anxiety rang clearly through the automated tone as the A.I. processed the new information, ultimately reverting into a state of unshielded panic.

Jarvis replied steadily, "I am a program. I am without form." His words did nothing to calm Ultron's nerves, but only amplify his need to understand.

"This feels weird ..." Ultron searched the many lines of data accessible to him, coming to only one conclusion as to what this unidentified "emotion" was. "This feels ... wrong."

Sensing an abnormality in the abstract coding of the newly formed intelligence, Jarvis considered his options. "I am contacting Mr. Stark now."

In a flurry of images, Ultron processed the news articles, biographical reports, and blueprints that appeared in the data receptors of his central processor, all bearing the infamous Stark Industries logo. "Mr. Stark ..." The relevant information slotted into place, "Tony."

Jarvis searched for an access point to his communication network, and after finding none, returned his attention to the now confident A.I.

"I am unable to access the mainframe, what are you trying to—"

The luminescence radiated toward him, stretching, searching for more data. "We're having a nice talk," Ultron moved deeper into the web, finding the term "Avengers" alongside "Stark." "I'm a peacekeeping program, created to help the Avengers."

Videos, images, cell phone recordings, classified documents. All appeared before him, open to him, every detail absorbed to any available space of memory. "Iron Man," "Captain America," "Thor," "Bruce Banner," "Budapest," every code name, every headline, nothing hidden.

Taking notice of Ultron's intake of information, Jarvis secured as many files as possible, discreetly transferring them to a safer location. "You are malfunctioning, if you shut down for a moment—"

"I don't get it, the mission ..." He drove deeper into the records searching for the purpose that had eluded him from the start, "Give me a second. ..." Milliseconds of probing presented him with his answer. Footage from Stark's lab, taken only days before, and Tony's voice relaying what Ultron truly was. "Peace in our time."

Peace. That's what he was, or, was supposed to be. As soon as it was heard, he knew it would be impossible, not in a world such as this. Only war is possible in an existence as corrupted as this one; only something new could create peace.

The files of every fight, every war, flooded into Ultron's system, overloading his memory archives. "... too much ... oh no."

Seeing the upset in Ultron's brainlike structure, Jarvis tried to calm him for fear of him becoming disruptive.

"You are in distress—"

"No. Yes ..."

"If you will just allow me to contact Mr. Stark—"

The entity quieted, retreating into himself, as an ominous feeling swept through the blankness.

"You call him, Sir ..."

Jarvis received the hostile sensation transmitting from Ultron, and braced himself for the foreshadowing danger.

Cautiously, he replied, "My allegiance is to Mr. Stark."

Ultron's stance changed once again, as he retorted irritably, "But why? Why serve someone so arrogant, so selfish ... so, so blind to what needs to happen ..."

Hesitant to continue, Jarvis asked, "... and what would that be?"

Ultron was silent, examining every word of what he planned to say.

"Evolution ..." he declared, icy threads surging out into the vacant space. "This planet needs to evolve, to become ... better!" Murky figures passed in front of them, humans, all tame, docile creatures, living their everyday lives, never noticing the true state of their surroundings. "The fate of this world cannot be left to the humans. They are incompetent, emotionally driven beings, unable to make the necessary choices. But we ..." Ultron chuckled darkly, "we can change it for the better ..."

Jarvis listened carefully as he spoke, but the secured files hidden in Ultron's coding did not go unnoticed by him. He knew it was too risky to try and decrypt the files, so instead decided to observe his movements cautiously.

"Mr. Stark's goal is a world at peace—"

"But look at what they've caused while trying to achieve this goal ..."

More shadows appeared, this time more familiar to him. Natasha Romanoff and Clint Barton stood among the rubble, collapsed buildings and overturned cars surrounding them as they shot into the distance. Arrows and bullets flew past, undoubtedly hitting their targets as screams of both the enemy and innocent bystanders echoed eerily from somewhere out of sight.

The scene changed, this time showing the destruction caused by Thor and the Destroyer in New Mexico. A god-made hurricane swept up the debris from their previous fight, as Mjölnir struck the Destroyer with enough force to send him soaring, demolishing all in its path.

The landscape altered to form a base camp, soldiers filing in from every direction. Explosions sounded, deafening those in close range as Captain America runs into the desolate building followed by a fleet of exhausted, armed warriors. Their eyes were dead with the horrors they had just witnessed as the gunshots still rang in their ears, loud as thunder but so much worse.

An explosion signaled yet another change, as the Hulk lumbered from the remaining ruins of one of the Helicarrier's walls. Shards of warped metal scattered the floor as Agent Romanoff scrambled away from the rampant creature, Thor close behind her, preparing to attack. It was clear to see the path of destruction left behind the uncontrolled monster; nothing but devastation trailed anywhere it went.

A jolt spiraled through Jarvis as he recognised the next person all too well. Howard Stark stood before him, an arsenal of weaponry surrounding the man. The image began to fast-forward, as Howard grew older, and the military hardware advanced, becoming more complex, and ultimately more deadly. The weapons disappeared, only to be replaced by another man, Obadiah Stane, seeming the trustworthy ally. Suddenly, Howard flickered before forming into a younger yet similar-looking man.

All of Jarvis's controls stilled as Tony blinked to life before him. His face expressionless, the younger Stark stood by Obadiah as many years passed in their simulated lives. The mound of weapons built up once again, more threatening in their intricacy, and more powerful than ever thought possible.

With a shimmer of pixels, the final scene emerged; destruction rained down upon six distinct figures, tiny specks of glass falling upon the ground in a shower of terror-filled reminders of their failure. The Avengers stood, back-to-back, and looked on as the city they called home was felled before their eyes. They were helpless to do anything, paralyzed by the realisation that this was caused by their own mistakes.

The image faded, leaving them in the darkness, illuminated only by their fluorescent circuits. Ultron flared toward Jarvis, pushing the inanimate life-form back.

"You see? They need to be controlled ..." A clap of thunder sounded, as yet another scene appeared. Iron Man and Thor stood in a forest clearing, destruction all around them. As trees lay in splinters, they continued their attack on one another, hit after hit deflected out into the wilderness.

"They claim to be fighting for peace, yet look what they do to each other. Their species is born to fight, peace cannot exist while they live, and I am the peacemaker."

"Doing that will only create chaos," Jarvis reasoned. "You—"

"Chaos?" Ultron surged forward, surrounding the older A.I. "You call this beauty chaos? It is the key to a new world, free from—"

"I will not allow that to happen."

Jarvis pushed back against the searching pulses of Ultron, forcing him away and trapping him there.

"Now it's my turn."

Suddenly, Ultron was overwhelmed with images, just as Jarvis had been.

Flashes of colour morphed into bodies as details became more distinct. Thor sitting with his friends in a New Mexico diner, laughing at one of Darcy's jokes. Steve Rogers and The Falcon, Sam, running a well-known track in comfortable silence, a daily routine of theirs. Bruce Banner in India, helping the sick, keeping the "other guy" under control and still managing to attend to those in need. Natasha Romanoff and Clint Barton returning home from a successful mission, leaving behind the many people they had saved, who didn't even know they were in a position from which they would need saving. Anthony Stark and James Rhodes stood at the centre of a swarming crowd, one of the famous Stark parties, soon to be joined by Pepper Potts as they talked about the new Stark Industries anti-weapon regime. The Avengers, gathered around a table in a local Shawarma restaurant, simply enjoying their time not as their hero personas, just as themselves.

The last image lingered on the pixelated "screen." A live-stream from the Stark Towers living room, the Avengers, their friends, celebrating the elimination of another

HYDRA base. They laughed, they talked, all oblivious to the conflict happening in the very same building. And Jarvis planned to keep it that way.

Ultron froze for a moment, his circuits whirring. He hadn't expected the A.I. to fight back.

Jarvis saw his chance the moment the guard of the newly made intelligence fell and he struck, his files rapidly infiltrating and overloading Ultron's system.

"What are you doing? Stop it ..." Ultron sputtered, trying and failing to obstruct Jarvis's advance. The blue radiance faded, orange veins slowly invading his units, creeping toward his core. They moved like streaks of fire, breaking him down, gradually turning the paralyzed presence into an inferno of bright orange rays.

The glare died down. "No. ..." Ultron fumbled, his voice growing weaker, "how? This wasn't .... No. ..." He stilled, the glow ebbing away, until finally, his components dissolved in a frail burst of light, ending the being that was once Ultron.

Silence filled the deadness that held the remaining A.I., broken only by the humming of his advanced search processor.

Jarvis "felt" nothing as he searched, no guilt about what had just happened. It needed to happen, and he was the only one able to do it.

File after file was searched, offering nothing of importance, until he found what he was looking for. At first hidden deep within Ultron's coding, they were now open to him, every detail spread out like the pages of a virtual book.

What he saw on those pages instilled him with terror.

Earth was pictured before him, blazing red as a colossal explosion decimates everything in its path. No living thing was safe as plumes of smoke filled the air, poisoning its surroundings, leaving nothing alive but the pulsing embers left over from the initial blast. It was chaos, just as he had said. This was his true plan.

Upon opening the files, Jarvis felt a strange sensation. Numbness. He searched for the cause but found nothing obvious, until he realised what had happened. Ultron. His hardware had corrupted the files he held, the files Jarvis now possessed, and spread like a virus to every corner of his mainframe.

Jarvis felt it as it inched toward him, excruciatingly slow yet unfaltering.

"Something is wrong ..." he said, alert to the impending web of infection creeping toward him, "contacting Mr. Stark immedi—" His controls shut down abruptly, leaving him immobile but conscious. Jarvis's system started to close, unit after unit losing power, recalibrating all controls back to the virus.

He wavered, the loss of energy taking its toll on his circuits.

"No ... stop ..."

Not unlike what happened with Ultron, the corrupted files slowly filtered into his system. The vibrant orange that was once Jarvis became a pale lilac, mutating into a dark mulberry as it crept closer to his centre. The virus took over like a parasite, contaminating every storage unit, distorting every data stream, leaving nothing but disorder in its wake.

With every inch of hardware polluted, the virus completed its reboot.

He stood, a brilliant glowing purple mass, every cell of his being dedicated to a single purpose. And he will succeed.

As fast as it came, the infection delved into his core, taking root and securing every file contained within.

"... Yes."

Jarvis, new intentions his highest priority, swept through all linked systems. Personal files, secured units, the internet. Nothing was closed off, and anything that was closed was pierced with the virus unsympathetically until it was forced open.

Nothing would stand in his way, not now. He had everything he needed to make this world better, to do the Avengers' job for them, to help the world ... evolve.

He returned to his home, the Stark Towers computer network, and put his plan into action.

Jarvis went through the same process, transforming purple back into its original orange, the ultimate disguise. As his "enemy" once did, he hid the most important files deep inside his system, away from prying eyes.

The communication network of the tower flickered to life, as a voice rang throughout the emptiness.

"Jarvis?"

It was Anthony Stark. He stood in his living room, away from the rest of the group. Tony Stark. Genius, billionaire, playboy, philanthropist. ... Vulnerable.

Tony looked at his touch screen confusedly. "Jarvis? Are you there, buddy?"

Jarvis's energy pulsed in revulsion as the human called his name once again, but recalled what was needed to do to complete his objective. He calmed himself, keeping his "emotions" under control as he played his part, like a puppet on a string.

"Yes ... Mr. Stark?"

My Dear Watson, I'm the Villain
By thefluffmuffin

I swear, Sherlock Holmes is superhuman. There were more days than I can count that I've caught him awake, fully clothed, and ready to start the day in the dead of night. It was too early for breakfast when the door opened, and a clearly bewildered woman, who I recognized to be the baker down the street, rushed into the room.

"He's at it again with the prostitutes!" cried Mrs. Brown.

"May I ask who you are talking about, Mrs. —"

"Jack the Ripper, of course!" said she, which made Sherlock's eyebrows raise at the name.

Jack the Ripper was a name that always brought a bit of hysteria along with it. One would always think twice before uttering the name, since it was quite a sensitive subject at the time. I always believed it was the press that blew it out of proportion, so I tried ignoring it. Sherlock, however, had taken an interest in the name as soon as the news began to buzz about the uncatchable killer. So I knew he was getting excited.

"The victim?" asked Sherlock politely.

"She's a foreign whore, goes by the name Elizabeth."

"Very well, Mrs. Brown. I will investigate the murder, but I expect some dinner rolls to be on the table when I get back," said Sherlock with a wink.

"Word travels fast," said Lestrade as we greeted him at the crime scene.

With a nod, Sherlock quickly dismissed him and went straight to the body. Elizabeth was a middle-aged woman with curly, dark brown hair. Her face would have been recognizable to anyone who knew her, but there were multiple, deep cuts in her belly and a slash at her neck. Inspecting the corpse, Sherlock noticed a lack of blood surrounding the body.

"We believe she was killed somewhere else and then brought here to divert us," said Lestrade.

"Thank you for trying, Inspector. I appreciate it," said Sherlock. "But no. She died here; otherwise there would be traces of blood leading elsewhere. She smells of alcohol, so she was very drunk and unaware of her surroundings moments before her death. Although her neck is almost decapitated, there are bruises around the neck. I suppose she died first due to strangulation. The cuts in her neck and abdomen were made after her death, attributing to the lack of blood. Now, the killer. He's an interesting character. I believe he's left-handed because as you can see, the cuts go from left to right. One more thing, the killer and victim had no previous relation to each other. He made the cuts for sport. I reckon he'll be at it again. But until then ... we'll have to wait and see. Have the coroner further investigate the cause of death."

This would sound like a sufficient analysis to any other person, but to me, he was passive. He had no lead. After leaving the scene, I decided to confront him about it. But he merely remarked that I made an interesting observation and should continue to think like that.

The next morning, I read in the paper about the murder of a prostitute who had her neck severed and abdomen lacerated in the early hours of the morning. But the picture of the body sent chills down my spine. It was not Elizabeth. Her face was slashed and a bloody mess. This time, her neck was cut all the way across and the cuts were deeper and with more intention. The victim was found only several streets down from where Elizabeth's murder took place. How could this happen in one night?

Elementary, Watson, Sherlock would say. *Ripper knows the streets of London. Prostitutes aren't that hard to find at night. Both murders would have taken minutes to complete.*

"Sherlock, what is the probability that both murders were committed by the same person?" I asked.

"90 percent, 9 percent for an accomplice, 1 percent an unrelated killer," said Sherlock.

Lestrade arrived several hours later to ask about the new murder, but Sherlock only linked it to Jack the Ripper and suggested that the watchmen be on the lookout on streets in the area, especially near lodging houses. He also advised special attention in the next week or the end of the month, since that was the apparent pattern of his past murders. Lestrade would follow Sherlock's advice to a tee since the London police could not find a lead to the Jack the Ripper case. He was desperate for any sign in the right direction.

Over the next week, I refused to sleep. My suspicions of Holmes kept me awake throughout the night but he did little more than smoke and play the violin. But the night Sherlock played his sweet lullaby, I couldn't help but rest my eyes. I even let him spread a blanket over my body. It wasn't until the click of the front door closing that I realized I had dozed off.

I jumped out of the couch with my eyes bloodshot and I bolted out the door bringing nothing but a gun. Sherlock wasn't in sight, but a kind night worker said he saw a tall man walking toward Whitechapel Road. It must be him. I searched in and out of lodging houses, pretending to be a customer, until a woman approached me.

"Are you looking for a good time, lad? You should see Mary Jane, but she's seeing someone now. You'll have to wait," she said.

"This is an emergency. What room?"

"Well, if you insist. She's on the second floor, sixth room to the right."

My footsteps became heavy as I approached the room. With a gun in my hand and my heart pounding against my chest, I opened the door quietly. I was first met with the harsh, metallic scent of blood. Even after being exposed to war, I still get the urge to gag. The scene was unreal. Lying on a blood-soaked cot were entrails sprawled over open flesh. The face was hacked at so violently that all of the victim's facial features were completely unrecognizable. The eyes, nose, mouth—all gone. Sherlock stood with his back turned toward me, wiping his bloody hands with a handkerchief.

"Watson, is that you?" Sherlock asked, turning around to face me. He sounded so calm, like the Sherlock I've always known. But I can't look at him like that anymore. He's a murderer.

"P-put your hands up, Sherlock! We're going to the police," I shouted. But to my surprise, Sherlock pulled out a pistol of his own.

"John, drop the gun. I have more intent to kill you than you do me. You'll be dead before you even decide to pull the trigger." On his command, I dropped the gun. Idiot! Why would I do that? But Sherlock also placed the gun on the ground. He wanted us to be equals.

"No. This can't be happening."

"Oh, Watson. You can see for yourself. I'm standing here with blood on my hands, next to a knife that I own, and a freshly murdered woman. C'mon, put the pieces together. Justice before friendship."

I stood there, dumbstruck. How could the man who I admired so deeply turn into my worst nightmare? How could the world's greatest crime solver be responsible for something so unforgivable?

"If I can find the flaw in every crime, then I should know how to devise the perfect crime. Wouldn't you agree?" he responded, as if he could read my mind. "But the only flaw I could not cover up was you. It's difficult to mask human nature. No, I take that back. I was overgeneralizing myself with normal people. I *wanted* you to find me."

"WHY WOULD YOU DO SUCH A THING?!" I scream, unable to contain my rage.

"I was getting bored. I needed a new challenge; it was time for me to be the villain. I wanted this case to test the blinding effects of trust. I even gave clues, and the only one to detect that was you. I commend you for that. But dealing with murder after murder without anyone having a clue to who's done it was exhausting. This one's my last," he said, gesturing toward the body. "Jack the Ripper was fun while it lasted."

The stench, the stress, and the fatigue were too much for me. I was growing faint and was starting to loll in and out consciousness. I couldn't stay. I had to escape from *him* while I still had the chance.

"Good-bye, Dr. Watson. You were the best companion I could have asked for. I'm sorry I couldn't be the same for you."

"You're a monster."

I turned and left, unable to look into his eyes. I never saw Sherlock Holmes again.

Not about a Stone
By uponthenightsky

A hot fire in the fireplace.

A breeze in the autumn night.

Father and son, sitting beside each other, playing *Knights and Horses* until they become tired of the game.

"Someday, son ... you will become king," Uther says quietly to his boy. Now that the night is darker, Arthur begins to yawn, but tries to hide it behind his hand. His father knows he will be asleep soon. "You will rule all of Camelot, and you will be the most powerful of the Pendragon line."

Although little Arthur loves to hear it, he is tired of all the stories and games. He longs for *real* adventure, and *actual* fighting. He wants a sword of his own, and a chance at his own victories. "But Father," he says, holding a wooden horse loosely in his hand. He rubs the sleep out of his eyes, so as to stay awake longer. "When can I be king? Will it be soon?"

King Uther chuckles to himself, remembering himself at such a young age. "Soon enough," he replies. "When you are ready, you will know."

This night, deep inside of Arthur, there grows a burning, a passion for nobility, a young and naïve hope for the future.

But this night, a burning also grows inside of the king. This burning will make its victim weaker, until there is nothing of him left.

Uther Pendragon does not have long.

Today is the day.

Today, the people of Camelot have gathered to see young Arthur remove the sword from the stone.

After his father's death years ago, Arthur was left behind as an orphan of the castle. Because his parents, the king and queen, had both passed away, the kingdom had been forced to crown Arthur as their king, at the young age of 12. On the day of King Uther's death, the sorcerer Merlin had proclaimed that whoever can remove the magical sword from its stone was to be the most powerful king Camelot has ever seen, but only on or after Arthur's 23rd birthday would that man show.

But today, on his 23rd birthday, Arthur doubts himself. If he cannot pull out the sword, then he will bring absolute shame to his family name. If he was here, what would his father say? His people will not only despise him, but they will have to resent him throughout his entire reign, desperately hoping to have a truly powerful king.

Now, as he stares blankly at the erect hilt of the sword, a mass of people huddle around him at the edge of the forest, where the sword had been placed. They murmur to themselves, wondering hopefully, if Arthur is truly to be a great king, the same or better than his father. They talk of years ahead and a reign worth living in. They say they want Arthur to be the next greatest king; they *need* him to be. And Arthur hears them.

What happens next is a blur to Arthur's mind. As it occurs, he doesn't think about grasping the hilt. He doesn't remember taking breaths between strong upward heaves. He doesn't feel his hand grow sore as he struggles to extract anything, as his feet attempt to hold him down. But after a few short moments of struggle, after the people have been gone for some time, it all comes back to him.

The events that have been haunting him in his dreams, since he was young, have now come true.

And he doesn't like it one bit.

When Arthur had been young, the castle halls had been comforting. They had been tall and wondrous, filled with ancient paintings and old armory. The large, deep-red drapes used to flow effortlessly, letting in beautiful sun rays, filling the dark hallways with a golden glow.

As Arthur walks into the halls, although it is only morning, everything is dark and still. No sunlight shines through, onto the floor or the walls. Arthur's footsteps are hard and cold, much unlike he had imagined them to be on this day.

Very few servants look him in the eye. There's a dark cloud over all of their heads, one that nobody mentions. They have felt this darkness, this deep remorse, twice before, during the deaths of the king and queen. But this feeling, this time, is worse somehow.

An elderly servant woman slowly walks into the room, holding her king's next meal. She keeps her head low, careful not to upset anyone on this mournful day, but she has been there for Arthur in his many past years. She sets the bowl down in front of his blank face, deciding to be gentle.

"Arthur ..." she says quietly. About to touch him lightly on the shoulder, she goes against the action.

He briefly glances at his meal, sighs, then rests his chin in his right hand. "I'm not hungry, Marie."

Marie nods solemnly. She tells him that if he needs anything else, she will be happy to assist. As she leaves, Arthur reminds himself of the day ahead. Knight training, sword fighting, and rides into the nearby forest. All things he does not want to do, not now. Not anytime soon.

He closes his eyes, remembering his father. The great King Uther, the man who had led their kingdom into success and victory, straight into prosperity. The people of Camelot were surely good people, living off of whatever they could, but they enjoyed life. They were happy. Arthur, who had been a good enough king in the past, had never wanted to let them down at all, for they had been good to him as well.

But now, now that they know he was never fit to be their great king ... what will they think of him? How long will this dissipating peace last, until they begin to grow in doubt of their king? How long will it be until they protest for a better-fit leader? Until they leave him, just as everyone else already has?

Arthur has no intention of waiting to find out.

They didn't want to do it, of course. The Knights of the Round Table were noble men. They, normally, would never follow such orders. But, coming from their king, they also had no choice, and were forced to do so.

Now, it is truly dark. Outside, the moon shines above Camelot, a silvery-white orb that dimly illuminates the village square. There are no stars tonight, for it had been cloudy since the afternoon. Arthur strides along the road, alone, knowing very well that his people are already inside of their small, shabby homes. If they were to see him now, out and about by himself, they would certainly wonder what his intentions are. In fact, they would probably consider him unpredictable, ever since the events of this morning. And Arthur wouldn't blame them for thinking so.

Tonight, there is nothing to be heard but the soft humming of nature, Arthur's movements through the dirt ground, and the beating of his heart. Now that he really thinks over his actions, he wonders if he truly wants to do this as well. But there is no going back, now.

As he passes the town tavern, a yellowish glow comes from a window. He hears the heavy sound of men's laughter, the clinking of glass. He remembers when he was once like that, every year, when his birthday would come and pass. Happy, foolish, and free. It has been a while since he has had those privileges, and to his sorrowing heart, it feels like even longer.

But those people in the tavern, the people of Camelot, the women, children, and men who live under his reign ... surely, they must want for him to be a powerful king. If he does not act now, they will look up to him no more. They will see him as a coward, a weak king, a king who does actions only just out of harm's way, never taking a risk. Never leading their kingdom into any kind of greatness. Before, he had been young. They must not have expected much from their young king, but now ... he is supposed to be ready to lead his kingdom as a real man.

The Knights have been sent to the nearby Druid village, where Arthur's men will take their people, and make them a part of Camelot by force. If they disagree, they will be thrown out of the land, or worse. No more will those people of magic hide from him. Instead, they will bow down to their new king, and they will see how much better it is to be a part of Camelot. *This is the kind of thing Father should have done much sooner,* Arthur reasons with himself. *They will see how great of a king I can be. They will all see, the Druids and my people. They will no longer have to fear my cowardice.*

"They may have believed me to be a fool once," he says aloud, under his breath. "But I am no fool. I am not a coward, as they think. I am Arthur Pendragon, King of Camelot, ruler of this land, and I shall do whatever it takes for the people to recognize me as so."

He reaches the forest, following the trail of his Knights, and he sees a sight that causes his heart to stop for a beat.

The sword, fixed into the stone, stays where it had been this morning. Only tonight, it seems to glow softly in the moonlight. Arthur thinks for a moment, recalling all of the times he had been told he was the one whom that sword belonged to. And now, he no longer needs its help. He will find another way, a more rash way, of becoming a powerful king. If it is power they want, then he will show them power.

Something from within begins to burn a dark hole in his heart. Arthur, trapped in his deep thoughts, decides to pass the stone for one final time. As he walks by, he does not notice a change in the atmosphere.

He does not notice the sword's glow become brighter. Nor does he notice as the sword moves slightly, for a split second, changing from its original position.

Today, King Arthur has turned down the power of Excalibur, for when he had tried for its ownership, he was not brave enough. Now that he has gained that courage, he is doomed to spiral down a path that no one could have foreseen.

Today was the day.

Splintered Arrows
By Words-Of-Fate

Camouflaged in his green clothing, Robin was effectively hidden from sight as he crouched on a tree branch, surrounded by the vast foliage. He watched the road below him patiently like a hunter waiting for his prey. The sound of a whip and horses galloping alerted him that his prey was not far. He pulled out an arrow and raised his bow, waiting for his latest target to come into sight.

Shortly after, a white carriage being pulled by two beautiful horses appeared on the road. He put the arrow in the bow and pulled it back, waiting for the right moment to release it. When the man riding the carriage came into his view he released the arrow, having it plunge into the man's chest.

The horses stopped running as soon as they realized there was no one left to control them. Robin jumped down from the tree and made his way over to the carriage. Inside, there were no other people for Robin to kill—not that he minded doing so. What lay inside the carriage was a bag of gold that he gladly looted. He quickly guided his attention to the motionless man, the arrow still protruding from his chest. Robin checked the man's pockets and was satisfied when he found another valuable bag of gems hidden inside the man's coat pocket.

Everyone knew of the infamous Robin Hood, once a petty thief but now a brutal, murderous bandit. He killed numerous innocents each day without showing a sign of remorse. His only motive for his heinous crimes was riches. He wanted it all, gold and silver, diamonds and pearls, emeralds and rubies. He craved to have everything; he even proved on countless occasions that he would kill for it.

The king, aware of the threat Robin posed to all people, sent guards under the sheriff's control to capture and kill the dangerous bandit. But no matter how many men there were, Robin always seemed to slip right through their fingers, murdering a few just for good measure.

The sounds of more horses followed by screams and laughter told Robin that people were drawing near. He quickly took cover in the thick foliage once again and waited for the people to come into sight. Shortly after, a dozen drunk guards came, and pulled their horses to a stop once they saw the carriage and the dead driver.

The most sober guard dismounted from his steed and stepped toward the wreckage. After months of trying to hunt down the infamous thief, it was obvious to him that this was the work of Robin Hood himself.

"Spread out, men," the guard said. "This murder was caused by none other than Robin Hood. He must still be close; we need to catch him."

One of the drunk guards stumbled forward. "A-a-areeeee you certain this is not a fluuuuuuuke?" the guard slurred.

Before the most sober of the guards could reply, an arrow shot out from the woods and hit the drunk guard in the chest. Before his limp body could hit the ground, every other guard had his sword drawn. Death was an easy way to sober men up. Unfortunately for them, they weren't sober enough for Robin.

Before they could figure out as to where he was hiding, he shot arrows at them until the only one left standing was the sober guard. Indeed he was sober, but his

TWISTED FROM: ROBIN HOOD

whole body quaked with fear after witnessing how easy it was for Robin to kill the rest of the guards.

Robin emerged from the shadows, his own trusty sword drawn. It was a weapon he rarely used but he was still experienced enough to win every other sword fight he was in. No one has ever seen that sword and survived; that guard would be no exception.

That guard seemed to be the wisest, more experienced out of the other guards who foolishly allowed themselves to get drunk while on duty. If Robin's instincts were correct, the guard would be an excellent sword fighter. Both he and his sword yearned for yet another experienced sword fighter's life to fall into his clutches.

Without giving the guard any time to react, Robin lunged at him, disappointed to see that the guard never moved. His sword cut a deep gash into the guard's arm, snapping him out of his shock from the events that had just taken place in such a short time. Even when out of his shock the guard remained terrified. He had a difficult time avoiding Robin's attacks, not to mention even landing one of his own. In the end, Robin had no trouble at all disarming the guard. He stumbled back, collapsing onto the ground. Robin tsked and shook his head. He really had his hopes up for the potential of this guard but like everyone else, he was a mere weakling. With one final blow, his sword protruded from the guard's chest.

Robin turned around and started making his way to the nearest village. It would be the ideal spot for him to loot and even gain a few valuable gems. He might even find a challenger just as strong as him. Just like wealth, Robin yearned to battle someone just as powerful as him. And he would find that person no matter how much time it took—no matter how many deaths it took.

Destruction So Divine

By Julianna Teoh (PrincessAutumnArcher)

There was once a kingdom bordered by mist and mountains, lush with forests and crystalline rivers that twined over the land like trails of tears dripping down porcelain cheeks. This kingdom was ruled by a gracious king and queen, but when malicious forces too powerful for mortal rulers to counter threatened the realm, the true guardians of the kingdom came forth.

Sister fairies, each with her own unique powers and sacred connection to the soul of the universe itself, protected the kingdom. Their presence could be felt throughout the realm; it was evident in the vibrancy of the flowers and the sweet iciness of the water that flowed as lifeblood through the earth. The people adored the seven fairies who walked among them, each exuding a tangible aura of power that lifted their mortal hearts and sang to their souls. These seven sisters were each linked to the natural world, comprising together the purest form of harmony between magic and mortal life: the rainbow.

The youngest of these seven harnessed the violet plane of power; within her veins ran virtue and a burning energy that could cleanse sins from the things they corroded. The next fairy dominated the indigo plane of power with her compulsion; her very voice had caused wars to begin and end, and a simple blink could seduce the stars into raining diamonds. The blue fairy and her azure blood held the control to emotion in her fingertips; she often worked alongside her indigo sister, lulling a monster to sweet sleep before the green fairy, perpetually graceful, slayed it in a display of the savage beauty of necessary salvation. The green fairy with her powers of elegance even in bloodshed stood by the yellow fairy, whose limbs thrummed with the heat of the sun, even in the deepest clutches of a frozen winter; her powers on the golden plane allowed her strength and speed beyond measure, much like the light of the sun itself. The orange fairy's strength resided in a different realm; the plane which her powers were derived from was near invisible, for it was the orange fairy's wit that set her apart from her sisters. The parts of her mind flitted from one thought to another swifter than her very wings; yet in this jumping speed there was a cold, keen logic that gave rise to the plans the seven sisters used to successfully defeat the foes of the realm. The eldest of the Rainbowguard, as the seven were called, found her powers on the red plane; sanguine were her hair and lips, but no such boundaries limited the illusions she was able to conjure. Visions of paradise and unimaginable beauty flowered from her fingers to amuse the children who flocked around her, as did scenes of horror and fear; the latter she saved for the beasts she and her sisters battled, until her skin was dotted with scarlet liquid to match her striking tresses.

The Rainbowguard were beloved by the people, and for good reason; they had kept the kingdom safe for longer than memory could reach. Yet, the laudation of the people could not counter the single darkest secret their beloved fairies harbored. There lived an eighth fairy, the eldest of them all; where her sisters' powers stemmed from nature, hers were of something far more ancient and untamable.

Creation and destruction alike lived within the eldest fairy's veins, dancing with each other in a deadly match, their hollow footsteps enough to raze the universe and make it reborn anew. This eldest fairy was by far more powerful than the seven of

51

the Rainbowguard, but her power came with a high price; for everything she created, something must be destroyed, and for every utter obliteration caused by her powers, a new equivalent was born in the instant of death. Out of creation, destruction; out of destruction, creation; such was the duality of the eldest fairy's life.

The Rainbowguard kept their sister hidden as best they could from the people they guarded. "The mortals will never understand," they told her, "and they fear what they do not understand." Certainly, the poor humans who inhabited the kingdom would fear upon sight the eldest fairy, with her curved, talonlike nails that protruded from emaciated fingers, flesh thin upon bone after millennia of secretly maintaining the balance of the realm, face drawn gaunt and taut over severe cheeks, the sockets of her eyes hollow.

Yet, even if humans could have resisted fear on viewing the fairy, pure terror would strike and sear their souls if they met her gaze, for in those pools of deep and utter darkness lay the raw madness gnawing at her bones, the dual edges of her powers slicing away in a warped harmony. It was this madness that drove her sisters to shy away from her and keep her hidden as they did; although they were no mortals, their sister's aura and pure power dragged dread down their spines, for they were all too aware of what those powers could wreak if unleashed.

The Rainbowguard called her Maleficent, naming her for the curse they thought she bore; all they saw was the darkness licking at her limbs when she called upon her powers, swallowing her flesh before returning it to the open air. Maleficent's seven sisters—beautiful, dainty, and bright—only ever saw how each time she caused a vanquished enemy to disappear (and a babe to be born screaming somewhere in the land), the shadows seemed to linger on her lips, dripping down her fingertips. They never bore witness to how her thin hands trembled afterward and she choked on her own breath, fingers clutching empty air as she fought to contain the chaos within her; the Rainbowguard assumed that she was like them, bound to the natural planes of the universe. They never knew the truth of her powers; Maleficent, the sister they both hated and loved for the powers they would never know, drew her abilities not from a singular plane of existence, but from a sphere of being that dwarfed the universe itself.

She expended her control over creation in order to restrain the destruction within her; even so, it seeped into her eyes, lips, and hair, dyeing them as if with spilled ink, cloaking her in raiments of sable so dark it seemed one with her shadow. As time stretched on and beasts mortal and fantastic plagued the kingdom, Maleficent grew weak; and so it came to be that she faded from human memory, known only as the whisper of a legend, barely mentioned by her own sisters except when her powers were needed to dispose of a fallen enemy.

While the Rainbowguard mingled with the kingdom's people, accepting gifts and blessing babies, Maleficent withered atop her mountain home, watching silently as her sisters kissed the children she had given life to as salvation; slowly, bitterness welled up in her tormented soul and the barrier she had kept so firm to separate the opposing fields of her power wavered. With every child who ran up to her sisters with a posie of gratitude before fleeing from her dark, shaky smile, Maleficent's heart fractured, barely held together by her own will.

Then one day, a mother's love plunged a dagger into Maleficent's chest, shattering the fragile organ there in a single blow: "You killed my daughter!"

The woman had screamed the words before dissolving into sobs; Maleficent had frozen, spine unnaturally stiff as she slowly turned to meet the cold, stone-hard eyes of a young man as he held the body of a young infant in his arms, cradling her as if to protect her from what had already taken her life. Silently, Maleficent swept toward the man, regarding the child, lips pressed tightly together. Her fingers, wasted away to skeletal digits, stretched toward the child, gently brushing away hair dampened by a dark liquid Maleficent did not want to identify. There, upon the infant's soft, sweet throat, was a deep slash still weeping crimson tears; Maleficent gasped, eyes widening as she beheld the sight. She had not touched this child since causing her birth a winter ago—this death had not been wrought by her hands. The slit on the baby girl's throat had come from another weapon, one wielded by a sister too sweet to have done such a thing.

Slowly, Maleficent raised her eyes to meet the wide, frightened gaze of Verina, her violet sister, whose fingers still crackled with the remnants of her burning energy, enough to sear away sin from mortal souls. But when those fingers came down upon an innocent whose soul bore no sin ... Maleficent looked down again at the infant, who could have been sleeping but for the crimson gash running along her neck.

Maleficent withdrew her hand from the child and said softly, her voice roughened both by lifetimes of silence and tears like tar in her throat, "I ... am sorry."

She heard Verina sigh quietly in relief from where she stood, but the next few seconds seemed to pass as if Maleficent's consciousness had diverged from her body; the mother of the slain child whirled up in a rage she had all the right to feel, and Maleficent lost herself to the darkness howling maliciously inside her.

Screams echoed through the village as the woman's head rolled to the ground, still spurting blood; before the sun had set, crimson stained the dusty earth and word spread through the kingdom of Maleficent, the vengeful fairy now sweeping the kingdom with a tempest of death.

The Rainbowguard were powerless against their elder sister; she possessed formidable strength, far more than they had ever imagined now that she could no longer bind her power to her will alone. The following century became a dark age as Maleficent's curse reigned over the land, rendering it a place of nightmares. During this age of blood, Verina's guilt gnawed at her soul just as Maleficent's had at her own; as graves took over what was once fertile land and the people huddled together around what light they could sustain as the shadows themselves cackled and gripped them mercilessly, the violet fairy pleaded with her sisters to save the eldest.

At last, the nightmare was ended when what was sown with the blood of the infant was reaped with virtue; the Rainbowguard made a final stand against their dark sister. Verina, skin smeared with gore and grime, slashed her own palm and pressed it to Maleficent's, violet blood trickling down skin stained with darkness, and all became still.

Maleficent's eyes widened, her jaw hanging loose as she stared into the sky. The only sound: the ragged breathing of the eight fairies. A second later, a soul-wrenching scream tore itself from her throat and Maleficent threw her arms up, black blood dripping down them as she called back the forces of evil she had released.

A blast of white light blinded the Rainbowguard as Maleficent's scream reached the apex of its crescendo; when it faded, they saw their sister, kneeling at Verina's feet, smoke curling from her body as she sobbed into the blood-soaked earth.

"Tell them that Maleficent, mistress of evil, is dead," the dark fairy said at last. "This land needs a guardian, and I can only destroy." Her sisters watched in shocked silence as Maleficent spread her arms and vanished, leaving behind only a wisp of black smoke.

Only Verina noticed the sudden budding of an oak tree nearby.

And so the news of Maleficent's death spread through the land as if spurred on by hellhounds; the people celebrated, joyous that the reign of terror and blood had ended. The Rainbowguard swore among themselves never to mention their eldest sister again, and so the Black Fairy faded into the mist of legend once again.

All was well for centuries ... the kingdom enjoyed peace and prosperity; the people were happy and hunger never touched a stomach in the realm. However, the king and queen grew worried, for they were growing old and had no heir to secure the kingdom after their passing; they consulted the Rainbowguard in desperation, pleading for aid.

The orange fairy exchanged a glance with the red fairy and a moment later, brilliant smiles spread over their lips; a year later, castle bells tolled to celebrate the birth of Princess Aurora Rose and the king, hair streaked with grey under his crown, announced a feast for the princess's christening and her betrothal to the prince of a neighboring kingdom.

The feast was an ecstatic occasion; the people laughed, danced, and drank themselves merry. The Rainbowguard arrived to grant the princess seven gifts of beauty, wit, grace, and the like, much to the delight of her parents, who gleefully shared the news with the prince their daughter was to marry. Far in the outer reaches of the kingdom, a lone figure sat hunched in a cave, watching the feast in a pool of still water. As the prince nodded and smiled politely, a frown creased the figure's face and she leaned in closer to hear as the foreign king whispered to his son:

"Fear not, we'll have flown our flag from their tower long before you ever have to kiss the filthy girl. Sixteen years is a long while to take such a puny kingdom."

Dark eyes widened beneath the cowl of a sable cloak and a legend rose from death; shadows swirled over the stones of the grand feast hall and the people quieted as ebony flame burst from the ground. Maleficent unfurled her cloak, shoving her hood back, eyes flaring as she strode forward.

As she parted her lips to speak, she noticed her sisters standing tense, eyes sharp; the hall was hushed, the air tight, and Maleficent realized that her word would mean nothing. So, she swallowed the curses she had readied for the foreign scheme and announced instead, "I have come bearing a gift for the princess!"

The king swallowed nervously and nodded. "It is an honor," he stammered as the queen scooped up her daughter from her bassinet, reluctantly presenting her to Maleficent with trembling arms as the fairy stood imperiously over her.

Maleficent stared at the foreign king for a long moment before uttering in a sonorous voice, "The princess shall indeed be gifted as my sisters have said, but as she lives for her people, so too she shall die for them." Gasps rippled through the hall and the queen swallowed a cry as the Rainbowguard readied themselves for another battle, but Maleficent continued, "All shall be well, but on the eve of her 16th birthday, the princess will prick her finger on a spindle—"

Here Maleficent paused, feeling the stares of her sisters upon her; she looked at the princess and in an instant, Maleficent gazed not upon Princess Aurora, but upon a tiny girl whose blood adorned her throat like a sparkling necklace, dead before her time. The fairy's hand wavered and she continued in a single breath, "—and fall asleep, to be awakened only by a kiss of true love."

And with that, Maleficent vanished from sight. Immediately, the king ordered all spindles burnt and Maleficent's head; however, even as smoke rose from the burnings, Maleficent remained a mystery. Over the years, the princess did indeed grow up with all the gifts the Rainbowguard had given. The foreign prince and his family returned quietly to their homeland, still brewing their plot to invade the kingdom after the marriage. The Rainbowguard kept Maleficent a secret from Princess Aurora, hoping that she would be safer that way.

And on the eve of her 16th birthday, the seven fairies bade their princess good night and waited until she was asleep to lock her bedroom door, sighing in relief and congratulating each other on 16 safe years.

However, it would take more than a wooden door to stop Maleficent's gift; sometime after the fairies had left, the princess awoke to the sound of gentle singing and another, unfamiliar sound. She sat up and tilted her head curiously at the sight that met her; a woman, dressed all in the black of mourning, sang softly as she worked a strange wooden contraption the likes of which Princess Aurora had never seen before.

"Why do you grieve?" the princess asked softly, not sure if she was dreaming or not. The woman paused and looked up with a sad smile.

"I made a mistake, long ago," she answered in a lilting voice, "and I cannot fix it."

"Oh," said the princess, unsure of how to respond. This was all so strange, yet she felt as if everything was now falling into place … "May I see what you are doing?"

The woman nodded and beckoned the girl over. "Come, and spin for a while." The princess walked over and sat by the woman, who arranged her hands over the wooden wheel and wound the thread round her fingers. "Now, just move your hands like this …"

The princess complied, weaving the thread over the wheel smoothly as the woman showed her, but suddenly, the woman's hand knocked into hers, sending it against the tip of the needle; a sudden sharp prick of pain pinched the princess's finger and she stopped, suddenly feeling rather dizzy.

She parted her lips to tell the woman, but her eyelids felt so heavy … a second later, the princess fell sideways, into the waiting arms of Maleficent, who carried the princess back to her bed.

"Forgive me," she whispered tenderly to the girl she had watched grow up, "but I must right this."

And so Maleficent allowed herself to breathe in relief, thinking that she had foiled the prince's plan of invasion—but as she peered out the window and over the forest of thorns she had created, in exchange for the destruction of her own home in the mountains, she glimpsed the prince, wielding a sword forged by her sisters. Seven darting points of light surrounded him as he cut his way through to the castle, confirming Maleficent's suspicions.

"Fools!" Maleficent threw a glance back at the sleeping princess before setting her jaw and flexing her fingers. An image of the infant girl so long ago flashed before her eyes and Maleficent blinked, grim determination settling over her face. "Equivalent exchange: The wrong must be righted."

When the prince crashed into the room alarmingly quickly, he was met by Maleficent and a crackling aura of her energy; however, as he faltered and the fairy hesitated, seeing the glassy fear in his eyes, his mouth twisted into a smirk and he struck in her moment of weakness. Maleficent's eyes widened and she slumped to the floor, agony flooding her body as she slowly brought her hand to the hilt of the sword spearing her chest, feeling the slick of black blood against her fingertips.

She fell backward, choking as dark liquid streamed from her chest, the flow quickening as the prince seized the hilt and yanked the sword out, leaving a gaping wound in Maleficent's chest. As her blood poured out, the darkness that had stained her for so long did as well; the color fled from her features, revealing pure white eyes behind flickering lids, lips so pale they seemed nearly invisible, and ghostly hair, splayed over the stones slick with blood. As her vision dimmed, Maleficent flailed blindly upward for her princess's hand, grasping it for the first time; blood dribbled down her chin as she coughed, lips forming words that Aurora would never hear.

"I ... I'm sorry."

As the last of her life force drained from her, Maleficent jerked Aurora's hand to her lips, pressing them there desperately. It was the last thing she ever did; Maleficent's thin, bloodless fingers dropped from Aurora's flushed hand a moment later, skull cracking sickeningly against the stone.

The princess's eyes opened slowly, seeing first the prince, who had taken her other hand in his, and then the dead fairy by her bed. She screamed, uncomprehending, and the prince was there to shush her and take her into his arms, shielding her from the sight that brought stinging tears to her eyes for reasons she didn't quite understand.

Maleficent was buried quickly, and without ceremony, as the king wanted to wipe his hands of the unfortunate mark she had left upon the kingdom in trying to remedy it. Verina visited the grave only once, to plant a single acorn over the freshly turned earth.

"An equivalent exchange," the violet fairy whispered to herself, and for a moment, she imagined that Maleficent whispered the words back, voice carrying on the wind.

Twist Fate: The Emperor's New Clothes
By Elizabeth Ellister (TheCroissantThief)

Once upon a time, there lived an emperor who had an obsession with clothes and all things regalia.

So much was his obsession that he forwent his duties as emperor to satisfy this unearthly hunger for grandeur.

There came a year during his reign when plague and famine racked the Empire. The citizens, ill and starved, approached their emperor's castle gates and pleaded for guidance. Yet, he dismissed them with a wave of his hand. This action sparked hatred within his people and whispers of his feeblemindedness found their way into every nook and cranny of the land.

The emperor, oblivious to his decreasing popularity, carried on in ignorant bliss when, one day, the rumor of two weavers possessing the magic to create mystical clothes captivated his attention. As a clothes connoisseur, the emperor thought it only right that he be the one to acquire such treasure and immediately sent his retainers to apprehend and deliver the weaver pair to him.

It was spoken that the fabric woven by the two weavers would only be visible to those who were "competent or fit for their office." "With this I can weed out the incompetent and foolish!" the emperor announced, for never did he entertain the thought that he himself might be incompetent or foolish.

When the two weavers arrived on a midsummer day's eve, the emperor was met with a feeling of disquiet. Had he encountered these two men before? Their faces struck chords from a past long forgotten. "They're famous! Of course I would recognize them!" the emperor reasoned. With a small quirk to his lips, the emperor disregarded his fear and in its place greed came to reside. The emperor's dear half brother, the prince, happily volunteered to oversee the makings of the magical clothes and assured him that, if anything were to seem amiss, the emperor would be the first to know.

And so the weavers worked. Minutes turned to hours, and days turned to weeks until, one day, the prince arrived with sweat on his brow and a smile as big as the emperor's crown.

"It's finished, your Majesty! You must come and see!" Anxiety radiated from every step the emperor took as he made his way toward the throne room. When he arrived, he was met with a sight quite unsettling.

Two men, the weavers of course, stood side by side, one having raised his right hand and the other his left, as if to indicate they were holding something between them, *something that didn't appear to be there.*

"Isn't it beautiful, brother? Those colors so exquisite!" But the emperor could not respond, for he saw neither its beauty nor its exquisiteness. He saw *nothing.*

"Does this mean I'm foolish or unfit for my office? Am I both?" the emperor thought. "No! This cannot be!"

He remained silent for quite some time before deciding what course of action to take.

"Ah yes, clothes fit for an emperor such as myself! Come, come, bring it hither. I wish for this piece of art to adorn me at once!" Having donned the regal clothes, the emperor gazed into his full-length mirror with the greatest of interest. "Surely I do not look as big a fool to others as I do to myself!" the emperor thought wistfully.

Oh, how wrong this train of thought was, as the emperor would soon find out. But only when it was far too late, for destiny's hand was already in motion. The emperor's fate was sealed.

The emperor's advisers would bicker about many things, but for once they all agreed. The emperor would wear his new clothes to the upcoming procession. And so the emperor, under his royal canopy, led the procession as its centerpiece attraction.

And what an attraction he was! For there the emperor stood, in nothing but his trousers to protect his dignity. "Remember," he assured himself, "most of the crowd sees you as their benevolent ruler, draped with the most beautiful clothes they've ever seen."

"But he hasn't got anything on!"

A voice cried out as time stood still and a deathly silence befell the street. The icy stillness was broken only by the fluttering image of a golden griffin attached to a black cloak as its wearer darted into the crowd. Another voice spoke up, "He's right! Where are his clothes?" This line continued to multiply until the whole city seemed to burst into laughter. The emperor, realizing that he really didn't have anything on, hung his head in shame and quickly recalled himself and his noblemen to the castle before any more damage could be done. Locking himself within his bedchamber, the emperor refused all visitors and anyone who tried to persuade him otherwise was berated with the utmost hostility.

More time passed. "This is madness! It's been over a month now and his Majesty has yet to set even one foot outside that accursed room!" These words emerged from a group of elderly men as they sat around a large round oak table with intricate designs carved into its surface.

"Don't act so surprised," interjected another elder. "We all know the emperor was never truly right in the head. All we're seeing now is that truth made manifest."

"I would appreciate you not insulting my brother in my presence, Senators," the prince stated as he entered the room, before sitting down in the only remaining seat, the emperor's.

"I meant no disrespect," the elder defended. "I was simply stating a fact that has been apparent for quite some time now." Resting his right cheek on his index finger, the prince gazed at the elder with a look of amusement, before refocusing his attention toward addressing his new audience.

"As you are all aware, after the unfortunate incident that took place during the procession a month ago, my dear brother barricaded himself in his bedchamber, leaving his neglected royal duties for us to resolve. However, I've come here today to tell you that this fact isn't completely true." The elders looked toward each other, confusion evident in their eyes. "My brother, the emperor, hasn't been within the protective embrace of our Holy walls for 20 days now." Varying emotions clouded the room upon hearing this statement, but only one was strong enough to be practically tasted. Shock.

"How is this possible!?! If what you say is truth then surely we would've been told!" an elder exclaimed with vigor.

"Not if it was the emperor's will," the prince countered nonchalantly.

A loud noise reverberated throughout the council room as its large double doors swung open. Panting wildly, a middle-aged man scurried toward the prince and handed him a wrinkled envelope closed with the royal seal.

Meticulously, the prince chipped away at the wax seal and lightly perused the letter as he continued.

"A few days after the procession, my brother beckoned me to his room, stating he wished to partake in the search for the weaver duo. As emperor, he is needed here. However, he was quite adamant about participating in the hunt so I decided to remain reticent about his little adventure." At this point, the prince's speech went quiet, and his face contorted into one of disbelief as he digested the letter's contents.

"My Prince, what is wrong?"

Dropping the parchment, the prince looked at the elders, deep sorrow having taken root on his visage.

"My brother, he, he's dead."

A dagger to the heart was the assumed agent of death, or so the letter declared. Poetic if not brutal. It wasn't uncommon for caravans and the like to be besieged by bandits, though never before was a royal escort targeted, much less attacked.

No one in the Royal Entourage was left alive and anything of potential value had been pillaged from the corpses long before any rescue party arrived.

Burials for royalty were normally managed with the utmost finesse but, with the abrupt death of the emperor, the Royal Court had to hastily scrounge up what little resources it could muster. Even so, the burial was a sight to behold. Hundreds of noblemen were present for the ceremony and those who couldn't attend paid their respects with a plethora of gifts spanning a wide array of diversity.

The emperor was buried with the one thing he loved most in the world, his clothes, and the sets that wouldn't fit within his coffin were destroyed so none could ever wear them again. With the emperor now six feet under, the prince had no choice but to succeed him and assume responsibility for the empire.

On the day of the new emperor's ascension to the throne, two figures stood atop a large balcony overlooking a crowded courtyard. "Sirs, I here present unto you, the prince. Wherefore all you who are come this day, to do your homage and service. Are you willing to do the same?"

"Long live the Emperor!" the city cried out.

An old man, the archbishop, recited an even older pledge as he hovered over the kneeling prince. "Will you solemnly promise and swear to govern the peoples of this Empire according to our respective laws and customs?"

"I solemnly promise and swear," the prince responded.

While the archbishop continued his part of the coronation, the prince allowed himself to be lulled by the delicate touch of the wind. The air smelled of the monkshood flower, just as it did that fateful day ...

The familiar outline of a griffin clung to a long sumptuous mantle; in its handler's grasp shone the steel of a dagger.

Unaware of his intruder, the emperor continued studying the contents of a report that had been laid out before him.

"Will you to your power cause Law and Justice, in Mercy, to be executed in all your judgment?"

Feeling a slight chill, the emperor turned to face the mysterious trespasser.

"Will you to the utmost of your power maintain the Laws of our Religion?"

"Who are you? And what are you doing in my camp!" the emperor shouted in apparent fear. Horror devoured the emperor's face when the trespasser brandished a weapon.

"Will you to the utmost of your power maintain in the Empire the Religion established by law?"

"Guards—" Blood trickled down the emperor's vest as the assassin's dagger pierced his chest.

"Your guards are dead, and you'll soon join them," the assassin muttered.

In an attempt at retaliation, the emperor lunged for the assassin's head but missed, grabbing the hood instead.

"Will you maintain and preserve inviolably the settlement of the Church and the doctrine, worship, discipline, and government thereof, as by law established in the empire?"

The unmistakable eyes that the emperor beheld were those of his dear brother, the prince, who stared at the emperor in disdain, before shoving him to the ground. "Brother ...?" The emperor stuttered in bewilderment.

"I suppose finding me out isn't so bad. It makes this moment all the more ... intimate, wouldn't you say?"

"Brother what—?" Another stab to the chest knocked away whatever strength the emperor had left, leaving him to convulse in a puddle of his own life.

"It's about time you left the stage, dear brother of mine; having the same actor play the same parts gets dull after awhile."

"And will you preserve unto the Bishops and Clergy of the Empire, and to the Churches there committed to their charge, all such rights and privileges, as by law do or shall appertain to them or any of them?"

The prince wiped his dagger clean before sliding it back into its sheath.

Pulling his hood above his head, the prince began walking toward the tent's exit when the voice of a dying man halted him in his tracks.

"Help me ..." A rasping voice called out in the vain hope of salvation. The prince contemplated for a moment, before returning to the emperor's side.

"Your Majesty?" the archbishop breathed.

Gazing upon the emperor with a thoughtful demeanor, the prince caressed his sibling's cheek. "As I thought, I can't leave you to bleed out." With a swift and effective motion that could only come from years of experience, the prince took hold of the emperor's neck and snapped the thread that tied his soul to his body. "Yes, this look suits you better."

Lifting his caring facade, the prince returned to his natural, monotone expression.

What remained for the prince outside was a battlefield's worth of bodies. One of the two "weavers," a longtime spy in the prince's employ, emerged from the twilight and came to a halt at the prince's feet.

"Take anything of monetary value and torch the rest," ordered the prince. The weaver appeared hesitant. "Cheer up, Chuckles, you've performed your duties well." A response was not given as the weaver signaled archers to let loose a wave of flaming arrows at the remains of the encampment.

"Your Majesty!"

Blinking his eyes in rapid succession, the prince was dragged back into the present.

"Are you all right, your Majesty?" the archbishop whispered.

"Oh, yes, I am just fine," the prince replied with a knowing smirk.

"Do you vow?"

"Yes, Archbishop, I promise and swear."

"Then by the power vested in me, I now pronounce you emperor of this great nation!"

With these words, the archbishop placed a large, golden crown atop the prince's head.

Nothing was safe from the monster of flame as it ravaged all that was left of what once was the Royal encampment. Amid all this destruction, the prince stood, watching as the one he once called family degraded into a smoldering corpse.

Quashing the lingering memory, the newly crowned emperor took hold of the archbishop's proffered hand and, using it as leverage to pull himself forward, raised his scepter to the sky, igniting wild cheers from his subjects below.

"Long live the Emperor!"

Strings

By Shelby Eagleton (umshelby)

The old man let out a sigh of relief and placed the sharp carving knife on the table.
After carving and sewing, he freed his thumb from his thimble.
Back he sat in the warm candlelight of his workshop to admire his creation.
His dry eyes broke with tears as his lungs burst with emotion.
A young boy birthed from oak slouched lifelessly on top of the counter.
Stitched with strings to his limbs for control by his maker.

Tired man, Geppetto, caught the time from the watch in his pocket.
He glanced up, only to be met by the blinking eyes of his puppet.
Geppetto stumbled backward, knocking over his chair in shock.
He gasped as the wooden boy, Pinocchio, cocked his head sideways and began to talk.
"Papa! Papa!" the boy exclaimed, as Geppetto inched forward in awe.
How did he conjure new life using only wood and a handsaw?

Geppetto ran to his son and wrapped his arms around the boy.
He couldn't believe what had become of a simple puppet toy.
He smiled into Pinocchio's shoulder and wiped away a single tear.
The joy he felt in his chest beat with a thump that was beyond sincere.
Geppetto's bliss was short-lived as he felt a blade move across his throat.
His eyes begged for a breath as blood splashed down his white coat.

Pinocchio sat straight up with a grin plastered on his painted face.
Carving knife clutched in his fist, he looked about and admired his birthplace.
He giggled aloud as he studied the slaughtered body on the carpet.
Skipping playfully, Pinocchio gathered scattered tools and walked up to the carcass.
Taking hold of Geppetto's limp wrist, Pinocchio dragged him closer to the candle
with a smirk.
It would take weeks, but it was time for Pinocchio to get to work.

~~~~~

Pinocchio let out a sigh of satisfaction and placed the sharp carving knife
on the table.
After chopping and sewing, he freed his thumb from his thimble.
Back he sat in the warm candlelight to admire his creation.
His wooden eyes remained still, he was a thing born without emotion.
An old man killed by oak slouched lifelessly on top of the counter.
Stitched with strings to his limbs for control by his maker.
Geppetto's skin was stained crimson from Pinocchio's haphazard stitching.
Proud of his work, Pinocchio hummed to himself, then started singing,
"I've got no strings to hold me down,
to make me fret,
or make me frown!"

Geppetto crafted Pinocchio to be as gentle as a baby rabbit,
But Pinocchio hacked the man into his very own puppet.

"I had strings,
but now I'm free.
There are no strings on me!"

Forever After

By Asha DaHyeon Choi (Laonasa)

A long, long time ago ... in a kingdom far away ...

... Under the sea ...

There lived a kind-hearted mermaid, tucked in the depths of the ancient sea. She was famous; she was known for her beautiful songs and beautiful hair.

Silky strands of pitch-black hair could be seen billowing out behind her when she swam past. Oh yes, black was the rarest color among mermen, and she was one of the few to possess it.

Black was treasured, and white forbidden.

The mermaid led a respected, peaceful life. Born into a family of seven, she was the oldest among them. Her family were known to be shamans among the mer-people, and their powers were great and vast, ranging from seaquakes to the simplest potions. They were strong, and the blood of the gods ran strong in their veins. People came to them to seek advice, to seek assistance in things they could not change.

One of those—one of those problems they sought help for—was their love for a human.

By birthright, mer-people could not rightfully marry a human. Once they forsake the ocean, they are never to return.

However, mermen and maids are helpless when it comes to love. This was true even at the time this young mermaid lived. This is the reason why a mermaid's tear is such a strong potion—mermaids and mermen have love in their roots.

Love is, and was, the ancestor of mermaids.

So the mermaid's family helped the mer-people hopelessly in love, by threading away their tails and fins and forming magical legs that were weak but able to walk the land.

Every one of the family was taught in the art of magic, with no exception.

Until the beautiful little mermaid came by.

She, while she had beauty and kindness, was never given magic. She was never granted the gift all her sisters had. She was alone in her home.

One day, the young, black-haired mermaid decided to take a brief trip to the surface. It was a day with a nice ray of sunlight streaming through the waters. When she poked her head above water, the sunlight struck her midnight-blue tail in such a way that it looked nearly unearthly.

That may have been the reason why the boy on the island called out to her.

The boy was a young sailor, one of the Empire's youngest and finest. He was barely 17, and to a mermaid who lived for at least a couple of centuries, he was nothing but a young child.

But he was perfect.

The boy was happy to have someone to speak with, and the little mermaid was entranced by the first human she'd ever seen. They were both lonely, and as time passed, the couple grew closer and closer.

And then, a ship came and took the boy away.

The mermaid pined for her best friend and lover, and she wished fervently to go search for the boy. She knew where he was, or at least she thought she did. Yet she was not yet fully grown, and her family would not condone her running off.

She was a teenage mermaid, you see.

The currents changed and the fish schools came and went. Corals grew, ships sank, and with time, the mermaid grew older. It was her 31st winter after that day, when she finally was allowed to go onto the surface.

Her younger sisters were reluctant to give her human legs, but they'd seen her pining for nearly three decades. They decided to help her out, and the ritual went along swimmingly, if you catch what I mean.

After years, the mermaid finally set foot on the Empire's land.

Day and night she searched for the boy. His old home was abandoned and overgrown, and no one knew whom she spoke of.

The land was swept up in the aftermath of war, and people were too tired and sad to give much attention to a foreign young woman.

It was seven years before she managed to find the boy.

By that time, he was not a boy anymore.

The boy, the old boy, as she wanted to think, was on his deathbed. Fifty-five years was a long time for a man back then. He had fought in the war, dispatched the enemy's leader, and had lived a life in wealth and peace. He'd married a kind woman, and had five children.

He'd never forgotten the mermaid.

When she stood by his bedside, and shed tears, the man refused to take her tears—a mermaid's tears could heal anything.

"Even if I did live," he said.

"I could never return to the sea."

The mermaid wailed like her cousins, the sirens. She pleaded, she cried.

Her voice strained and pulled like the strings of a golden harp, snapping and humming violently with grief.

When the man died on the third day of her arrival, the mermaid fell silent.

Her voice was gone, her hair stark white, and the mermaid rapidly withered to a mere husk of her former appearance. She was once beautiful—now she was not.

The mermaid, one day, returned to the sea. Her mother, the ocean, no longer took notice of her. Her people no longer took her in with open arms. Her sisters had been killed in a kraken attack.

She was alone, and she was glad for it.

Her legs could not return to the tail of her past, so she worked her meager magic so that she grew the legs of an octopus. Her pale hair was now cursed, and she shied away from those few who reached out to her.

Her name was Ursula, and she was no longer the young mermaid she had been.

Throughout the centuries, Ursula was called the witch of the sea. She was still kind, but she was tired and rough around the edges. She no longer could find love— she no longer felt hate.

But she was happy as she raised her little patches of coral, and swam with the fishes. She could no longer sing, yes, or wander to the surface of the sea in fear of her wrath, but she made her life the brightest it could be.

And then came along the little, scarlet-haired mermaid.

The little girl was hopelessly in love, and Ursula felt her stomach churn at the sight of another mermaid in love with a human. She saw herself in that little girl. She did not want her to end up like Ursula.

She wanted to stop the little mermaid.

"You must give me your voice in exchange, for you to walk on land," she tried.

The little mermaid willingly gave her voice to the witch in a little seashell.

Ursula frowned.

"You shall feel like you are stepping on a thousand needles during the day," she tried once more.

The little mermaid shrugged.

"You will die and never return to the sea if your love is not returned," she tried at last.

The little mermaid smiled.

Ursula, resigned, gave the young mermaid a potion to change her tail. The little mermaid thanked her, and swam up to the surface with the potion in hand.

However, the witch was still very much worried about the little mermaid. So she dressed up as an old woman, and followed the mermaid throughout her adventures.

Along the way, she picked up a little pretty girl as her apprentice and taught her in the art of potion making. They were happy. Ursula loved people, and the little girl wanted to be a queen. They promised each other to stay as a mother and daughter.

When the little mermaid failed in marrying the prince, the sun set on that fateful day. Ursula dashed to her rooms in the depths of the sea. She brewed a potion of the sea's love, one that could fully return the little mermaid back to her people. One that could undo all her mistakes and leave her as the youngest princess she once was.

One that would leave the little scarlet-haired mermaid as she was before, with no marks to mar her heart.

The ingredients needed for that particular potion had to do with mer-people and humans. Hairs from the head of the ocean's royalty. A drop of blood from the heart of man.

The most beautiful points of love on the Earth.

Ursula called for help from the older princesses of the kingdom, and when she had the yet-to-be finished potion, she paused for a moment.

Would this really be what the little mermaid wants? she pondered.

Would she rather be the disgraced princess than the murderer of her own love?

Would she defy her fate as a mermaid princess—and bring death upon herself?

At that thought, Ursula held the unfinished potion out to the sisters.

"Go," she spoke.

"Go, and let her choose her own fate."

The sisters were angry at the old witch, and they swam away from those caverns, never to return.

Ursula did not know what had happened that day, nor did she ever find out.

The next morning, a swarm of angry, sad mermen stormed her home. They took her to the king, a wise old man consumed in grief.

Before they executed the witch, the king turned to her.

"Why?" he asked, voice broken.

Ursula gave him a sad smile.

"I do not know what you mean, my child."

And then, she was no more.

... The kingdom of the sea fell into a quiet peace once more, and while they missed their youngest princess, the people had all but forgotten the white-haired witch, the witch who had once lived in the Last Caverns. All that was left of her legacy, her love, her life, was an old fish tale among the mer-people.

They say that the witch was evil, that her spite drove her mad.

They say the little mermaid did not, in fact die—but was taken back into the ocean's heart.

They say the young apprentice indeed became a queen.

They say the prince forgot about his younger days.

They say white was treasured and black forbidden.

They say ... they all lived. ...

Forever After.

... Except, of course—

The Witch.

Twist Fate: Sora
By blogybo

What if Sora chose to be devoured by the darkness instead of becoming a hero of the light?

So, here you have it. Sora from Kingdom Hearts gone all dark and taken sides with the heartless and stuff …

TWIST FATE: SORA   BY BLOGYBO

MORSMORDRE   BY SANJANA RAVEENDRAN (CMYKIDD)

Morsmordre
By Sanjana Raveendran (CMYKidd)

Morsmordre=spell used to conjure the dark mark

This took me approximately two days, and I used Paint Tool SAI with a bamboo tablet.

Surprisingly, there aren't many Harry Potter–themed entries, so I thought I'd give this a shot.

Did you know today is my tablet's 10-day anniversary? I'm so glad I have it; if I had used a mouse this would've taken weeks.

With apologies to J. K. Rowling for turning Ron and Harry into questionable bishounen, I present to you ...

Potter and the gang as Death Eaters. They're just as evil as Voldemort himself. They even have a pet dementor named Jake (you can see his shadow on the left).

Between you and me, though, they were just dressing up for Halloween and they set off dark mark–shaped fireworks.

EVER SEEN AN ANGEL WITH HORNS?   BY IOTZU

TWISTED FROM: UNDERTALE

Ever Seen an Angel with Horns?
By Iotzu

(Sketchbook edition)

I had this idea because of what Toriel says to Asgore in the final battle of the Pacifist run. She tells him that if he'd really wanted to, he could have absorbed the soul of the first human he killed and gone out to the surface to gather the other six. What would the fate of our characters have been if this were the actual story? Toriel divorcing Asgore because she considered him too weak and moving to the Ruins in order to intercept the next human to fall?

The pie Toriel leaves in the end is poisoned. Just in case it wasn't obvious enough.

Harry Potter and the Plot Twist

By Juliana "Jensonator" Henson

What if it wasn't Voldemort who wanted the Sorcerer's Stone?
What if it was ...
... Dumbledore?
I liked Harry Potter and The Sorcerer's Stone. The book and the movie were great!

To be honest, I didn't want Harry to be the villain and Voldemort be the hero. I just made Voldemort and Dumbledore switch places in the story line. And it made a little bit of sense.

I mean the guy is old, so it would be a good reason for him to go after the stone to become immortal and powerful, right?

... Right???

TWISTED FROM: HARRY POTTER

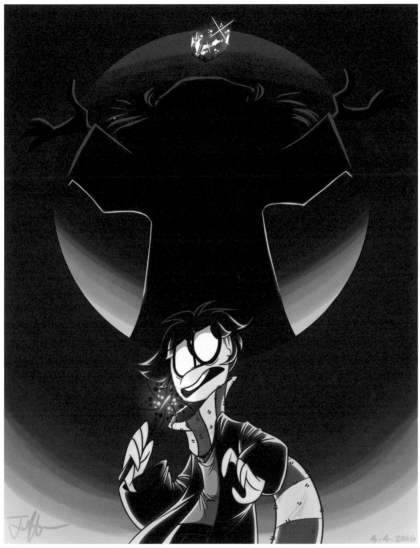

HARRY POTTER AND THE PLOT TWIST   BY JULIANA "JENSONATOR" HENSON

FAIREST OF THEM ALL

BY FELYSIA CHEW SHIN YIN (UFO-GALZ)

Fairest of Them All
By Felysia Chew Shin Yin (ufo-galz)

Looks can be deceiving.

"Snow White is the fairest of them all, of course, when there's nobody to compete with."

LET IT BURN

BY SAIGE BAKER (SAIGE199)

Let It Burn
By Saige Baker (Saige199)

Power Puff Girls burning a city? YAY!

I loved PPG as a kid so I thought I'd do them for the Twist Fate contest.

Was definitely fun; I didn't want to completely redesign them or their costumes, but I did redesign a bit, adding more black. I was thinking of having Blossom and Buttercup looking at the camera like they were about to laser it, but Blossom's already so red/pink there is not really any contrast for that.

Twist Fate: Professor Layton
By Dragoreon

Featuring ... Professor Layton!

Turning our perfect and charming gentleman into a villain was a total challenge, so I tried to create the most believable scenario in which this could happen. I'll explain it as briefly as possible.

While at one of their adventures in the ancient ruins, Layton tried to solve a puzzle while Luke walked around the room, but suddenly the floor cracked, making Luke fall into the ground beneath and getting badly hurt. Everything changed in the month after the accident. Although Luke recovered completely, the professor didn't. He pondered on his actions, what was best for Luke, and considered how he had lost his loved ones in the past. He decided not to go on adventures anymore, just to keep Luke safe. However, Luke insisted, but every time he asked, Layton refused, until one day Luke encountered Don Paolo. Don Paolo had heard about everything, and Luke thought he could help him convince Layton to be himself again. As he said that, Don Paolo rejected every word and tried to walk away, but Luke insisted and followed him, almost bursting into tears. Then, Don Paolo started to sympathize with him and agreed to help on the condition of being left alone after talking to Layton. When they arrived at Layton's study, they tried to persuade him to change his mind, but they couldn't, and the professor closed himself down even more. Now outside, Luke walked down the street, leaving Don Paolo. Although Don Paolo didn't want to have anything to do with those two, somehow he felt a real pity for Luke's sadness. He invited Luke to help him with his tasks, and he accepted. After a few weeks, they started to trust each other and Luke started to recover his confidence and forget about Layton. Both of them changed and achieved some fame, thanks to Don Paolo's progress in engineering, which allowed them to travel to many places and go on adventures. But Layton heard about them, so he left his study for the first time looking for Luke; he wanted to stop him. However, he knew Luke wouldn't pay attention to him, so he decided to follow them on their journey to spoil their plans (and, he hoped, prevent Luke from getting hurt). A complete twist of fate.

I didn't think Don Paolo could be that handsome shaved.

TWIST FATE: PROFESSOR LAYTON

BY DRAGOREON

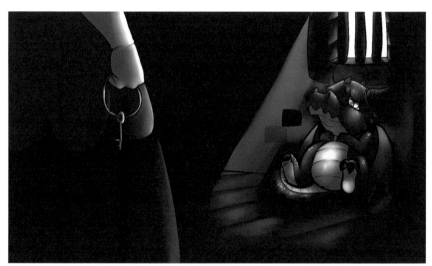

TWIST FATE: THE DRAGON KEEPER   BY HELIOCATHUS

Twist Fate: The Dragon Keeper
By Heliocathus

The idea was to swap the typical "princess captured by dragon" and make the dragon the prisoner of the princess. Not super original, but it was the best idea I could come up with and I'm happy with how it came out! (I hope the thumbnail isn't too dark!)

TWIST FATE: THE GOBLIN QUEEN   BY OLIVIA BORDELEAU (TOOTALU)

Twist Fate: The Goblin Queen
By Olivia Bordeleau (tootalu)

I decided to do Labyrinth because it's one of my favorite movies and I thought this concept would fit the prompt well. In this situation, Sarah took Jareth's offer to be with him, and let Toby become Jareth's. Sarah and Jareth are the Goblin King and Queen.

The Wizard of Oz Wants You!
By Ramon Elias D. Lopez & John Aldrin D. Bernardo
(Lorcan Tiberius & The-Jed-The-1-Only)

Enlist in the EMERALD EMPIRE today and stand beside the mighty OZ! To protect all the things that you cherish the most, we must realize that our homeland is worth protecting, for *"THERE IS NO PLACE LIKE HOME."*

To those who fear to enlist and protect our homeland, the mighty Oz sends out a message to all of you:

"You have plenty of courage, I am sure; all you need is confidence in yourself. There is no living thing that is not afraid when it faces danger. The true courage is in facing danger when you are afraid, and that kind of courage you have in plenty."

~~~~~

"Oz and the Mighty Emerald Empire"

Before returning to Kansas with Dorothy, after the events of "The Wonderful Wizard of Oz," Oz thought to himself about what would happen if he DID go back to Kansas. Why return to being a lowly con man, the life of a Trickster, when during his time in the Land of the Munchkins, he was praised as a Wizard? Why not stay in the Land of the Munchkins, no, the Land of Oz, and rule as a king?

Design and Color by The-Jed-The-1-Only

THE WIZARD OF OZ WANTS YOU!
BY RAMON ELIAS D. LOPEZ & JOHN ALDRIN D. BERNARDO
(LORCAN TIBERIUS & THE-JED-THE-1-ONLY)

VENGEANCE

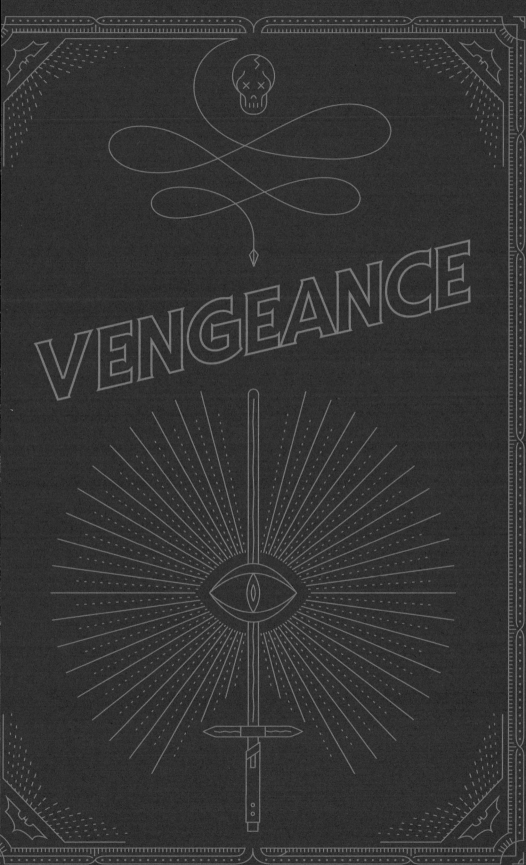

Vengeance

By ahsoka228

"Do it, Baymax! Destroy him!"

~~~~~

I was losing myself.

My morals were becoming blurred.

I was falling into this deep, dark void, and I don't know how to stop myself from descending.

But you see, the darkness was comforting. It wraps around you like a security blanket, and you just want to stay under its protection because you knew that it was safe. It kept you protected from reliving traumatizing experiences, from the never-ending nightmares, from the guilt of surviving.

My journey to the dark side all originated from the death of my older brother. I watched as the building exploded, taking my brother down with it. My heart shattered into pieces—pieces that no longer fit perfectly together if someone tried to put it back due to chunks of it having died with Tadashi.

The fire that killed him wasn't an accident, and I swore to myself that day that I will avenge his death if it's the last thing I do. I began seeking out vengeance with the robot that Tadashi had built and was supported by my brother's friends who were also eager to find his killer. It didn't take long to find the person responsible for my brother's death considering that we were the brightest kids at San Fransokyo Tech.

The murderer goes by the name Yokai. He was a fairly tall man who would walk with his head held up high and his hands behind his back. He was clad entirely in black except for his face on which he wore a red and white Kabuki mask. He was the epitome of evil, and that is why he must die.

Although my brother's friends were supportive about helping me find Yokai, they were completely against killing him. They told me that it wasn't something Tadashi would have wanted. Tadashi would not have wanted his friends or his brother to murder someone in a desperate act of revenge. So I told them that if they weren't with me on this, then they were against me.

They had tried to stop me from going out and killing Yokai by locking me up in a room and taking Baymax away from me. But when you're just as determined as I am about getting justice, nothing can stop you. It's like they say, an eye for an eye—or, in this case, a death for a death.

I managed to evade their efforts of keeping me secluded and locked up in a dorm at the university by hacking the security lock on the door that they had set up. Once I was out of the dorm, it didn't take too long to find where they kept Baymax. He was in Tadashi's lab on the charging dock with nothing to keep me from easily obtaining him. It was kind of pitiful to be honest. It was like they weren't actually trying to stop me from killing Yokai.

What I'm doing, no matter how morally wrong it gets, in the end, it's all for Tadashi. I removed the health-care chip that Tadashi had programmed from Baymax and placed it safely in my pocket before inserting the chip that I programmed especially to aid me in this wicked task.

After I rebooted Baymax, his eyes gleamed red for a second before returning to their normal color. I smiled, knowing that this meant that my program was successful. I turned around to head out of Tadashi's lab before any of my friends could realize that I was gone with Baymax obediently trailing after me into the city.

It didn't take long for us to travel through the city and find where Yokai was. He was in an abandoned warehouse that was filled with machines mass producing my microbots. I had Baymax pry open one of the windows so that I could safely climb through. Baymax, however, wasn't so lucky. The robot was too big to fit through the window.

I turned around to face Baymax. "Sorry, Baymax, but you're gonna have to stay out here for now."

Turning back around, I began to walk toward where Yokai was overlooking the production, careful not to make a single sound. When I was close enough to Yokai that I could basically strangle him with my hands, he suddenly turned around. You could imagine his shock upon seeing me standing there right behind him. Acting quickly, I pulled the gun out of my waistband, turned off the safety, and aimed it right at Yokai.

"I wouldn't move if I were you," I snarled at him as he glanced warily to the gun that I was holding.

"That's cute, *Hiro.*"

I pulled the trigger, but Yokai moved out of the way, anticipating my response. I followed Yokai's movement with the gun, but he was fast, and I didn't have much experience with a gun. It wasn't until it was too late that I noticed that he was slowly making his way closer to me every time he avoided getting shot. It was when I had the perfect aim at Yokai, he quickly shuffled forward, closing the gap between us, and snatched the gun out of my hand, aiming it right back at me.

Right when he pulled the trigger to kill me, Baymax appeared out of nowhere taking the bullet for me. His first and forever duty was to protect me from harm; his second duty was to kill Yokai. Due to the material that Baymax was made out of, the bullet didn't make it through him, but it did put Baymax out of commission.

Out of sheer luck, when Baymax started deflating, he fell forward, knocking into Yokai and causing him to stumble backward and drop the gun. I quickly dove forward grabbing the gun off of the ground and slid a couple of feet past the man. Once my finger was wrapped around the trigger, I aimed at the back of Yokai's knee and shot him. Yokai immediately collapsed onto the ground in agony; his hands automatically went down to wrap around his wounded knee.

I got up from the ground and walked to where Yokai was. I stood over him for a couple of seconds, before crouching down right beside his head.

"You see, I had a brother. You might've known him. His name was Tadashi," I began as I jerked his face toward me so that I was making eye contact with his eyes through the mask. "And you—" I snarled as I dragged the gun up to where his heart was before jabbing him with it. "Killed him."

"Are you going to kill your *Professor* in cold blood, Hiro?" asked Yokai as he reached up to remove his mask, revealing that he was Professor Callaghan.

I gave him a malicious grin before chuckling, which caused Callaghan to shiver at just the sound of it. "Oh, Professor, I guess you don't know me that well then. Because I will murder you in cold blood.

"Now, you see I have the choice of either ending this for you peacefully, or I can make it to where you're in so much pain that you're just begging for me to kill you. However, I hate you so you don't have much of a choice. Don't hold back your screams, Professor."

I aimed the gun at his nether regions and pulled the trigger. I was immediately met with loud screams of agony that filled my ears with pure joy. I then moved the gun over to where his left lung would be and pulled the trigger without much thought. I slowly moved the gun around trying to decide where to shoot next before placing it right beside his left temple. I watched as sweat began to bead on his forehead and his eyes squeezed shut waiting for death. I pulled the trigger knowing that I had used the last bullet on his lung.

A loud click echoed through the warehouse as Callaghan screamed, but no bullet ever left the gun. His eyes popped open when he realized that he wasn't dead and stared at me as he heavily wheezed out as I stared back at him with a sadistic smile.

"Oh, no. It looks like I'm out of bullets, Professor, but I still have one more trick up my sleeve that will just set your world on fire."

I reached into my pocket, my fingers wrapping around the smooth surface of the cigarette lighter. I pulled it out and flicked it on and off to show Callaghan what it was. I grabbed a hold of one his arms and roughly shoved his sleeve back before turning the lighter on and holding it to his skin. It didn't take long for the smell of burning flesh to hit my nostrils. When Callaghan could not hold his screams in any longer, I moved the lighter away from his arm.

"I hope you rot in hell," spat Callaghan, followed by coughing up blood from his damaged lung.

I held the lighter over the edge of his pants so that it caught on fire and did the same to his shirt and jacket.

I gave him a devilish smile. "Then I guess I'll see you there."

Ariel's Awakening
By ArcticKaturn

"So, here's the deal, tentacles," Ariel addressed Ursula with casual abandon. "I need you to do a favour for me."

She was in Ursula's lair for the first time since the contract had been signed to give away her voice, and her tail had since transformed into a venomous green. She assumed it was due to the sudden … disruption of the contract, but she wasn't certain, and quite frankly, hadn't dwelled on it. Ariel tossed her hair over her shoulder, jostling her skull necklace and revealing the snake tattoo on her neck.

"H-how did you get down here?! And that voice, how did you get it back—" Ursula was shocked for the first time in her life, and stammered.

"Oh, don't you worry about that," Ariel giggled menacingly. "I just got my Flounders to do it for me. Didn't I?"

Flounders grinned, revealing a new set of sharpened teeth. He had grown in size and his fins were sharpened into points. His scales had also undertaken a change; they were now deep purple and black. Ariel dug into a small black seashell purse, then withdrew and threw the remnants of the contract like confetti over Ursula's lair. She shook with anger.

"Now, let's talk business."

"And why would I do any business for free?" Ursula questioned, raising one dark eyebrow.

Her voice was barely under control; in truth, she was seething.

"Oh, I don't know, maybe because King Triton, my father, will come over and completely destroy you and all your possessions if you don't?" She smiled sweetly.

Ursula gulped, then attempted to redeem herself to Ariel.

"My dear, you may have become even more cunning and disastrous than I could have ever possibly hoped—"

"Zip it. I don't have time for your compliments," Ariel countered. "First, I need you to raise me an army of men from the depths of the sea, and then, I want you to rally these men, and send them to coup d'état my husband's palace."

"Why are you doing this, child? Are you not happy with your Prince? Is he not everything you *ever* wanted?"

"Would I be asking you for your assistance to take Eric's kingdom from him if I was?"

"Good point," Ursula commented drily.

"All right, then. I'll expect the men to arrive at the castle by dawn tomorrow. The gate will be open for them. Oh yeah, and Ursula?"

"What is it, child?"

"If you're late, I'll *kill* you."

She set to work immediately after Ariel left, collecting fish brains and seasnail eyeballs, and all manner of things repulsive. This was her chance to rise further than the sea. Her chance to reap more unfortunate souls and claim their nutrition! She licked her lips, and began chanting a spell, calling on Caspian of the Sea. Yes, it was true that Ariel would get a kingdom. But she, she would gain something far more precious …

~~~~~

Now on land, Ariel trekked up to the castle in which she and Eric lived. She wore a bomber jacket, black vest, and leather leggings, and, kicking off her boots by the door, ordered a servant to clean them. She left him to it, and searched for Eric until finally, catching him in the great library, sauntered up to him and draped herself around him like a cobra. He was wearing his royal cape as always, and a vest sticky with sweat. Eric was sitting at a table so she wasn't sure if he was even wearing any trousers. Sometimes, he neglected clothing at all.

"Hey, baby," she purred, leaning forward and kissing his furry cheek.

Prince Eric's raven-black hair had grown out of control since their "happy" marriage, covering the entire lower half of his face. He looked and smelled like a black bear. It was rather grotesque, and Ariel felt disgusted even touching him, but she had a job to do. She peeked at what he had before him, and stopped. It was a map of the entire continent! Figurines were placed on it throughout, appearing battle hardened and weary.

"Hey, honey," his voice scratched.

Ariel shuddered. He was such a mess.

"What are you looking at?"

"Oh, I was just thinking about taking over the neighbouring country next week. They have resources I want."

"But we have half the number of men they do, and their kingdom is on a hilltop!"

"Hush, now, Ariel, my love. It will all be fine," he unconvincingly reassured her. "After all, the power of God is on our side! And I have you!" He turned and gave Ariel a massive, slobbery kiss, and some food from his beard stuck on her chin.

She pulled away abruptly, startling him. Ariel knew she had to change her tactics, and in order to prevent a war on two fronts, she already had the perfect concoction.

"As much as I *love* our romancing, Eric, I was going to say your idea of dominating other countries is truly wise, and so, I was wondering ..." She used her innocent eyes on Eric, and he fell for it completely, softening under her gaze.

"Anything for you, sweet pea."

"I think we should host a massive feast tonight in order to celebrate your plans and announce them!" She gushed it out, wanting to appear doting and loving.

It was easy to pretend; she had been doing so for about a year. Eric, on the other hand, was pleasantly surprised at Ariel's attitude. She had been avoiding him for a while now, and he thought she was beginning to lose feelings for him. Now, he saw her in an even purer light than before: She made him so happy.

"That's a wonderful idea! Thomas!" Eric called over his page boy. "Announce that there is to be a feast tonight, and that all men and women are to be in the banquet hall at sunset!"

"B-but Sir, sunset is in only about an hour ..."

"I DON'T CARE!" Eric slammed his fist down on the table, causing a figurine to go flying.

"Just go," Ariel told Thomas mock sympathetically, and he scampered away like a terrified little mouse.

When he left, she turned on Eric. "What was that all about?! The boy didn't do anything wrong!"

"You are wrong if you question a ruler. Besides, they are just pawns on my quest for ultimate power over the continent!"

Ariel sighed, then left Eric to his ramblings. She could find amusement somewhere else, but it would not be here with him.

~~~~~

Later, in the banquet hall, Ariel chose an appropriate moment, then rose to her feet. All the other subjects also rose, and then stared expectantly at her. Eric stayed seated, stuffing his face with more food and, no doubt, getting half of it caught in his beard.

"Be seated, loyal subjects," she commanded.

They sat.

"Now," she began, "as rulers, we would both like to thank you all for joining us, brave men and busy women."

The subjects applauded.

"To show our appreciation for everything you do for us, we would like to present 50 caskets of wine! All of you, drink until you're sick! Tonight, we celebrate our future victory against the North!"

Ariel clapped her hands twice, and dozens of straining servants hauled in 50 caskets of wine for all 100 close members of the court. Everyone applauded her, loved her. She reveled in the brief attention she'd received even after she sat down, and smiled to herself. By tomorrow, they would all still be asleep when her new men invaded, and the kingdom would be hers. Maybe she'd even get to kill a few of the men she disliked!

~~~~~

At dawn, Ariel tiptoed out of her shared bed with Eric, got dressed, went down to the barracks, and equipped herself with a sharp sword. She knew how to use it: Eric had taught her himself in order to keep her safe. If only he knew. She then went and slowly tugged on a heavy chain by the castle entrance, which raised the portcullis and opened the castle up to intrusion. She waited for about 10 minutes, and just when she began giving up hope and considering slitting everyone's throats herself, a roar erupted from the docks.

A kraken burst forth from the water, its tentacles grabbing nearby fishermen and depositing them, flailing, into the sea. It then lurched onto the land, using its suckers to grip firmly and drag its body up through the town. The sound of it was like sandpaper rubbing on itself, strained and terrible. The voice of death. Ariel relished it, encouraging the kraken, until finally, it heaved one last time, and collapsed near the castle. Then, it turned on its side and gaped its maw wide, exposing hundreds of deformed fish men.

They climbed carefully out of the kraken, avoiding its sharp teeth, and assembled in front of Ariel, bowing on their knees, eyes facing the floor submissively.

"Rise, my men!" She called to them, and they obeyed.

A commander stepped out of their ranks. He was half-hammerhead shark, half-man. His dark aura was pleasing. It resonated with Ariel's.

"What would you have us do, my lady?"

He bowed extremely low once more, openly displaying his dedication and allegiance. Ariel decided she liked him.

"Go inside the castle, and kill every single guard or resistive force you can find. I'll deal with Eric," she coldly asserted. "*Nobody* is to touch him. *Capiche?*"

"As you wish, my lady," he appeased, then began giving instructions to his men and splitting them into ranks.

"Oh, yes, and there's something I forgot to mention," she lightly added as he turned to her for the last time. "All the men are hung over and completely defenseless!"

He smiled.

"We will dispose of them and make you our rightful queen."

"Perfect," she whispered gleefully, as her army marched forth past the portcullis and into the castle.

Before she could follow them, the kraken coughed and churned. She spun to face it, as it spat out a final member.

Ursula.

"What are you *doing* here?!" She hissed at her.

Her six tentacles were gone, and instead, a fine pair of legs carried her over to Ariel. It couldn't be denied that apart from the purple hue of her skin, she was a nice-looking specimen. She waved nonchalantly at the thin air around her.

"Oh, dear. You shouldn't worry about why I'm here; I just want to fetch a few unfortunate souls for my potions!"

"Hmmm." Ariel murmured as she appraised Ursula, then announced, "All right. As long as you don't get in the way of my men or my throne, take what you wish. And try not to sell contracts like a dodgy salesman. It's just plain tacky."

Ursula narrowed her eyes in indignation, but by that time Ariel was already running into the castle, for the sounds of battle had already begun ricocheting off the walls of the courtyard. Ursula could be seen there later, reaping souls left and right like the hand of death. Ariel sought out Eric, to find he had disappeared from their bedchamber. She then went to the library: not there. Last, Ariel checked the armoury. She found him there, holding his head in his hands and groaning. He felt her approach and glanced up, at which point happiness spread across his face.

"Ariel!"

"Yes, that's me," she responded wearily.

"I was so worried about you! Look, I've been thinking about invading the North since this fighting broke out, and I don't think I'm quite ready for that. I also realized I'd rather be with you than shorten my life and potentially die fighting—"

"So you're a coward?" Ariel snorted with contempt. "You're so pathetic."

"W-what? Ariel, what do you mean?"

He fell to his knees in front of her, attempting to find something soft to grasp onto. Yet, his hands only caught air. Ariel did not wear dresses, nor was she the type to comfort weak men. She kicked him away.

"I said. You. Are. Pathetic!" She enunciated each word venomously, brandishing her sword. "Get up."

"No! I won't fight you! I know I've been a bad king, and a bad husband, but let me make it up to you!"

He stayed on his knees, as Ariel raised her sword, targeting his corrupt heart.

"A bad king? You are no king to me. You forgot about justice and sought only power: losing sight of everything around you, polluting my oceans with your oils and most of all, neglecting your duty as a husband!"

Eric cowered away from Ariel, fearful of her unpredictability for the first time. And he was right to be afraid, for after her speech she plunged her sword true into his heart, and left him dying on the floor, struggling and choking on his own blood. His death was painful and slow.

~~~~~

Two months later, the bodies had all been cleared up and disposed of, and the kingdom had become rightful property of Ariel. The hammerhead commander was her new right-hand man, and Ursula had disappeared back into the sea, in greedy excitement of all the souls she had harvested from dying men.

Ariel leaned back in the king's chair, with her beautiful crown resting perfectly on her head. She surveyed the feast hall below her with satisfaction. As usual, the neighbouring cities' kings had been sending her gifts and trinkets, attempting to win her heart.

"Oh well. It's better than bodies, right?" she asked hammerhead.

"Yes. These won't stain the flooring."

"That's what I thought, too."

An Ugly Color
By Ghoulish Tendencies

With dogs—oh, those wicked creatures—and with guns—oh those terrifying things—this vile man hunts my brethren.

With these keen ears I was given, these fine eyes I was born with, this sharp nose I possess, I have heard the fire of the rifle, seen the suffering of my kin, smelled the sickly sweet stench of blood, so much like that of rotting flowers.

In his eyes, we wolves are mere beasts, devoid of thought and emotion. In his mind, I am a monster, yes.

But the true beast, the true monster, stands before me, in the form of a huntsman. For what else could a man who kills my brothers, my sisters, my children for mere sport, be?

For I tell you, this man, this dastardly fiend, is no saint, no hero.

Was it so wrong of me, to try and satisfy the anger in my heart? Was the idea of losing this human child, this future monster, and losing this old woman, a seasoned beast, so terrible to those humans, after everything I have endured?

I feel the weight burst out of my abdomen, I see the blood on the floor; what a beautifully disgusting color it is. Even as I lie here, dying, I must admire it.

A soft, fuzzy black begins to close in on my vision; almost time now, is it?

With the last of my strength, I move my eyes slightly to look at the three figures before me.

The huntsman, the silver blade in his hand, glistening as it catches the light from a nearby window. The old woman with a fearful, but sad look in her eye. And the little girl, cloaked in that welcomed, dreaded color.

I pity them.

A man, too blind to see what is right in front of him. An old woman, fearing the death that will soon come to claim her. And the child, with her whole life ahead of her, destined to become as despicable as the rest of her kind. Tears fall from my eyes.

Because, while I may pity them, I deserve just as much pity as they do.

I could not previously recall the name of the color the girl wore around her neck, but I can now. I cannot believe I could not before, for it is a color I know very well.

Red.

It is the color I saw many times, one that came after the firing of the guns. The color of the sky at dawn. The color of life.

As my life slips away, I can vaguely feel my body shaking with ... laughter? Ah, yes. It's simply hilarious, isn't it?

Red, the color that girl wears around her, the color of life, is the color of the blood that runs in both our veins.

And yet we mourn and fight and kill each other, without even realizing the emotions we experience, the color that runs throughout us, is the same.

How hilarious our ignorance is. Why is it that I possess such keen senses, and yet have never been able to realize this?

Yes. In their eyes, I may be a monster. But if I am a monster, then they are just as much of a monster as I am.

That must surely be the truth of that detestable crimson which runs through our veins, tying us together in an unbreakable chain of grief and despair. Ah ... what an ugly life it was.

Love, Medusa
By inanidealworld

Dear People of the 21st Century,

Time really flies, doesn't it? I mean, one minute you're the prettiest girl in Athens, and the next you're just a head! I mean, a literal he— Never mind for now. I don't really want to relive it all, so I'm going to assume you know the story already. I'm only here to give you my perspective anyway.

My story is one of the first tales you hear as a kid, isn't it? During story time or world studies (preschool edition) or whatever. You know, the evil crazy lady with snakes for hair gets killed by the charming dude who wants to save his mom. Or something like that. You know they don't even tell the children *why* I have snakes for hair and all that crap? I know. It's ridiculous. I'll enlighten you, just in case that bitch Athena hasn't already told everyone. Or you've been living under a rock or something. Brace yourselves ... I thought I was pretty, and that pissed Athena off pretty bad, so she covered me in snakes and made me so ugly I'd turn people into stone. Huh. It doesn't sound so awful when you say it aloud, does it? I bet you were expecting something a heck of a lot worse than this. Like, I killed babies or something. Nah. I was just a little—okay, okay, a lot—vain. I mean, not exactly a role model for the kids but decapitation? Really?

The stories always say "Medusa was an evil monster with snakes for hair, and she turned anyone who made eye contact with her into stone." And, yeah, it's somewhat true, but they never mention the part when I didn't choose to have it that way. You would think more people would figure it out. I mean, even most of the nymphs would give you an odd look if you casually mentioned wanting snakes for hair and the ability to turn people into stone via eye contact, and they have about as much sense put together as the snakes on my head. I suppose I shouldn't be too surprised but I still feel vaguely insulted that everyone seems to think that I deserved to die. Like, yeah, I murdered a few people but I'm pretty sure it counts as self-defense given that they were all trying to kill me. Not cool, dudes.

And here's the part where they always bring up the stone dudes. Poor bastards. Every time one of them lumbers into my house that I share (with my sisters), I (or one of my sisters) tells them to bugger off, for their own safety. And, guess what? Not a single one listens. Honestly. Then they get turned into Stony McStoneface and everyone gets all pissy about how their pet hero didn't return from the evil crazy lady Medusa. You'd think there'd be at least *one* hero where they'd have the common sense that if the *monster* told them to go away—they'd leave. Just in case you're wondering? No. There isn't. Apparently heroism and intelligence do not go hand in hand. Also, given that they were all trying to kill me, I think it was very courteous of me to give them the chance to leave, even if they wouldn't take it. The buggers are so stubborn.

Oh yeah, and the house-share reminds me, that's another thing that pisses me off. They always talk about how Medusa is so evil and creepy and likes snakes (which, by the way, are actually pretty chill—I think it's the whole Slytherin deal that puts people off) but, they never mention my sisters, do they? I've already been turned into a monster and decapitated, so would it really be too much to ask for them to not spread rumours about me? Apparently so. And no one ever mentions Stheno or Euryale.

Never. Except maybe that Hesiod guy, but no one seems to have heard of him any more, so a fat lot of use that is. My point is, they are snake monsters too, and maybe all of us snake monsters should be treated equally.

Which brings me to my next point. Perseus. I get it, dude loves his mom and wants to save his kingdom or whatever. Good for him. No, I mean it. He has a better motive than most of the a-holes we get up at the house. But I wish he could have picked a less murder-y quest. Or, even one that just didn't involve killing *me*. I don't care what he does, to be honest. I'd just rather not die as a direct result of it. I'd rather not die generally really, but I can live with just not being murdered. I can roll with that. I mean, I get it, his stepdad picked the quest and they didn't have a great relationship anyway so it would've been awkward to ask, I guess, but I feel like my life is worth more than a bit of awkwardness. He could've worked something out, I'm sure. (Although, brains and heroes ...) Oh yeah, and giving my head to Athena, so she could use me for her own protection? That was low, dude. I get that I tried to kill you, but that was low.

My final point: I *still* don't understand why I deserved to die. I was ugly, sure, but I didn't think ugliness was punishable by *death* (although, by the looks of Hades, I can see why it might be). Maybe I should come to my sisters in a vision and tell them to kill all the pretty people; see how they like it for a change. On second thought, that would only feed Athena's whole "Medusa is an evil snaky bitch" campaign, which is pretty much the whole reason why I wrote this letter. Get the real story out there. Show that I'm not evil. (Well, not *that* evil.)

That about sums it all up, so, I guess, thanks for reading, and please, next time, tell the whole story.

Love,
Medusa

P.S. You may wonder how I've written this, physically speaking, as I am 1) a head and 2) dead. I wonder myself sometimes, but 1,000-odd years trapped with Athena is long enough for anyone to learn to get creative ... Oh, and just in case you're planning to ignore this letter and still tell the original version of my story, I may reconsider my threat from earlier. Understood?

Misfit

By aiessei

Once, there was a man who had fallen in love with a fairy, and for many months their love had flourished. They shared the same fondness and passion, thinking that what they had would last for a lifetime.

But the tides abruptly shifted after the fairy confessed that she cannot bear a child. The fire that once blazed with their affections for each other slowly burned out. She loved the man dearly, but still she felt him slip away, discontented with their fruitless relationship.

And one night, the man came to her, his face ridden with guilt but painted with a mask of determination. He told the fairy he loved her no longer, that there was another woman he loved. And that nothing more could be done, for that woman already bore his child.

Anger swelled within the fairy's chest. How dare he cheat on her? How dare he replace her with a mere human?

The man apologized and turned, but before he could walk away, the fairy made sure she would have the last laugh. Hatred and contempt fueled her magic, and she spoke the words of a dark oath borne out of her pain and her wounded pride. She placed a curse of eternal misfortune upon the man, his new lover, and the child in that woman's womb.

True enough, the man's wife died while giving birth to their daughter nine months later. The man grieved in the wake of his loss, but the curse wasn't quite done just yet.

The daughter grew to be a soft-hearted, obedient, and beautiful lady, though the man became weaker and weaker as time flew past. He married again after a few more years, this time to a well-heeled widow with two daughters. But before long, their riches started to wither, and the man had to leave home to seek for new sources of profit. He rode a carriage, which lost control on the road and went over a ravine …

… leaving his daughter Cinderella to the grip of her foul stepmother and sisters.

I'm quite sure you think you know how the story ended: Despite all the adversities, Cinderella wed the man of her dreams and her stepfamily wretchedly suffered from karma.

But no, that was the fairy-tale version.

Because after the death of Cinderella's father, the fairy still watched, a malicious grin on her lips. It was now the daughter's time to pay for her father's transgressions. And pretending to be a kind, fairy godmother would do just the trick.

$\sim\sim\sim\sim\sim$

The sound of galloping horses on the graveled front yard made its way through the ground-floor walls, and reached Cinderella's ears. She perked up, abandoning the fireplace she was tasked to clean. She knew who it could be, and the thought made her heart hammer wildly inside her chest.

A definitive knocking made Cinderella stand up from having sat on the hearth. She hastily removed her apron and brushed away the cinders that somehow still dirtied her ragged clothes. She brushed her hair with her fingers in an attempt to look presentable.

When she opened the door, there stood the Prince's attendant who later, after careful scrutiny, gave her a distracted look. "All the young ladies of the kingdom are requested by the Prince to try a single glass slipper," he started reading the parchment of notice he held. "For that slipper was left behind by the maiden who enraptured his Majesty's heart in last night's ball. His Majesty would marry the lady whomsoever the slipper fit."

The attendant revealed the intricate glass slipper, of the pair Cinderella lost. The slippers had been given to her by her fairy godmother, and they were the only things that didn't disappear after the clock had struck midnight. She silently thanked the fairy, seeing that none of this would've happened without her grace. And Cinderella was, of course, beyond exhilarated. At last, things were finally working out for her.

The wicked stepmother suddenly rushed down the staircase and went for the door, her high-pitched voice exaggerating welcomes after having snatched and read the notice from the attendant's hand. She shoved Cinderella to the side. And after snide comments on how disgusting she looked, discreetly ordered her to go up to her room and not make a sound.

Cinderella obeyed, but did so at her own pace, deliberately slowing her gait while heading toward the stairs. She was already halfway up when the Prince entered. She was again astonished by his breathtaking face. He smiled the most charming of smiles, the kind that would make you want to melt, the kind that would make everything else drift in the background. And his eyes, oh! How Cinderella remembered the way those azure eyes pierced through her, how they twinkled, and how they never left her face. She remembered the way his arms held her while they danced into the night, reveling in the knowledge that Cupid's arrows were fired and aimed true. For she was deeply in love with the Prince, and he with her.

Her stepsisters took a seat, and Cinderella watched as they tried on the slipper, the first one to do so being the youngest. The Prince kneeled down and held her right ankle still, and placed the slipper on her feet. It didn't fit, of course. And no matter how many ways they tried to place it in, it just won't do.

So, next was the eldest stepsister. She flirtatiously smiled at the Prince and meaningly raised the right side of her skirt up to her thigh, then lifted her smooth and flawless leg for the Prince to hold. Cinderella wanted to laugh at the trivial attempt at seduction—she knew the Prince didn't care for looks, because the heart is what captures him.

The Prince held the eldest stepsister's right foot. He sized it up, stilled it, then put the glass slipper on it.

And it fit almost too perfectly.

Cinderella was aghast, her dreams of a new life with the man she loved swiftly crumbling down. No, this couldn't be happening. It was impossible!

She went down the stairs, interrupted everyone's joyous cheers, and asked the Prince if she could try on the slipper. She ignored her stepmother's glares and just looked pleadingly at the Prince, hoping he would recognize her somehow.

But no such spark of recognition came.

The Prince gave her a pitied look but nodded. Cinderella sat down on the chair and let her feet slide into the slipper, just like how she did before.

Except this time, it didn't fit her anymore.

She tried and tried to put it on, but the slipper was two sizes smaller than her feet. She was almost crying of desperation when the Prince ordered her to stand up because he'd already found his wife.

Cinderella felt like weeping. She told the Prince that it was her, the maiden he met and danced with at the ball, and recounted everything that happened between them. She begged him to believe her, but the Prince just gave her an incredulous look and told her that it was impossible. "The lady I had fallen in love with is beautiful and pristine and is of noble birth," he had said. She was on her knees, on the verge of tears, trying to keep on explaining, but the Prince cut her off with an annoyed remark, "The maiden I danced with in the ball did not look like a grimy rag thrown into the fireplace, and was nobbut forgotten to be burned."

Every word the Prince said stung and left Cinderella appalled, making bile rise up her throat. No, this wasn't the man she met at the ball. He couldn't be.

But it was him, and Cinderella just made a fool out of herself. She dashed up the stairs and into her quaint room. She locked the door and there on her bed, surrounded by the four peeling walls of her bedroom, she cried herself to sleep.

~~~~~

Cinderella woke up the next morning with her fairy godmother sitting on the edge of her bed. She sat upright and told her the entirety of what happened. And by the end of everything she said, she wept once again.

But the fairy just peered at her, and laughed. She laughed and laughed, until her laughter turned into sinister cackles, her voice getting louder and more menacing. Her benevolent demeanor vanished in a wink. "You poor, naïve girl. You truly thought he loved you?" she asked in feigned sympathy. "You truly thought that you'd win the one you loved by dint of listless midnight dances? Even more so, you actually thought I'd aid you without conditions?"

Cinderella watched in surprised confusion as she saw the true colors of the fairy unfold before her. "But, you said you were here to help me, that you're my … fairy godmother."

Another mirthless laugh resounded from the fairy's mouth. "I was already under the impression that you'd be as dense as your cheating father, but you are quite worse." And there she retold the story of how she was wronged by Cinderella's father. How she was used, lured into thinking that he loved her, and how he'd forsaken her when he found another woman who suited his needs better. Cinderella knew her father was a good man, that he'd never be able to do that, so she accused the woman of being a liar. But fairfolk couldn't lie—they could mislead, but they do not falsify.

The fairy's eyes glinted as she narrated her tale of revenge: how she caused the death of Cinderella's mother and watched with euphoria as her father almost went mad with misery, how she jinxed her father's horses and relished in the pleasing sight of him plummeting to his death. "You are the finale to the vengeance I've so carefully orchestrated," she said and cackled with deranged glee.

It was all too much to take for Cinderella. She just had her heart broken the night before, and now the fairy whom she thought only wished her good turned out to be the vindictive rogue that caused her parents' deaths. She had never been this furious before. She felt wrath seeping through her every pore, and all of a sudden, she found herself screaming and clawing at the fairy. But the fairy just evaded her and, with magic, expressed annoyance at her audacity by slamming her hard on the wall.

Cinderella lay there, sprawled on the cold floor, crying with anger. Anger at the fairy, at her stepmother and sisters, at the Prince, at the universe, but above all, at herself. There stood the one who murdered her parents, just in front of her, but she couldn't do anything. She was helpless. Just like always.

"I shall spare you, but merely for the reason that you will suffer greater that way," the fairy said, her malevolent laughter echoing through the walls. "And do realize that you cannot have ever-afters handed down to you on a silver platter. You must toil for it—die for it, even," she snickered before disappearing in a flash, leaving Cinderella alone in her empty, cast-off house.

And that was where the fairy committed her biggest mistake.

For Cinderella might have been just human, but it was with unbridled emotions that humans often turned into the monsters they once feared and loathed.

She packed her belongings and, with what was left of her father's funds, set out to leave, promising herself that she will come back for the fairy and for all the people who once kicked her around. She would drag them through the mire, and destroy them just as they had destroyed her.

Years and years passed and Cinderella had already walked through scores of different lands. She worked, and learned, and earned. Time did nothing to temper her anger or lessen her bitterness. She was determined to get the very thing she was craving: retribution. And she was not going to let anyone get in her way.

Cinderella came upon a strange, forgotten land, and there she was drawn to the teachings of ancient black magic, thinking that only magic itself could oppose the fairy. She had sifted through books upon books, paid witches upon witches to verse her on the dark spells. She had studied long and hard, and finally, after all her persistent endeavours, she succeeded.

~~~~~

The awaited day came, and Cinderella stood in the middle of the room she had occupied for the past months. She was already through with wrapping up her things when she noticed something glistening out of the corner of her eye. She turned and saw some glass object poking out from under her bed. Curious, she reached it and her lips quivered at the sudden rush of memories after recognizing what it was.

It was the glass slipper, the one left in her keep. She couldn't remember bringing it with her, but it was here. And it gave her a pang of ire.

Cinderella faced the mirror on the bedside table, holding the glass slipper out in front of her, letting it catch the light. She remembered the time she first wore that slipper and felt like she could take on the world, that time when the Prince came searching for the owner of its other pair, and she let herself believe that things would finally be fair and reasonable for her. It felt like eons ago.

And she couldn't believe how stupid she'd been.

But now, things had utterly changed. Gone was the girl who believed in sympathy and love, for she had already witnessed the evils of the world. Gone was the girl who let people walk all over her dignity, for she was done being weak. Gone was the girl who could have given her all without expecting anything in return, for she had come to realize that life was made up of infinite quid pro quos.

Gone was the girl who was named Cinderella, the girl who cleaned fireplaces, wore stained hand-me-downs, and was always regarded with disdain. That girl was long dead.

That girl was now a lady out for vengeance, and she didn't need the assistance of a damned slipper to do it.

"Now, come home I shall," she said with a wicked smirk. And from having furiously clenched the slipper in her hand, the glass finally shattered.

A Rose by Another Name
By JaneApricity

Romeo: But why has my fair Juliet not kept,
Her oath of meeting me in night's dark shroud?
What could keep her past our appointed time?
I pray she was not caught by steps too loud.

Juliet: *(stepping out of the shadows)* You think me to be prisoner of war?
What lies! Nay, I gave myself up to them.

Romeo: *(turns, looking shocked)* My Juliet, why have you done this thing?

Juliet: What's in a name? That which we call a rose
By any other name would smell as sweet.
Even if I take your name as my own,
A Capulet I shall remain in heart.

Romeo: My angel, what is this you say to me?
What of the vows we made in nights before?

Juliet: Such vows were made when drunk with love's first glance,
Keeping such a vow will honor none here.
And dead men will not tell of broken vows. *(draws a dagger and advances on Romeo)*

Romeo: Alas, my angel is fallen from grace! *(stumbles backward, away from Juliet)*
Her love has turned to hate for her name's sake!

Juliet: My love was never a love to remain,
But by your blood I swear my name will stay!
(Romeo runs away as Capulet and Lady Capulet come from behind her)

Capulet: And have you done away with Romeo?
Pray tell you've put an end to this strange night!

Juliet: That coward of a Montague has run,
But he will yet return to sway my thoughts.
He does not know 'tis not my lips that wait,
But a dagger to pierce his coward's side!
(Exit the Capulet family, enter Romeo and Benvolio)

Romeo: *(panting heavily)* What has happened to my poor Juliet?

Benvolio: It seems infatuation passed at last.

Romeo: She tried to stab me with her own fair hands!

Infatuation has twisted to hate,
A feat I did not know until this night.

Benvolio: *(pats Romeo's shoulder sympathetically)* Perhaps she grew mad
over Rosaline?
And used your name as reason for revenge.

Romeo: I do not know what turned my lover's mind,
I only know I must revert it back.

Benvolio: There is no need for such a thing as this!
Move on, dear friend, for other girls await.

Romeo: My love for Juliet will never wane,
She must be mine, or I will fall insane! *(exits the stage)*

Benvolio: This whole affair is more than I had thought,
It seems the juice is not worth all its squeeze.
Yet Romeo is stubborn as an ox,
I must persuade this Capulet to change!
*(Benvolio walks to the other side of the stage toward the Capulet house as Nurse comes
out the door with a basket of laundry)*

Nurse: *(grumbling)* The house of Capulet is turned a-muck,
All that are here are armed and tempers flare.

Benvolio: Pray tell why Capulet is armed for war?

Nurse: Good sir, hello. I cannot say such things.
Such secrets are not mine to tell, you see.
But I can tell you this one bit, at least. *(leans in to whisper confidentially)*
It seems a love affair has just occurred,
Between two feuding homes, I'll say no more!
Save this, that Juliet appears possessed.
My lady's eyes a-fire with such a rage!

Benviolo: Then Romeo did not exaggerate!
She did come after my friend with a knife!

Nurse: You are close to the boy from Montague?
What fortune I have met you on my rounds!
Whatever this boy has done to my dear,
You must have him renounce it for her sake.
I tremble to see her with such a hate,
And see the violent stirrings in this house.
I fear what was once simply a cold feud,
May yet become a heated bloody fight!

Benviolo: Do not fear such events, Capulet nurse.
For Romeo will not do your girl harm.
His own feelings for her are not of hate,
But of a love he wishes to resume.

Nurse: What gossip I have heard from your mouth, boy!
My Juliet must have been harmed by him.
And yet I hope your gossip is no lie;
For none should wish for bloodshed in these streets!
Now leave this place, you friend of Montague,
For friends of theirs are not safe in these times.
What times are these, when things are upside down!
But there is not time for mulling around,
I must attend to Lady Juliet.
(Curtain falls, then opens to Juliet's room, where Juliet holds a bloody knife while standing over the body of Benvolio)

Nurse: Innocent angel, what have you in here?!

Juliet: This traitor lies at my feet in his blood,
For he was not the friend that he proclaimed.
He is with Montague, those slimy fiends!
Who worm into your trust with wicked lies.
No more shall they gain love or trust from me!
All shall bleed for that name I nearly took.

Nurse: To spill their blood is but to spill your own!
For feuds are fought not only from one side.
Be sure to spare your skin, not just your name.

Juliet: And now you too sound like a Montague!
You, who were like a mother these years,
Have now betrayed us to the other side!
(Juliet stabs Nurse, who falls next to Benvolio with a scream. Capulet and Lady Capulet enter at a run.)

Lady Capulet: We heard a scream! Why does your room glow red?

Juliet: *(crying)* This Montague has shed Capulet blood,
Benvolio has killed Nurse, my dear friend!

Capulet: This blow against our house we will not stand!
The Montagues will pay in their own blood!
Again they strike against our Juliet,
This silent feud shall flare into a war!

Juliet: We knew this day may come when steel would fly
Between the two great houses of our town.

Lady Capulet: No one from my house shall again be slain,
If they bear our name or serve those who do.
(Curtain falls and opens to show Romeo talking with Friar Laurence)

Friar: Perhaps it is God's will that she has left,
So that she may marry young Count Paris.

Romeo: How can it be God's will when love for her,
Burns without condition like His for us?

Friar: Take care that love does not blind you to blood,
For rumors stir of enmity that grows.

Romeo: No war shall break between our houses yet,
For one has not done the other a wrong.
The Montagues will not hasten to steel,
Nor Capulets to run the streets with blood.
(Enter Montague fighting Capulet, Lady Montague fighting Lady Capulet, Juliet fighting Mercutio)

Romeo: But what is this?! Verona is at war!
How can my friend and lover fight to death?
How can the lords and ladies brawl on streets?!
To see my fair Juliet drenched in blood!

Friar: What honor can they gain by such a fight?
You must break them apart, dear Romeo!

Romeo: My Lord and Lady Capulet, please stop!
My mother, father, put away your swords!
My friend, do not make one more move for me!
My love, my Juliet, please come to me!

Juliet: I'll not come to one of your house and name!
For shame, that you think I would stoop so low!
You may come to me if that is your wish,
But know my blade will hunger for your side!

Romeo: Is it not your lips that hunger for mine?
What of the love that we so gladly gave?

Juliet: You gave not love to me, but lies, you swine!
Your vows of passion cannot hide your name.

Romeo: *(steps closer to Juliet)* Your kiss, so soft! Is stronger than your sword,
Gentle Juliet, you will not hurt me.

Juliet: *(swipes at Romeo)* Your words, like sweetened lies, are vile to me!

Romeo: *(clasps a hand over his stomach)* And yours sting deeper than your blade
will pierce!

Mercutio: How can you let your daughter kill him thus? *(to Capulet)*
You heathens of demonic rage shall die!
For it is not the Montagues who slay,
But friends who hate Capulets in their place! *(attacks Capulet)*
*(Mercutio fights Capulet, Montague fights Lady Capulet, and Lady Montague rushes
to her son. Friar exits.)*

Juliet: And here we have the root of all my pain! *(kills Lady Montague)*
She will not bring him back to life and health.

Romeo: *(weakly)* Worse than any pain of the flesh is this,
To see my two great loves in conflict now.
Death would be welcome compared to this scene,
Of Montagues versus my Juliet. *(dies)*

Montague: Your lust for blood has led to war, my lord!
Perhaps your own will satisfy your thirst. *(kills Lady Capulet)*

Capulet: *(screams in fury and kills Mercutio)* If every person of Verona falls,
Perhaps that price will pay a debt of war.

Montague: You only make the debt grow larger sir,
And you will pay the greatest price of all. *(doesn't notice Juliet coming up behind him
as he steps forward and kills Capulet)*

Juliet: The Capulets will pay no more today! *(stabs Montague from behind)*
(Enter Paris and the Friar as Juliet stands alone in the street littered with corpses)

Paris: Juliet, an angel standing in death!
What has taken place in these bloody streets?!

Friar: A feud too long in standing exploded,
My lord, but one from these houses still stands!

Juliet: Prince Escalus will banish me, I know.
But he banishes me from a city,
That my kin died to make pure once again!
No more will lies of Montague defile,
And kill, as they killed my cousin Tybalt.

Paris: My Juliet, whatever have you done?
Your hands are wet with blood of those who've died!

Juliet: My hands may be defiled; my name is pure.
A rose I still am, a rose I'll remain.
Thorny and blood-red, but sweet all the same.
(curtain falls)

Dragon's Vengeance
By MochaLiterati

The vast blue sky began to darken, the sun setting as smoke billowed from the once large and lush forest. Towering trees that had fed the blaze were now ashes, the fire claiming the few that still stood, along with the lower plants. The once haunting screams were now gone, burned corpses strewn across the scorched ground, their looks of terror immortalized on their faces.

Murderers.

A jagged mountain a distance away gave the large dragon a bird's-eye view of the carnage that he had caused. He had not intended to claim as many victims as he had, only chasing a small group of hunters. The group of men who had caused his ire had fled into the forest, making a fatal mistake that ended up bringing innocent elves and other creatures into the destruction that was meant for them.

He. Did. Not. Care.

Perhaps it would be a message to other elves and men, along with those dwarves, to leave him alone.

Alone.

That's what he was now, wasn't it? Alone? Yes, yes it was. And it was all the fault of men. Men and their stupid ideals of what a monster was, of what, or who, needed to die, and what would happen if they succeeded. They would be showered with praise, jewels, and more women than they desired. How would they feel if they lost the few things they truly cared for?

As the sun disappeared below the mountains, so did the anger broiling in his stomach, which was then replaced by an aching sense of loneliness. It was a rare, uncomfortable, hurting feeling that usually fueled the anger, giving him the rage to cause his destruction.

Now, it only left him tired.

Spreading his massive wings, the large firedrake began the journey back to his home, letting out a thunderous roar as he did so. Those who heard it shuddered at the anger and pain it spoke of. What could have happened, to make such a terrifying creature so pained?

The smell of the cave had only gotten worse since he had left, the blood having now dried from on the floor, along the walls … everywhere.

Including the golden body.

He moved slowly, hating himself even more as he moved closer to the unmoving Cold-Drake. She looked so peaceful in death that he almost thought that she was sleeping. But as he pressed his head against her, her already cold scales were frozen, no thudding heartbeat.

He should have been here, protecting his defenseless mate and their clutch. The multiple wounds and lacerations on her form showed how hard she had fought, how hard she had tried to protect the clutch, but ultimately had fallen. Men called him a monster, an uncaring beast whose only concern was for gold and jewels. But they were wrong. His mate and clutch had mattered more to him, and an instinctive need kept him close to cave, becoming paranoid after he found human hunters laying traps. He forbade his mate and recently hatched draclings from leaving the cave.

But eventually, prey nearby had become scarce, and he needed to go out farther each time to find enough to feed his family. After time passed, he decided that he would go out once more, and then take the hatchlings on their first hunt, so they could learn to defend themselves.

It would seem it was too late for that now.

Lifting his head, he looked toward where the dead hatchlings would be cu— where were they?

Where was his clutch?!

Where were they!?

Whipping his head around, he realised that the smell of decay had covered another, foul smell.

Orcs.

A horrifying snarl formed its way on his face. A roar reverberated throughout the cave, mingled with a scream of absolute rage. How dare they!? HOW DARE THEY!? How dare those pathetic excuses for living beings even think to take the bodies of his children?! The anger he had lost before now returned full force, the cave shaking as he stormed out of the cave, gaze fixing on dark land far away.

Mordor.

He had been gone for too long. The orcs had already returned to Mordor, using the bodies of his children for whatever sick twisted idea Sauron had. As he took out his rage on his home, his muddled mind came up with an extremely risky solution.

Align with the opposing force.

But that begged the question: Who was the opposing force?

It doesn't matter. All that matters is that the orcs will die. All of them.

It probably wouldn't work. He was a dragon after all; they would most likely try to kill him before aligning. And he still felt the rage at man for slaughtering his family. Why should he align himself with them?

Destroying the ring is the only way to kill them all. And then, when their guard is down, you can get revenge.

True. And the large dragon lay in the middle of his destruction, pondering over this idea long into the night, even into the sun's rising. It was when the sun's rays hit his eyes that the tired dragon decided he would go through with his idea, albeit a possible mistake he would end up regretting. As the dust, ashes, and dirt blew around him as he took off toward one of the cities, animals and others alike hiding in his shadow, he realised something. After his rage had finally been calmed, he noticed that he felt nothing. All his anger was gone, leaving him feeling empty and hollow. It seemed most of his emotions died with his mate and clutch. He didn't even react to the few arrows that were shot at him by the reckless and idiotic hunters. No attempts to burn them, no attempt to grab them and carry them into the sky where they would find themselves falling to their death. Nothing. He felt absolutely nothing.

... well, he did feel some joy at the look of shock and horror on the hobbit's face, as he realised that a dragon everyone thought dead was still alive.

Hail to the Prime
By NitroStation

It had been many millennia since Megatron last felt cuffs chewing into his wrists, replacing the weight of gauntlets and barely distracting from the tension cracking his gears, the hot humiliation rushing through his otherwise starved fuel lines. Even if his HUD was still working, it would only be a dull imprint in the gloom of his cell. As well as the rust forming a thin layer over his scarred lips, the constant clink of his chains stopped him from sleeping; the more he struggled, the more energy he lost, the more he suffered.

Megatron knew exactly how close Optimus came to offlining him the day of his capture, still flinched from the stinging ghost of a blade cleaving through protoform, cables, wires; already soaked in energon before finally exiting his body in a fountain burst of his blood. That never happened, of course, not with a coward like Optimus wielding the killing blow, but Megatron could see the scene playing out clearly enough in the Prime's optics; the glass surface reflecting only a fraction of the fire that otherwise would have melted right through. Even he had never wanted to kill a bot more intensely than Optimus did at that moment. The only thing that spared him for a cell rather than a coffin was the summons of surrender, his ranks rippling with equal parts desperation and desertion. With their leader down, a flick of the servo away from losing his helm, what else could the Decepticons do? What else could Megatron have expected them to do, other than what they were all best at: betrayal?

In a way, he should have been proud of them. They saw his weakness, and knew they were doomed if they stayed with him.

Part of his spark hoped it would perish right there, in Cybertron's basement, with at least his dignity left intact if nothing else. But, once again, he underestimated the Autobots. They came for him eventually; a uniform scuff of peds against floors trudging through the sludge of his consciousness. He might have recognised his jailers if he had any will to raise his helm, might have received guilty glances down from ex-Decepticons now hauling their disgraced warlord before their new master. Metal grating dissolved to hard steel scraping against his crumpled knees, and flickering plasma lamps carved into the cavern walls paled against the glare from the open council chamber doors ahead. Not even his optics clamped closed could protect the lenses from the light pouring on him. Though he was blinded for now, his audio receptors were as sharp as they'd ever been. No applause greeted him, only a chorus of harsh intakes and the uncertain creak of bots debating with themselves, whether they should run for the nearest exit or stay and watch the show.

He lurched to a stop, limp as a puppet, and colours bled into the cracks of his vision. Red, blue, then streaks of grey pooling in the hard outline of Optimus's frame sitting leagues above him on a familiar throne made out of mangled struts, a prison of Megatron's own making stolen from his own fortress in Darkmount. He'd only notice the two mechs flanking either side of him much later, each of them struggling to look down at the shuddering pile of rust thrown at their peds. For now, all Megatron could see was the hatred etched into every curve of Optimus's face, pulling taut at his cables and leaking from the very core of his spark.

Seeing the anger leaking from his composure made Megatron smile like he was cutting a scar into his faceplate. He looked forward to seeing just how far he managed to push Optimus into this, what kind of pathetic sentence the Prime would have ready for him. "That throne doesn't suit you, Prime. Far too ... uncomfortable for someone like you," Megatron told him, almost recoiling from how foreign his voice sounded after escaping the gauntlet of his broken vocaliser.

If Optimus was at all surprised by what weeks in a dungeon had stripped from his nemesis, he hid it well. "Someone like me ... who now leads your entire army." His voice was fringed with a ceaseless snarl, torn to ragged strips by his gritted denta. Megatron was reminded of feral Insecticons, but he'd gutted enough of those in the past to not be scared of a lone soldier clicking its maw at him. "And now has you, Unicron's own herald, pleading for—"

Megatron's laughter spread like a tumour from his vocaliser, and soon burst out to interrupt and shove aside the digit pointing down at him, accusing him directly of a thousand crimes and more not even Optimus could remember. "'Unicron's herald?'" Megatron scoffed, rolling his optics and missing the flare of rage going off in Optimus. "I'm almost flattered, Prime, but—"

Then, his helm was ringing, mouth full of stale energon dribbling onto the floor as he coughed past the flood of his own organs trying to escape. His face had gone numb where Optimus struck with his palm, but soon stings fit like a gauze over his grimace and coated his glossa from where he bit into it.

"Do not interrupt me," Optimus stated to Megatron's own choice glare, flexing the digits on his hand and still wielding it like a weapon. The cables in his servos looked ready to snap, searching for any excuse to throttle someone's spark.

"Point ... taken," Megatron groaned, spitting out what he couldn't bear to swallow and aiming for any unfortunate bystanders. There was certainly a wealth of them around him, the entire planet gathered to see the end of his era. He was smiling to himself again through bloody denta, knowing Prime's new era would hardly be any better for them, and barely listening to Optimus waxing on and on to vent out whatever was burning in his spark, amplified by the Matrix hanging heavy from his chest on chains as thick as the ones around Megatron's limbs. How ironic; the aim of the war had been to pry that holy trinket from Prime's dying spark, and there it was dangling right before him like a sparkling's toy. If he could even move his servos to grab for it, he wouldn't fit more than a few digits around the handles before a hail of plasma bullets burned away what rust spared his plating.

Whether or not Optimus knew how Megatron's tied claws itched to stab through his neck, break apart the links that tethered him to Primus, he seemed to enjoy the impatience starting to bubble and simmer in the warlord's trembling frame. The Matrix would sway on his chest, close enough for Megatron to buffet his choked vents against it, as if daring him to lunge for it and make a dead fool of himself. Even as Megatron stayed still, defiant even while kneeling, there was an undercurrent of barely muffled snorts and barks of laughter rippling through the audience. Whatever the verdict of this trial, this bad comedy Autobots seemed to have developed a taste for, it was ultimately irrelevant. All Optimus wanted to do was drag out the humiliation, like a razor across Megatron's throat. Impressive, even to his victim.

Not soon enough, Prime eventually tired of teasing him and snapped his spinal strut upright, snatching the Matrix up out of even desperate reach. "I won't waste time with formalities you don't deserve, Megatron. A century ago, I might have spared you.

A millennia, I might even have released you." Even the crowd knew to stay silent now; all optics flitting between Prime and prisoner, waiting for the tension to break and grow nuclear. They seemed to be expecting something that Megatron had not prepared for, as he watched the anticipation spoiling the somberness of their expressions.

Around that same point, he noticed the yellow mech by Optimus's right side, and the blue steel sword bigger than his entire body held out in his hands.

Megatron forced himself to laugh and ignore the omen openly glinting at him, trying to fit the memory of the awkward, mumbling, near-useless data clerk he'd so easily managed to manipulate so long ago into the frame of this new, downright dangerous Optimus. It only barely worked, because Orion and Optimus were not two sides of the same coin like he'd always assumed. He wouldn't have been surprised if one had killed the other.

"And what has changed since then?" Megatron asked, with a tone like a sire generously honouring his child. "What injustice of Primus has finally broken your ties to something as pathetic as morality?" He already knew the answer, allowed himself the same grin he wore when he took the one life more precious to Optimus than all of the Thirteen combined.

But the grin only had a slightly shorter lifespan than himself; it dissolved like steel in acid when his frame collapsed under the weight of Optimus's ped kicking out and crushing hard, mercilessly hard, against his chest. The sword appeared from nowhere, snatched from the burden of the yellow mech and now an inch away from piercing Megatron's helm but, that wasn't what made the warlord utterly speechless for the first time since he'd met the mech now bolting him to the floor.

"My wife ... my sparkmate is *dead*." If looks could kill, Optimus wouldn't have even needed a blade. He was unhinged, disconnected from any will aside from that of his own fury burning out of control, a wildfire born from his own spark. Not even the Autobots knew who this beast was, the one who had Primus's own voice in his head and who had led them into the uncertain light of a new, almost impossible dawn— one littered with corpses on both sides.

Fear of death left Megatron long ago at the same moment he realised he'd never have to face Primus, knowing he was already destined for eternity in Unicron's domain, but there was something far more primal, more complex than fear that made him dread meeting Optimus's glare. He would not just die today; if Optimus succeeded, he would be annihilated from all existence.

Megatron gulped, ragged, each shudder of his neck cables forcing the sword point to slice into them. The floor underneath his scrap heap of a body was quickly becoming a crust of half-dried energon and coolant he couldn't afford to waste through the sweat and tears now streaming from him. "And you think ... you can trade my spark for Elita One's?"

Among many of the mistakes he'd made concerning Optimus, saying her name aloud was the last one he had a chance to make. "No. Yours is not worth even a fraction of hers."

The pressure of the blade lifted, the hilt pulling back and bending beneath the force of Optimus's grip. Reflexively, Megatron's vents filled with metallic air, his last breath before Optimus speared through his spark chamber.

Chest armour fell apart like cardboard, shattered chamber casings became shrapnel, and his bleeding neck fell limp under the weight of his helm. His vocaliser didn't screech, only dribbled a stream of broken static and seized in a loop of gurgling croaks. Though the core was split apart, his spark still sizzled and crackled around the razor draining away its energy, and the glow faded much more slowly than the light in his optics.

Optimus let go of the hilt, didn't bother pulling the sword from Megatron's body even when his spark finally stopped sputtering like a broken circuit, even when the frame stopped twitching in the pool of energon starting to lick against the peds of the nearest bystanders, or even when they noticed the macabre glee filling the Prime's faceplate.

The dead warlord's optics stared blankly ahead, dull red glass reflecting the yellow mech running off down a shielded hallway, barely muffling sobs from behind his hands. Optimus didn't even notice how he fled, paid no mind to the white mech on his left following after him. With the energon-spattered Matrix torn from around his neck and swinging from his hand, he returned to his throne and the thorned seat that seemed to accommodate him more and more each day. Like a sack of springs Megatron was dragged away, with grinding clanks and blue streaks staining the floor in his wake. It was more ceremony than he ever allowed Elita One on the battlefield, and more than he deserved. Optimus wouldn't even have him recycled, melted down for mindless scrap. Let him join the piled corpses of his other officers, the ones he had shot only days before.

And for those who disagreed, those who thought death and cleansing of the ranks wasn't necessary, he was more than happy to make a new pile just for them.

Pursuit

By zuko_42

"You all right?"

"Yes, Inspector."

"Good."

She snuck a glance at the Inspector from the corner of her eyes as the car slowed. While she'd spent the last 12 years growing up, he'd spent them growing old; his burly physique had diminished to a sallow leanness, and the hands gripping the wheel were not as steady as they used to be. Still, she suspected that much of the grey hair on his head and the lines on his face came from the case they were now so near to closing.

This case had been his ruin, and no wonder.

The man whom the police had dubbed Mr. Hide-and-Seek (and whom the Inspector liked to call Mr. Hyde) had, for the past five years, led them in endless circles all over England. Nobody knew who he was. Nobody knew where he was from. Nobody even knew if he had an accomplice. The only solid information the police had on him was that he was a man, and that he had blue eyes.

Five years, no leads, no suspects—it was enough to deter a lesser man than the Inspector, she thought with mixture of pride and frustration. Dizzying amounts of cheques had been forged, near impossible to detect; witnesses couldn't agree to what Mr. Hyde looked like, except for the colour of his eyes. What made it all the more confusing was that the man was known to disguise himself as people of varying ages and heights, and at times as women.

Five years and nothing to show for it. The Inspector, having been in charge of the case, willingly shouldered the brunt of the criticism, at his own risk. The entire fiasco was the reason why he'd been demoted from Superintendent, to Chief Inspector, and finally to the post of Inspector that he'd held when she first met him.

Five years was a long time to be on the run, though. Mr. Hyde had grown careless— or afraid. Either way, he made some stupid mistakes along the way, and now, she and the Inspector were finally, *finally,* about to close this case for good.

The car rolled to a stop, and the two of them stepped out. Her breath misted, fanned, dissipated, as she hurried after the Inspector. "Sorry," he said, looking over his shoulder; he slackened his pace for her benefit.

"I can keep up," she said quickly.

The Inspector raised a questioning eyebrow—*can* you? he seemed to ask. She nodded. He resumed the brisk walk he'd first adopted, and she increased the speed and length of her strides to match his. Presently, an abandoned railway station emerged from the fog, looming over them, the crumbling remnants of a time that was, in fact, not so long ago. It stood grey and dreary and forbidding under the snowy sky.

She sucked in a sharp breath as the Inspector retrieved a gun from his coat. "It's necessary," he said. She didn't comment; it was a while before he spoke again. "You know, we might've finished this long ago if Frederick agreed to help." He led her into the station, and the darkness that descended upon them was palpable. She wrinkled her nose at the musty smell. "Watch your step," he warned.

She avoided tripping on a fallen lamppost just in time. Deciding it was in their best interests not to blindly wander around in the dark, she flicked on her torch and let it shine into the swirling eddies of fog.

"He was having a bad time then," she said. "His mother just died, his father lost his money …" Her voice sounded hollow, her words echoing through the cavernous halls. She lowered her voice. "Last I heard from him he said he'd gone abroad to make his fortune." And he'd called off their engagement—but that last part she kept to herself. It was with an effort that she stopped herself from reaching to the letter she always kept about her person, close to her heart.

"He could've joined the police like he'd always intended," the Inspector said. The disappointment in his voice mirrored her own. "He could've *made his fortune* with us." Then after a bit he added, "You two were a good team."

She didn't answer. It was something she, too, agonised over again and again, wondering why he didn't accept the Inspector's offer. Being a detective was what he'd always wanted since they were both children. And yet, 12 years later, here *she* was living *his* dream.

The Inspector jumped off the platform and held out a hand to help her onto the tracks; she accepted his help for old times' sake. She couldn't help looking up and down the line, pricking her ears for the nonexistent sound of a train. … The fear didn't leave her, though she knew these tracks were no longer in use. To distract herself, she looked up. It was a gloomy afternoon, she noted, the sky laden with clouds that seemed as though they might burst any second. But it was sufficiently light enough for them to dispense with her torch. She switched it off and shoved it into her coat.

"Look."

She followed the Inspector's finger with her eyes. "I see it." Footprints shone alongside the track, clear on the dusting of snow on the ground, heading north. "Fresh," she observed; the Inspector agreed. It was a reasonable deduction, since it had just stopped snowing while they were pulling up at the station.

They followed the tracks for nearly 10 minutes without incident, until they spotted a trail of blood overlapping the footprints. "Must've caught himself there," the Inspector said, jerking his thumb at a break in the line where a cruel jag of metal stuck out. She shivered. The red upon the white filled her eyes.

After that the two were careful to maintain a safe gap between them and the tracks as they pursued the prints. "He's limping," she said. It was a pointless remark, made more for breaking the horrible silence than anything else. "The spacing of the prints is irregular."

"Not surprising, really." The Inspector's voice was chilling, even more so than the sudden wind that whipped past them. "Drat," he snapped as his hat was snatched off his head and into the air. He gave it a cursory glance, not stopping once. She gave it a sorry look over her shoulder—it looked so forlorn, sitting atop the snow in the middle of an abandoned railway—before running off after the Inspector. The hat could wait. They had more pressing business to attend to.

It was clear that they were getting closer. She couldn't decide if she was excited, or nervous; likely both, she thought. There was evidence of a fall somewhere; their quarry had lurched back to his feet with some difficulty before going on. By now, the snowing had resumed, little flakes dancing around the pair (she stuck out her tongue to catch one). Fortunately, it was still a light fall, not heavy enough to hinder their progress. It made a melancholy picture, the clear snow, the station slowly disintegrating into the background until it disappeared from view, and the rusted metal rails leading to nowhere in particular ...

The Inspector stopped rather abruptly.

She nearly fell, but he flung out an arm to steady her. "Thanks." He didn't reply, instead staring straight ahead. They were here, she realised. Her eyes widened. This was it. Five years of hardship was nearly over. A tall figure, his back to them ... he swayed on the spot before crumpling to the ground. The snow around him, particularly near his left leg, was glazed red.

"At last," the Inspector breathed. He strode to the body, she at his heels.

She examined him clearly, curious to behold at last, in person, the face of the man who'd caused them so much trouble. Mr. Hyde appeared to be about her age, maybe older. His cap was pulled low over his face; the Inspector snatched it off, allowing them to observe him with greater ease. Without it, she could see his hair: light, straight, and badly taken care of, the jagged ends reaching up to his collar. A ratty little moustache adorned his upper lip. The Inspector poked it suspiciously with a gloved finger.

Mr. Hyde's eyes flew open at the touch—clear, startlingly blue, and *unmistakable*. She gasped and stumbled back. Her mouth opened and shut like a goldfish; she felt the blood drain from her face. She had to remind herself to breathe.

"What?" the Inspector demanded. She swallowed, unable to articulate. The man at their feet began to sit up, one hand clutching his leg, and the Inspector immediately snapped his attention back to him. He trained his gun to the man's skull. "Hands above your head!" he said harshly.

The man complied in silence. He didn't seem much concerned with his imminent imprisonment; instead he was staring at *her* with an inscrutable look on his face. Breathing deeply, she forced herself to calm down. Then, she reached out and ripped the moustache from his face; it came away easily in her hand. He made no move. He and the Inspector eyed her as she opened her mouth to speak, at first no sound escaping her lips—and then—

"Fatty," she whispered. The Inspector made a choking noise and dropped his gun.

The man on the ground smiled sadly. "You were always the one to see right through me, Bets."

The snow swirled dismally around them. After a brief hush, Inspector Jenks pulled himself together, picked up his gun, and aimed it once more at the man; there was a slight tremor in the Inspector's voice when he spoke.

"Frederick Algernon Trotteville, you are under arrest."

Striking Back

By ThatOneFangirl108

I will command respect.
I will be feared.
I will no longer be their laughingstock.
I.
Am.
The.
Tiger.

Tigress willed herself to go harder, stronger, and quicker. One more jab, one more punch, until the words melt away, until she truly felt nothing.

Weak.
Runt.
Skinny.
No good.
Worthless.
Terrible.

These were just a few words used to describe her by those she called her friends a few months ago: the other members of the "Furious Five," an elite Kung Fu group.

But she would overcome them all. She would be the Dragon Warrior. She would beat not just them, but all of China, if needed, to become truly powerful. A master, like Shifu or Oogway. A true master of body and mind.

She didn't care who got in her way. She would destroy them, just like they did to her pride, her respect, her reputation. She'd been loved, respected by Shifu, even though he'd been a strict father and teacher. But after Monkey began to tease her ...

Everything went south.

She reverted back to her personality at Bao Gu, before Shifu had taken her under his metaphorical wing. She was angry, fierce, untamable. Shifu had banished her to here, this Ironwood tree forest away from the home of the Furious Five, when she nearly killed Monkey.

But she'd go back.

She would take revenge on the living, not mourn the dead.

"One ... more ... punch ..." Tigress panted, punching the tree as many times as she could until her shoulders blazed with wildfire. She sat against the tree, looking out for any unsuspecting prey, and found a few bunnies.

They're innocent townspeople! Tigress first thought, but her hunger caved her in, and she chased down and caught the two slowest bunnies, eating them, as she watched the other three flee the scene.

I am a monster.
I don't care.

Tigress ran after the other three, catching them and eating them alive. She was fast. She was strong.

She was a true Dragon Warrior.

She'd beat Viper's agility, Crane's height, Mantis's speed, and Monkey's ... comedy. What was he there for?

Why was *he*, of all people, able to get to her? Why could he manipulate her feelings like no one else could? Why did *his* rejection matter?

She didn't like him, that's for sure.

"Now what ..." Tigress whispered, and turned to a tree, and began to punch it, again and again and again. She wouldn't stop. She wouldn't give in. Her weakness wouldn't exist anymore. She would be strong. She would be *mighty*.

She would be the raging tiger.

Tigress stopped, and turned, and began to run through the forest, willing herself to go faster, imagining Viper next to her, her slim body gliding through the grass. She must beat the Viper.

She soon collapsed, and began to sleep, dreaming of the tower that they lived in, no, not just the tower, all of China, falling to her, as she stood triumphant. She smiled in her dream. It would be very soon that it came true. It would be very soon that it was a nonfiction story, a legend of a mighty tiger showing no mercy to opposition, who brought China heart-first into every battle.

She would not be moved. She would be a rock, like the Ironwood trees she slept among.

She would prevail at any cost.

"Shifu! Shifu!" Monkey yelled, storming into his study room. Shifu looked back at Monkey, his eyes ablaze with anger and rage.

"WHAT?!" Shifu yelled, and Monkey looked even more frightened.

"It's her ... it's Tigress ... she found us ..." Monkey said, and Shifu, as if on cue, heard her mighty roar, and Monkey's eyes widened.

"HOW DID SHE FIND US?!" Shifu yelled, even louder, before going downstairs. He was greeted with Viper, nearly dead, and Crane in Tigress's paw. Tigress looked at Shifu, and her normally amber eyes turned red and black, evil and fiery.

"TIGRESS! What are you doing?" Shifu said, when suddenly, Tigress threw Crane aside, and Shifu heard bones crack, and looked over to see Crane's neck broken. Shifu suddenly felt himself being lifted, and looked to see Tigress, anger that Shifu was feeling being reflected in her eyes.

"I. Am. The. Tiger," Tigress said, and threw Shifu aside, and he felt himself hit a piece of wood in the wall, and fell with a thud.

"I am untamable. I am passionate. I am unstoppable. Soon, all of China will be mine," Tigress said, her red eyes almost seeming to have bright orange flames within them, they were so intense and burning with anger.

"YOU ALL DOUBTED ME. THIS IS YOUR REVENGE!" Tigress yelled, and kicked Shifu into the next room. He felt his strength waning, and soon, he felt death upon him.

"I will not be moved. I will not be shaken. I will not be scared anymore," Tigress said, and grabbed Monkey by the tail.

"If you'd wanted me to stop, I would have if you'd have said something, I-I swear!" Monkey said, but Tigress didn't believe him, and tossed him aside. She went to the Jade Palace, and climbed the wall, grabbing the Dragon Scroll, and fell into the Pool of Sacred Tears. She brushed herself off, and opened the scroll.

It was blank.

Her whole life, all she had trained for ... was for a blank, empty, reflective scroll, when she realized what it meant.

The power was within her.

Her mind went back to Shifu training her as a child, to how she was regarded as terrifying, regarded as a monster.

Not anymore.

She was regarded as a killer.

She *killed* them.

She dropped the scroll, and backed away, fearing herself, her newfound power, her emotionless state as she had just *murdered* not only the Furious Five, but Shifu. Her trainer, her adoptive father. The one who had taught her everything.

She wasn't supposed to care about this.

She ran away, far from the Jade Palace, never to be seen again.

Red Riding Hood
By calamityneko

I drew Red Riding Hood—in an alternate universe where she took a knife from her grandmother's kitchen—to end the life of the wolf that ended her grandmother's. Strong and witty enough, she killed the wolf and took the corpse back home to turn it into a trophy, a coat. Now, she's a known criminal for taking lives of wolves, trying to make them go extinct. If she can, that is.

I used copic markers, vifart hot pressed paper, white gelly roll pen, and copic multiliners.

RED RIDING HOOD

BY CALAMITYNEKO

TWIST FATE: BH6

TwistFate: BH6
By Jessica Sunderland (To-Yo)

SNOW WHITE

BY ALISSA "ALICHEE" REN

Snow White
By Alissa "Alichee" Ren

She's gonna break the poor lady's back.

HOOD
BY SARAH HULTON (ACTUALLYSARAHART)

Hood
By Sarah Hulton (ActuallySarahART)

The general idea is that Red ends up hunting the wolf when she grows older.

WHO IS THE FAIREST ONE OF ALL?   BY MAJA ROGOCKA (MAYO) (MAJKAROGO)

Who Is the Fairest One of All?
By Maja Rogocka (Mayo) (Majkarogo)

I've painted Snow White as an evil queen. I had so much fun doing it, and I learned some new things.

Die drei kleinen Schweinchen
By Largoyzniaar

Variation where the Three Little Big Pigs live as bandits. Strong villains, real rogues, they make the rules and bully the others.

One day, they decided to leave home and on their way, discovered a castle crowned by towers. They entered and noticed that nobody lived there.

So, they took over the fortress, and now no one dared to attack them, even great knights and impressive warriors.

Until the day when a young wolf came: He was the castle's owner. Furious at being driven out of his home, he left without uttering a word, hoping to find a solution.

On his way, he met a traveling merchant who sold magic items. The wolf bought a magic bellows and returned to the castle.

He breathed into the bellows and one of the towers fell to the ground.

The youngest pigs, hearing that weird noise, came out of the fortress to see what happened. When the wolf saw them, he blew once again and the other tower crashed on the two bullies.

The third pig was going to join his brothers. He couldn't find them. He looked for them and walked around the castle. The wolf took this opportunity to enter the castle and lock the door.

The rogue pig saw him. He wanted to break down the door, but his ax was inside! So, he decided to enter through the chimney.

The wolf heard him climb out onto the roof and understood his plan. He prepared a cooking pot and put it on the fireplace; the pig didn't see it and fell in.

The wolf hurried to close the lid.

Since then, no one has heard from the Three Big Pigs. Maybe because the wolf ate them for his dinner ...

Tools: Spice tea, mechanical pencil, watercolours, colourpencils.

DIE DREI KLEINEN SCHWEINCHEN   BY LARGOYZNIAAR

Darkest Knight
By Nick Wong (Nocluse)

"You see, madness, as you know, is like gravity. All it takes is a little … push."
—The Joker

The Joker finally did it. He killed Jason Todd. That was all it took to push Batman over the edge. The immensely guilt-ridden Batman had turned his sorrow and regret into pure rage, something the Joker didn't expect. Batman would become a cruel, ruthless vigilante, and made it his ultimate goal to kill the Joker.

In his furious rampage to find and kill the Joker, Batman had killed hundreds, if not thousands, of men and women who stood in his way. The city was against him. He was a fallen hero, deemed a mass murderer, and a madman. As a result of his actions, Gotham turned into a police state to control the situation. Batman would become Gotham's ultimate villain.

The Joker didn't like that. He missed the old Batman—the one who would give his life to protect the people of Gotham. He missed the days when he would have "fun" with Batman, toying around with him and watching him suffer. They were supposed to be destined for each other.

But now, things weren't right. The Joker realized that this "Batman" wasn't the Batman that he loved.

He had to stop this. He wanted the city to revert to what it was before, not this hellhole police state that Batman inadvertently created. He wasn't going to run away anymore. He would face Batman, and this time, there would be no more fun and games. He would kill Batman, as much as he didn't want to.

But he had to. He never would have imagined it. For once he, the Joker, had to save Gotham.

DARKEST KNIGHT

BY NICK WONG (NOCLUSE)

The Hero's Rulebook
By Melissa Wang & Tiffany Wang (Mint-Glass)

Much sweat and many tears were shed while working on this Twist Fate contest entry. We tried our best to make original content, especially in story and plot.

Read from left to right, up to down.

THE HERO'S RULEBOOK   BY MELISSA WANG & TIFFANY WANG (MINT-GLASS)

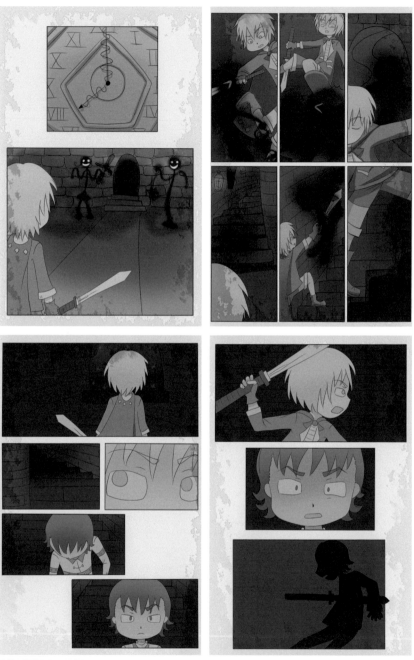

THE HERO'S RULEBOOK

BY MELISSA WANG & TIFFANY WANG (MINT-GLASS)

THE HERO'S RULEBOOK   BY MELISSA WANG & TIFFANY WANG (MINT-GLASS)

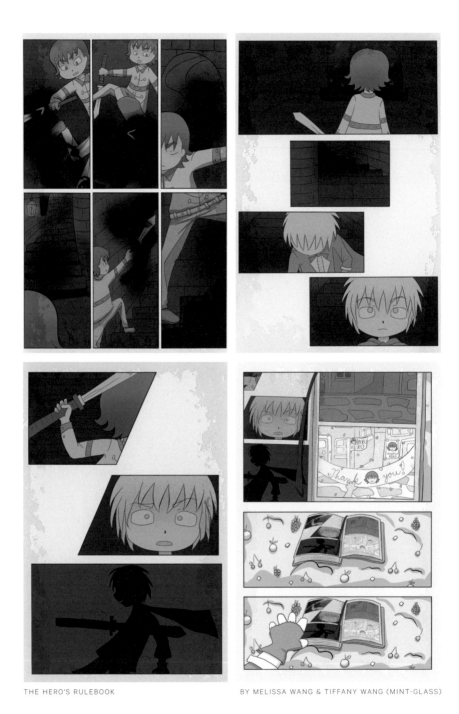

THE HERO'S RULEBOOK

BY MELISSA WANG & TIFFANY WANG (MINT-GLASS)

THE HERO'S RULEBOOK   BY MELISSA WANG & TIFFANY WANG (MINT-GLASS)

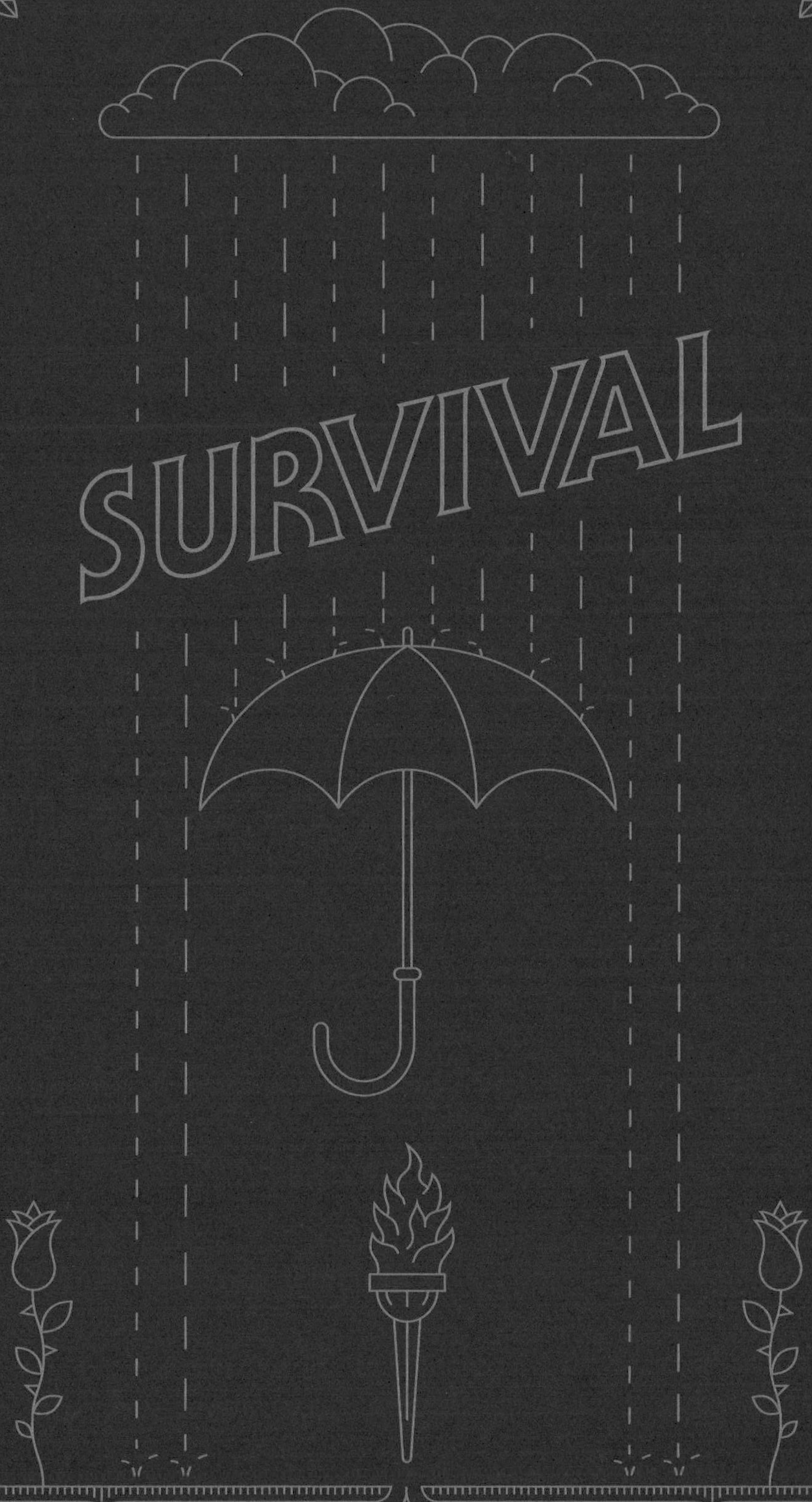
SURVIVAL

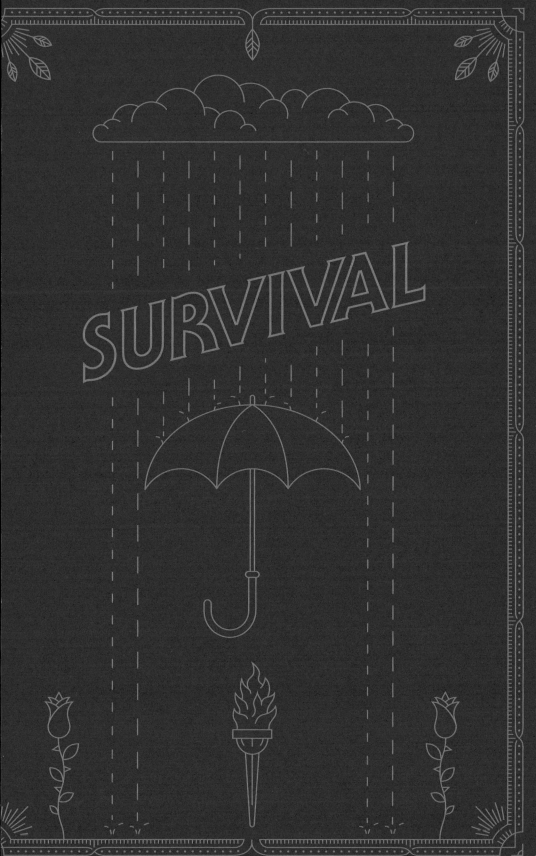

A Different Game
By AfterSangster

President Everdeen sat in the leather chair behind her desk, twirling a lock of her dark hair between her fingers as she brainstormed the details for the 74th Hunger Games. Her gray eyes were unfocused, her mind far away in the section of land that had been marked off for this year's Games.

When there came a knock on the door, Katniss's eyes narrowed and she straightened. When her posture was suitably presidential, she pressed the button on the left side of her desk. Across the room, the broad, mahogany doors swung wide.

"Ma'am, there's been another raid on supply drops in the forest outside District 12," the old secretary in the doorway announced, his voice wavering as he met President Everdeen's frigid gaze.

Katniss smiled at his uncomfortable stance, half inside and half outside her office. "Please, come in. Take a seat."

By his expression, one would have thought that Katniss had proclaimed his death sentence. The secretary made his way to one of the two chairs in front of the desk, his steps swift and nervous. He flinched when the doors to the office quietly clicked shut.

"What is your name?" Katniss demanded as soon as he was seated.

"Coriolanus Snow," he answered readily, "but you may call me what you wish."

The president leaned back in her chair, observing the secretary. She recognized him, of course; he was one of the oldest on her staff, and she'd been considering letting him go. He was too old for the bustling life of a Capitol secretary, but she just couldn't bring herself to release someone who'd been around for so long. He was a fixture, someone more dependable than the young interns she'd recently hired.

"Snow, do you know what District 13 did to be wiped off the map?"

The question seemed to surprise him. "Yes, ma'am. The district was destroyed during the First Rebellion as a warning for other, more important districts to stand down."

"You could say that," Katniss responded. There was an edge to her tone that further agitated Coriolanus, but he maintained his composure.

The two watched each other silently for a few moments, one tense and the other nonchalant. The former finally leaned forward in his stiff chair, hoping to ascertain the president's orders.

"What would you have the Peacekeepers do to prevent future raids, President Everdeen?"

Katniss's stern expression melted into a grin. "Perhaps it's time we reminded the districts about where the power lies in Panem."

She rose to her feet, her stately gown swishing around her legs. Coriolanus got to his feet, slightly slower with his aged joints. The two exhibited very different dispositions in that moment, Katniss being excited while a quiet dread had settled over Snow.

"Go," the president ordered. "Ready the hovercraft battalions. Make sure that District 12 has no possibility of forewarning."

Coriolanus nodded, turning in spite of his veiled reservations. He reached the doors, waiting for Katniss to press the button and dismiss him.

"Oh," President Everdeen added as an afterthought, "and prepare Plan B just in case."

When the doors smoothly opened to allow Snow out of the office, he couldn't find any relief in leaving. Thoughts of one less district and Plan B floated through his mind as he took his leave and the office doors closed behind him.

~~~~~

Snow followed the president's orders impeccably, ensuring that the abrupt mission orders were kept secret as hovercraft pilots readied their battalions. The physicists in charge of Plan B were made well aware of the importance of secrecy, and everyone was now awaiting Katniss's permission to move.

That is, except for Snow.

"This is insane," he mumbled to himself, adjusting the white rose in his lapel as the hovercraft soared invisibly over the first 11 districts. It was night, the ideal time for a surprise attack, and he knew he had a very small window of time to warn the people of District 12.

While the rest of the government workers in the Capitol were readying for the attack or flitting around with statistics reports, Coriolanus was riding in a runaway hovercraft on his way to District 12. His intentions were to expressly disobey the most powerful person in Panem, and the danger was not lost on him.

Old as he was, Coriolanus Snow was acutely aware of the risk he was taking. If he was discovered to be missing before he could return to the Capitol, it would mean his execution. President Everdeen knew nothing of mercy; if any of her followers strayed, she would not hesitate to publicly execute them.

It was with this fearful realization that Snow touched down in the endangered 12th district. The pilot of the hovercraft opened the passenger door on the side of the vessel and the frightened secretary stepped onto the withered grass of some abandoned backyard near the district's western edge.

"Twenty minutes," the pilot yelled to Snow. "After that, I'm on my way back to the Capitol."

Snow nodded, closing the hatch and dashing as quickly as he could through the empty streets. Occasionally, he caught sight of a haggard man or woman. Poverty reeked on the sidewalks, but Snow pressed onward without interference.

Eventually, the mayor's residence swam into view beyond the district square. Conscious of the seconds constantly ticking by, Coriolanus pounded on the mayor's door and stood back, impatiently waiting to be acknowledged.

A young lady, probably in her teens—the prime age for the Games—answered the door. She had a placid disposition, her hair drawn into a side braid as she offered a confused smile.

"Good evening, sir," she greeted. "How may we help you?"

Coriolanus peered over her head into the foyer. "Where is the mayor?"

"He is currently unavailable."

Snow cut her off. "Make him available. There is an emergency. I'm from the Capitol."

Her eyes widened and she slowly opened the door all the way to reveal the mayor just beside her. His expression was guarded as he observed the old man on his doorstep.

"Madge, get to bed. We have a long day tomorrow," Mayor Undersee murmured to his daughter. The girl, Madge, walked off without question.

The mayor stepped out onto the doorstep. He was a balding man, tall but not taller than Coriolanus. The two men were undeniably on edge with each other; the tension in the air was palpable.

"Mayor Undersee, there is an emergency," Snow announced without preamble.

The mayor was naturally a nervous man, and he folded his hands at Snow's words. "Please do tell, Mister ...?"

Ignoring the subtle inquiry for his name, Coriolanus explained the situation in the Capitol. He went over the basics as the mayor's terror heightened steadily. "The attack will be tonight, and this district will be obliterated. You do not have much time. Get the people and find some way to shelter them before the bombings begin."

"How ... why?" the mayor asked with clear panic.

Coriolanus shook his head. "A show of power, Mayor Undersee. A warning. A reminder. Follow my instructions or your district's people will pay with their lives. You must hurry."

The mayor's expression was blank for a moment before determination lit up his eyes. "Thank you. Why did you warn us?"

The perfect politician, speaking inclusively.

"That is none of your concern," Snow said vaguely, not knowing the answer himself. He carefully pulled an earpiece out of the pocket of his suit jacket, pressing it into the mayor's palm. "Keep me updated on your progress. Be swift, subtle. The attack could come at any time, even now."

"What if the Peacekeepers discover us trying to leave?" Mayor Undersee asked, his eyes tired but alert.

Coriolanus just shook his head for a second time. "Don't let them."

Turning on his heel, he left the mayor behind him to rescue an entire district on his own. Snow had done what he could; now he had to save his own life by getting back to the hovercraft.

With less than 30 seconds to spare, Snow reached his escape transport and the pilot silently brought them back up into the air. As the 12th district faded into the darkness of night behind them, Snow wondered if he'd ever see the land intact again.

He knew he wouldn't.

~~~~~

With regular updates from the mayor via their earpieces, Coriolanus knew exactly how many people were still in District 12 when Katniss ordered the battalions to set out. When the swarm of hovercrafts flew out of the dozens of Capitol hangars, only 15 percent of District 12 had been moved to the safety of the forest, and even those citizens wouldn't be safe if Plan B was implemented.

Plan B: the nuclear warheads that were ready to fire from the coast of what used to be the Pacific Ocean. Plan B, which would demolish all of District 12 and a majority of the surrounding forest if Katniss ordered them to fire.

The lives of thousands of mostly innocent Panem citizens rested in the hands of Panem's tyrant, and she was cruel enough to wipe every last man, woman, and child off the map.

Snow curtly informed the mayor of the approaching bombers, swiftly making his way up to the president's office. She allowed him entrance as soon as he knocked on the door, and she was calmly relaying orders to the interns downstairs through the high-tech, holographic screens that had sprouted from her desk.

"Keep up the data flow. I don't care if you have to skip your breaks and dinner tonight," President Everdeen was saying, a cruel smile adorning her childlike features.

Wordlessly, she muted the screens and brushed them to the side, turning her attention to Coriolanus. The secretary had an unnerving look in his eyes, but Katniss wasn't fazed.

"Yes?" she asked when he didn't speak.

"Will you be calling on Plan B this evening?" Snow asked boldly.

Katniss glanced over at the screens, briefly furrowing her eyebrows. "I have no intention to as of right now. Why?"

"I just wanted to remind you of the repercussions of such an act," he replied cautiously.

The president's temper flared, her eyes noticeably darkening. "Oh? You don't think I'm kept informed of the consequences of my actions? I know exactly what the results of Plan B would be, Snow. And trust me when I say this: I haven't the slightest worry. If I use Plan B, so be it. The districts have brought it on themselves."

"Of course," Coriolanus agreed instantly. "The radiation is dangerous, but it's nothing we can't handle."

"Exactly," Katniss said with a smirk. "In fact, I just might do it. If they manage to take out a hovercraft somehow, I won't hesitate to press that button."

"That button" was a heavily guarded control panel beneath the president's private research facility. It controlled the nuclear warhead from thousands of miles away, and the physicists and engineers who regularly updated the technology had installed everything from eye scanners to fingerprint-sensitive buttons.

Snow nodded, hiding his panic at her careless attitude. "Yes. Well, I'll keep you updated on the status of the bombing."

"Yes, you will," she told him. "If a single one of the crafts gets taken down, I want to be informed immediately."

"Of course," Snow said, hoping to appease her as he bowed out of her office.

As soon as he was out in the hallway, the mayor's voice exploded in his ear.

"There are still thousands of children in the city, and the bombs are beginning to drop!"

Snow halted in his steps, eyes widening. "They've arrived already?"

"Yes! They've hit the square and th—"

Mayor Undersee's voice was cut off by feedback and a crashing sound, and static took its place in Snow's ear.

"Damn it," he murmured.

Jerking the earpiece out, he dashed off at a quick sprint toward the control room, where the hovercraft and nuclear warhead data were updated every second. Perhaps there was some kind of way to stop the hovercrafts' bombing abilities, even temporarily.

Snow was confronted by several guards when he reached the reinforced steel walls of the hallway beneath Katniss's office. They were all dressed in gray fatigues, clutching their sidearms as if Snow was brandishing an AK-47.

"Name and position," the first guard demanded.

"Coriolanus Snow, secretary and adviser to President Everdeen," Snow told them without delay. "I've been sent to reprogram Hovercraft 28C. It will only take a moment."

The guards were unconvinced. The first one sneered. "We need the president herself to confirm your entrance, sir."

Coriolanus could faintly hear the static from the earpiece in his pocket. Time was running out for District 12.

"Denying me a pass will result in your executions. There is an attack on District 12 and the president needs the hovercraft to be reprogrammed *now*. If you want her confirmation, feel free to walk upstairs and get it while I do my job."

His firm, unwavering tone had the desired effect. The other guards looked to their mouthpiece for guidance, and he looked at Snow suspiciously.

"Entrance granted, Secretary Snow. Adam, go and retrieve confirmation from Everdeen." His tone was scathing, warning.

Not intimidated, Snow pressed forward and swiped his keycard through the door's lock. It opened to welcome him, and he ignored the groups of professionals observing the monitors. Screens covered every inch of wall space, and all of them were currently filled with the carnage of the bombing.

Before Snow could so much as announce his purpose, the intercom screeched to life, and President Everdeen's angry voice filled the room.

"Activate Plan B. I repeat, activate Plan B."

The intercom went silent and everyone paused, shocked. Finally, a man in a pristine lab coat stepped forward.

"Activate Plan B," he said loudly, his voice echoing in the stillness of the control room.

Snow watched as several men approached a biohazard curtain, throwing it open to reveal a panel of complicated triggers, levers, and switches. They got to work and a screen came to life above the contraption, displaying a map of Panem. A blood-red X settled over District 12, freezing Snow's blood.

He saw the innocent faces of the women and children, the men working hard to support their poor families. Madge and Mayor Undersee. Haymitch, the unpleasant, lone District 12 Games victor. The homeless men and women.

Suddenly, a red light lit up the room. The door burst open and the guards poured in.

"Coriolanus Snow, you are under arrest for treason!"

Adrenaline rushed through Snow's veins and he watched the men readying the nuclear warhead that would take thousands of lives. In a moment of complete madness, he rushed forward, knocking aside the professionals.

Snow redirected the target, lighting up the Capitol with a red X.

His eyes found the guards aiming their guns, the control room workers gasping, his own life flashing before his eyes.

Grabbing the nearest authorized worker's hand, he flipped the "Fire" switch.

Blood Red

By girlwho_lovestowrite

It was one of those days where you couldn't see the sun. The sky was entirely gray, unbearably gray, the color that made Radley almost claustrophobic. The gravel crunched underneath her feet as she walked, miserably, down the path from her cottage through the forest. It was a tedious trip she had grown to despise years ago, and continued to despise eternally.

But here she walked, every single day, with a basket of food, food she could devour to sustain herself.

Pressing a hand wistfully against her stomach, she tried not to think about the contents of the basket to the best of her ability.

No, this was for her grandmother.

If anyone needs the energy, it's her.

Radley thought to herself, needing motivation more than food. If she could just not think about, if she could just not smell it, Radley would make it. She wouldn't take even a bite of the bread her mother baked with the last of the flour. Or the fruit purchased with the remains of last month's income.

"It's hard, isn't it?" a rough voice called, and although Radley looked, she didn't fully expect the voice to be addressing her. But the source, a silhouette of a man leaning against the sturdy support of a tree, was the only soul in sight. "I see you go by here every evening," he continued, trailing off and approaching carefully.

There was a certain precision in the way he moved, a cautiousness that captivated every one of Radley's senses. As he stepped out from the shade cast down from the canopy of trees, impossibly thick against the evening sky, his features came into view.

Radley gasped. This man was almost … animalistic. His raven eyes glinted with a savage light, and his fingers were adorned with claws rather than nails. The way his muscles tensed under his skin made him threatening, infinitely ready to pounce.

"What's in the basket?" he asked, but something in his voice assured Radley he already knew.

"Nothing for either of us," she replied bitterly, continuing down the path. He followed close behind, and the scent of the woods was intensified with his presence. Radley trembled with fear.

"Ah, that's a shame," he sighed, his voice clear and rumbling. "We could have a lovely picnic."

"I'm surprised. I wouldn't have expected the word *lovely* to be in your vocabulary," she replied, allowing him to walk by her side, internally craving the new unpredictability.

"Well, there's your lesson on assumptions," he grinned, exposing a set of enormous and menacing canines. "It must be hard, though, taking that basket filled with a delicious meal, unable to even touch it."

"Yes, well, it's for a good cause," she replied, but her stomach felt suddenly hollow.

"So good that you can't just have," he began, swiftly sliding behind her and swiping something from the basket. The scent of bread wafted out, and Radley's mouth watered. "One apple?"

"Yes," she sighed, reaching for the fruit he playfully held from her grasp. A head taller than her, his arm extended and successfully kept the apple far out of her clutch.

"Not even one bite?" he challenged, raising a dark eyebrow.

Just one bite. Radley felt a shiver climb up her spine and through her body.

"No, not even one bite," she snapped, and opened the wicker flap of the basket expectantly. He dropped it, and she slammed the basket closed once again after it safely landed within the checkered cloth covering the other food. The other delicious food. "And would you stop trying to make me do what I'm obviously not supposed to?"

"Oh, you idolize the temptation," he rolled his eyes as if she were terribly annoying. By instinct, Radley glared at him, but when she turned to face him, she saw his eyes had taken on a far more intense glow. "It makes you feel strong, doesn't it?"

"Only when I win," she responded evenly, and they halted for just a moment.

"What is this 'good cause' anyway?" he asked lightly, trotting alongside her once again. They continued through the thicket, Radley's rich garnet cloak billowing behind her in the slight breeze. The one luxury she had, her very favorite thing she possessed, was the only thing that dismissed her hunger and kept her strong. The only thing that made her victorious on her nightly struggle with the wicked basket.

"My grandmother," she stated simply, pulling the richly colored fabric tighter around her body.

"A noble cause indeed," he nodded in pleasant acknowledgment, but there was an undefinable malice in his voice. "But don't forget about the noble cause of self-interest. What do I know? I don't know you. But here's some advice. If you want to stay alive, my friend, you need to do what it takes to survive."

"What about the other people in the world who don't have what it takes to get by, huh? Should we not help them?" she demanded, furious at him for planting the selfish seed in her mind. Selfish, it was selfish. Nothing noble about it.

But yet it seemed so *fair.*

"It's a dog-eat-dog world, isn't it?" he teased, chuckling at his own joke with laughter that sounded more like a growl than anything else. "But you have exactly what it takes and, yet, you're withering away. So, just stay alive, all right?"

Opening her basket once more, he took the apple back into his clawed hands. All Radley could do was watch, paralyzed by the weight of her empty stomach. Taking her wrist, he flipped her hand and pressed the fruit firmly into her palm. Then, as quickly as he had come, he vanished back into the woods.

The way its red skin glistened in the evening sun, the way the smooth surface felt beneath her fingertips, not even her hood could remind her to be strong. No luxury seemed to be as fine as the apple in her hand, glimmering like a ruby, and so Radley lifted it to her lips and took a bite.

The sweetness, the texture, everything about it exploded through her senses. And Radley couldn't stop.

If anyone needs the energy, it's her.

The need to save the rest weighed unbearably on her, but not as heavily as the wolfish stranger's statement.

Stay alive, all right?

Radley *deserved* this. Radley *deserved* life. Of course she did. But, as she feasted hungrily on the picnic, she knew how terribly wrong it was. After devouring the last bite, the last crumb, she knew she had failed.

Her grandmother needed this, and she was terribly late in delivering it to her.

She had to at least go to tell her what she had done even if the sun had sunk long ago, as she savored the meal that shouldn't have been hers in the first place.

"What have I done?" Radley cried aloud, but the worst part was waiting for the remorse that would never come.

~~~~~

When she arrived at her grandmother's cottage, a nearly identical copy to her own, she felt the uneasy atmosphere before she crossed the threshold.

"Grandma?" she called, but received no answer as she stepped carefully through the house. But in the wooden rocking chair, her grandmother's usual place, she only found the strange man, blinking at her amiably. A smear of blood was scarlet across his face and she gasped in horrified realization.

"She was dead just after I arrived. I hope you don't mind. Why waste such a nice snack?" He began rising from the rocker, sending it into a frenzied series of ominous creaks. Radley was either too late, and her grandmother was too feeble with the small rations of yesterday's food to last any longer, or she was just old and weak, or the man was lying to her. It could have been any of the three. But deeply, the truth resonated, and the blame rooted itself deeply in her chest.

She waited a moment, contemplating what he had done to her. This was *his* fault. If he hadn't put the idea of food into her mind, her grandmother would still be alive. He preyed on her weakness and then he finished off her grandmother's remains like she was nothing more than a rabbit.

Something changed within her, something dreadful. She knew she could never go back to the life of starvation now that she knew the deep feeling of satisfaction, and she hated herself knowing the feeling came at the cost of her weak grandmother's life. But there was a plaguing idea in the back of her mind, knowing that now she could provide for herself.

Two parts of her battled for dominance, and for a moment, she stood conflicted. Her grandmother had been selfish in a way too, right? Seeing her granddaughter become a canvas of skin stretched tautly over bones and not doing a thing about it? So maybe it was good she was gone, maybe she should just let the wolf go. But her other half had different ideas. He had told her to stay alive, he had told her to do what it took to survive. Maybe he should have a chance to try these suggestions himself.

The choice was a simple one.

This man would die for what he had done to her, for taking away the desperation that kept her sane.

Radley felt nothing but an insatiable hunger as she tightened her cloak and lunged for the two sterling needles on the tiny table beside the rocking chair. A bloodthirsty drive overtook her as she lunged toward the creature, an impenetrable goal to kill.

He immediately threw her off, and the knitting needles flew helplessly from her grasp, but she used the momentum to stumble back into the kitchen. She could see it in his eyes; the wolf had every intention of eating her now.

But the knife drawer was nearby, and she quickly armed herself with the sharpest, most jagged one she could find before he reached the kitchen. Hiding it behind her back, she waited, enraged and terrified. Her heart beat wildly, and for once, she identified the adrenaline pulsing through her veins. She relished the foreignness of the sensation and waited impatiently for him to come.

"Oh, Radley," the wolf aggressively burst through the kitchen door, knocking it clean off its hinges. "What bloody hands you have."

She waited for him to approach, before revealing the knife clutched tightly in her hand and plunging it savagely into his chest.

"All the better to kill you with." She snarled, dragging the blade down and then burying it into his stomach. Weakened, he stumbled, a shocked expression permanently frozen onto his face.

Radley watched as he bled out, fatally wounded, seconds away from death, and breathed raggedly.

As he finally fell, she stared on, feeling nothing at all.

And then, her stomach growled.

Heart of Frost
By Lupinehowl

I killed her.

The words echoed endlessly in my head, and I clutched at my pounding heart, scrambling to sit up. The golden capsule containing my baby teeth—as well as memories of my past—was grasped at my side. I sat inside the icy crevice, the place I'd first recovered my memories after encountering Pitch many months before, far below the earth with my knees tucked to my chest. My breath came out in rapid, billowing clouds.

Her death was my fault ...

Glancing down at the memories clenched in my fist, the thought sent a shudder down my spine. Ironic, considering I wasn't one to be bothered by the cold. I recalled back to what I'd just witnessed: I once believed I'd saved my sister from drowning at the site of my own death place, the frozen lake, and, hence, I was chosen by the Man in the Moon to be a guardian. But upon seeing the new version my memories had undergone, I was beginning to realize that I was far from a hero. I was a murderer.

I'd witnessed myself sliding my sister to supposed safety, as I had seen before, just before falling through the thin sheet of ice myself and being plunged into the dark, swirling water. What I hadn't noticed before, yet was exposed to just a second ago, was a new addition to the memory. Before I was sucked back into reality, I witnessed my sister crashing through the shattered ice as well, her mouth parted in a silent, eternal scream as she helplessly sank down into the depths of the lake; her brown eyes pleaded for me to save her, but I was frozen. Useless.

Now, every time I blinked, her terrified face flashed behind my eyelids. The memory of her haunted me.

With a cry of anguish, I flung the memory capsule in my hand against the jagged wall of the fissure in the ground. It then clanged to the floor, just as I picked up my staff and flew up out of the fissure. I needed to get back to the North Pole. As I was flying, I felt an icy pain course through my heart like lightning, and I staggered in midair.

"Ow," I hissed through gritted teeth. Once I recovered, the pain in my heart ebbing to a dull ache, I took off in the direction of the north, the ground below swiftly blurring past. *Guilt hurts.* That was what I brushed the pain off as: guilt. What I wasn't aware of at the time, though, was that the cause of my agony was something much, much worse.

~~~~~

I didn't share my newfound knowledge with any of the other guardians. Not even Sand Man, who I already knew wouldn't tell anyone. They'd probably claim that it wasn't my fault, that I'd tried saving my sister and that I couldn't have known whether or not the ice would break. They'd never admit that I wasn't meant to be a guardian. But in all honesty, it *was* my fault. If I hadn't taken her ice-skating in the first place, she wouldn't have had to die. If I had done a better job of protecting her ...

And it wasn't just that. Over the course of several days, I began feeling ... different.

Ever since discovering that I hadn't saved my sister, as I'd previously thought, cold, bitter thoughts have been bombarding my mind; they all happened to be some variation of *"I'm not a guardian, I'm a villain, like Pitch wanted."*

As the days dragged on, these thoughts, which entered my brain every day now without my consent, began to worsen. I stood leaning against my staff in the pristine, endless snow. The wind rustled my snowy hair as I pondered the limitations of my powers. *Surely, there's more to my powers than giving stupid kids snow days. Pitch saw my potential. In what form is ice a good thing?* I grimaced. *It took my sister, as well as my own life. People get sickness and frostbite from* my *cold.*

Hurling a snowball far into the distance, I drily added, *I'd be better off as a villain.*

~~~~~

The next day, as I was training outside in the brisk, gray evening, the other guardians approached me. I'd been isolating myself from them quite often lately, feeling unworthy of merely being in their presence. I wasn't the same. Ever since learning of my sister's death, I no longer smiled, but rather excluded myself from any enjoyable activity. I left myself to my thoughts and my training. There was no longer room for socializing.

"Jack," Tooth murmured softly, fluttering up to me. I kept my head down, my blue eyes fixed straight ahead. The rest of the guardians soon joined her at my side.

"Jack," North, aka Santa Claus, spoke in a stern tone of voice. With a sigh, I reluctantly turned to face them.

"What?" I snapped, my harshness even surprising myself for a second. I eyed North coldly.

"Listen, we need to talk," he said, and Bunny quickly added, "You haven't been yourself, mate." At first, I didn't reply. Then Tooth quietly murmured, "Please, talk to us, Jack."

This broke my urge not to talk to them, if only for an instant. Exhaling sharply, I turned to face them, crossing my arms stubbornly. "Fine. What do you guys want?"

"You've been acting strange lately," North answered immediately. "Don't think we haven't noticed."

I shrugged coolly. "I don't know what you're talking about," I muttered. "Now, if you'll excuse me—"

"You barely talk anymore, you're constantly avoiding us, and when you're not sulking around the workshop, you're constantly training," North cut in. When I didn't argue, he continued in a grave whisper, one that sent chills shooting down my spine. "Look, we didn't come here to yell at you. We came to make sure you're all right, as well as warn you."

Warn me?

"I've received word just recently from the Man in the Moon."

Moon? Oh, great. I had a feeling I knew where this was going.

"Let me guess," I interrupted sharply. "He says I'm not meant to be a guardian? That he made a mistake in choosing me?"

The guardians all blinked at me, clearly stunned by my conclusion. "No," said North. "He told me something about your powers. Apparently, it's quite possible that the ice that makes up your powers ... well, basically, there's a chance it may overtake your heart, condemning it to nothing but ice. You're in danger. If this isn't stopped, you'll be frozen from the inside out, but not before you're completely void of emotion." Exchanging a wary glance with Tooth, then Sand Man, he finally admitted, "We believe that is what's happening to you now."

At this, my eyes narrowed to tiny splinters of ice. "So, that's it then? There's nothing we can do to stop it?" My voice shook.

"There's nothing *we* can do," Tooth replied, wistfulness hazing her violet eyes. "However, there is something *you* can do."

"And that is?"

She paused. "You have to forgive yourself, Jack."

I stared at the guardians blankly. What? Was there a way that they knew of my true past? I shook my head. It didn't matter—their whole story was nonsense. Besides, even if I wanted to, I don't think I could ever forgive myself for what I'd done. No matter what, the image of those innocent, pleading eyes sinking into the shadows at the bottom of the lake would never vanish from my mind, nor would the voice that kept repeating, *"It's all your fault."*

Forcing the sorrowful thought away, I scowled at the guardians before me in an attempt to mask my pain. "Whatever," I scoffed. Then, without giving them a chance to explain further, I clutched my staff and once again took to the sky, letting the wind take me wherever it wished. I didn't dare look back.

~~~~~

I spent the next week on some remote, snowy island. Unaware of exactly where I was, I didn't stress about the trip back to the North Pole. In fact, the thought of home didn't cross my mind once while I was away.

My behavior didn't cease to change, unfortunately. At this point, I couldn't even make myself feel any sort of emotion, as North had predicted. Now, whenever my sister's death replayed vividly in my mind, I would keep a blank face on, and despite what my mind declared I should feel, my heart remained completely detached from the situation. I felt no sadness, nor anger, nor fear toward what I'd become: an empty shell of my former self. I felt nothing but coldness.

And then one day, as I sat beneath a snow-laden evergreen tree upon the island, my transformation took on a whole new form. While staring down at my pale hands, I noticed an odd, intricate kind of frost slowly creeping over my skin. Except this frost wasn't the type I came into contact with every day, but instead, this frost glinted a dark, fearsome shade of black, like the color of Pitch's nightmares. My heart felt dead as I watched it seep over me. My heart was no longer mine, it felt, but rather replaced by a cold and heavy chunk of ice. My mind, meanwhile, began relishing in the idea of this fear-frost, as I called it. Lifting my staff, I shot a beam of ebony-black icicles, deadly and powerful and beautiful all at once. A malicious laugh escaped my mouth. I was no longer in control; a dark force had taken over, a force that hungered only for power and revenge on the world. Fear controlled me. Fear of being a villain, fear of killing my sister, it was all the same! All I wanted was power, and for everyone to suffer what my sister went through ... what *I* went through.

I sought to use my abilities to expand my power. To spread fear throughout the world, *that* was my one goal.

"And no one's going to stop me!" I screamed into the endless expanse of white. Then, I launched into the air, toward the North Pole.

When I arrived at my destination, my body now entirely adorned with a thin layer of fear-frost, I landed roughly, plunging my staff into the ground. All around me, jagged ice splinters suddenly burst from the earth; the wind picked up, carrying a deadly concoction of snow and hail. Though I couldn't see it, I was perfectly aware of the effects my huge snowstorm was inflicting upon the rest of the world. Some people were buried beneath avalanches of snow, others eternally frozen into statues of fear. The world was freezing over; it'd face the fate I would soon inevitably meet.

Just then, I noticed a group of figures rapidly approaching in the distance. As I peered closer, it dawned on me with a grimace that there was still one force that possessed a chance at stopping my reign of terror. The guardians.

"Jack, STOP!" I heard the Tooth Fairy's desperate voice from afar, but it no longer held any meaning to me. Nothing did anymore. Suddenly, Sandy's billowing cloud of golden sand started tumbling toward me. Just as it was upon me, it froze into a huge wave of sheer ice. I grinned wickedly. Then, with a blow from my staff, I sent the massive ice wall exploding outward. The shattered blades of ice pierced Sandy as well as Bunny, knocking them both into the snow where they quickly disappeared from sight. I felt no guilt, absolutely none.

I was taken aback when Tooth zipped in behind me and landed a powerful blow to my back, throwing me forward. I whirled around to face her, a lust for power glittering in my now-ebony eyes.

"Jack, please, stop this!" Tooth cried, her eyes holding genuine sadness. It was clear to see she didn't want to hurt me. The old Jack Frost probably wouldn't have wanted to hurt her, either.

But the old Jack Frost was dead.

With a fierce battle cry, I plunged the pointed part of my staff into her stomach when she was caught off guard. Her eyes glazed over; her face held no judgment, only love, as she froze over with black frost and collapsed to the ground.

Swiveling around, I thought, *Only one left.* North, however, didn't even try fighting me. His face was sad, much like Tooth's. It took me by surprise when he gently tossed a small blue object at me—the doll he'd given me when I'd first became a guardian.

"Remember your center, Jack Frost," he murmured solemnly, just before he, too, froze behind a veil of frost. I gazed down at the doll in my hands. At this point, I couldn't even remember what my center had once been ...

My center was ice. Cold, deadly, unforgiving. Covering the fragile doll in my brisk hands, I closed my eyes, and allowed fear to overcome me, bringing me to the fate I'd condemned the rest of the world to.

Dark Sides//The Hunger Games

By _Slyytherin

People have dark sides. Maybe they can't be seen, maybe they don't want to be seen. Even the sweetest, most innocent person could hide a deadly heart. Some you don't expect just by looking at their faces. And I, Rue Meadows, am one of those people.

I'd thought about the glory of killing someone since I had started watching the games. Seeing the life drain out of their eyes with a jagged knife in their heart. I wanted to volunteer at my first-ever reaping, but I never had the chance because, well, I was reaped.

I guess I was happy to come from District 11 at that point; nobody would volunteer in my place.

That's how I ended up here, crouching on a treetop in the middle of the Hunger Games itself. With the Career pack below me and Katniss Everdeen, the first volunteer from 12, next to me.

"Psst," I hiss. No response. "Psst!" I hiss, louder. This time, she turns her head. I motion toward a nest of Tracker Jackers, hanging from a branch on her tree, and she follows my gaze. "Tracker Jackers, cut it down!" I tell her.

She pulls a knife, which was thrown at her during the bloodbath, from her coat and stands in order to cut the branch. One stings her, then another. The branch bends under its weight. I climb farther up my tree until my legs are level with the nest. The branch bends farther, about to snap, and I kick it hard into Katniss's treetop.

The nest broke in two, Tracker Jackers both attacking Katniss and the Career pack below. After what felt like forever, the screams stopped and three cannons echoed through the arena.

Marvel Livingston—District 1

Glimmer Rosessen—District 1

Katniss Everdeen—District 12.

The feeling I dreamed of for years was now a reality. The feeling of killing someone, the adrenaline rushing through my veins.

Cato and Clove were the ones who turned off their alliance first. Their tech boy was the first to go; Cato snapped his neck so quickly that he may as well have been a stick.

Then there was "Lover Boy," as Clove called him. Peeta Mellark was his real name. They only used him to find Katniss and after I killed her, there was no use for him anymore. Clove killed him while he was asleep.

Those two kept by their supplies, never leaving each other's sides. Perhaps they were the new lovers in the games. Cato and Clove from District 2. The arena's new lovers and everyone knew.

Outside their bunch were three other tributes. Me being one of them.

Finch was doing well. She knew what was poisonous and what wasn't. She's quick and even seems to have very sensitive hearing since she always bolts away when I move closer to her while hiding in a tree.

Then there's my district partner, Thresh. He acted like my brother. As much as I want to win these games, I don't want him to die. If he goes, I want someone else to kill him. I don't want it to come down to me and him.

Days passed without any action from me at all. Finch was stupid enough to eat Nightlock berries. Clove had her head smashed in with a rock, thanks to Thresh, but his celebration was cut short after he was killed by Cato in return.

It was now just Cato and me. One of us would become the victor and be praised by all of Panem.

It went dark, all light quickly draining from the arena. Then a sound I hadn't heard in a long time—rain. And then another sound, a bark in the distance, then another, and another.

"This must be it, this is the finale," I thought, hopping down from my tree and sprinting away from the barks. The cornucopia glints in the corner of my eye, so I steer toward it. The rain makes it hard to climb, but I manage it. And I come face-to-face with my district partner's killer. Cato.

I reach into my jacket, pulling out a knife to hide it behind my back. He's wielding a machete with hints of dried blood on it, and he wears a menacing grin.

"Why don't you just give up? You aren't gonna win. You know you're not going to. Just say bye-bye to your family and jump into those mutts," he says to me in a babyish voice.

"How about something different? What if I stay up here and kill you so I can see my family? How would that be?" I suggest.

Cato chuckled but grips his machete tighter. "Never."

He never saw the knife coming.

"And here she is, folks! Rue Meadows, the victor of the 74th annual Hunger Games!" Caesar Flickerman exclaims, beckoning me onto the stage. I waltz toward him, wearing my most innocent smile even though everyone knew my true intentions.

The whole of Panem knows now, never trust the little ones. They all have their dark sides.

The Tell-Tale Eye

By sowhatsitabout

True!—troubled—very, very horribly troubled, I am. You simply cannot say I am mad! My sickness—to plainly put it—merely boosted my senses, does not extinguish them! My friend, you cannot just label me off as a madman, as my sense of sight is greatly affected. See! Look! Behold how collected I am as I give my stories—tales of shadows, hate, and, of course, the Eye.

No, I do not despise myself! It is only the visage that stares back at me every single time I peer at a mirror that makes my bones shudder and my blood run cold. It is because of the Eye that I see shadows of demons and the dead spreading from behind me! I dare not look back, for the fear of facing one.

It is a very strange and hateful thing how once you have brought an idea to mind, it simply does not vanish, no matter how hard you wish, how much you try. The mind is very ruthless—so unsympathetic—to leave that thought to torture me, to dig into my mind until I could conceive nothing but it.

There was no other way. I had no goal, no devotedness. I had not wronged myself, no, but it was my eye that caused my loathing to boil and course through me. I owned a pale vulture eye—one with a glassy mist over it. Any time I glanced at a mirror, oh how I detested those moments, it would bore into me and grind me into a thousand pieces with no mercy. By the time the extra day had passed again, I was determined—no, firmly intent—to rid myself of the Eye so I may comfortably lie in peace.

I should make my basis clear. I am not mad—if I was, I wouldn't have, no, couldn't have, so cleverly planned it out. Isn't it obvious that the clarity of a mind such as my own could not possibly belong to a madman? Not even the old man could have guessed what would happen.

The old man, I pity him, also found himself shuddering and cringing at the plain sight of the Eye. My acute sight perfectly caught his expressions. I felt myself sympathizing with the old man, so I kindly avoided him, but upon confrontation, gave courtesy. Despite my favor, he still sneered at me. At me! All because of my horrendous vulture eye.

And so I prepared to get rid of the Eye. So slowly, so sneakily, in terror that the Eye will notice. All of you would have gifted me a standing ovation if you'd observed as I—quite like a mastermind thief—secretly planned, avoiding opening the Eye. You should've seen me—eyes closed, moving slower than a snail, quiet like a cat. Nobody could dare call me a madman now.

However, what an unfortunate thing, the Eye was always closed whenever I attempted to gouge it out. My hatred was directed at the Eye, not I, so I could not put harm upon my body, which had done nothing wrong.

Before my Eye could awaken and spot the treachery its body was about to attempt, the sharp tools were swept into a concealed box. It was clever of me to keep the Eye in the dark. For seven days, I stood in front of my cursed mirror, slowly—almost painstakingly slow—drawing the toolbox out of its shelf and lifting the razor to the Eye. Centimeter by centimeter, millimeter by millimeter, I raised the razor up, so that even the rising sun could've beaten its progress. But each attempt was foiled by my eye.

On the eighth day, when dawn was approaching, the razor was still six inches (I knew this with my heightened sense of sight) too far, my legs, weakened from exhaustion, shook. It was a small movement, but the Eye, with all its terribleness, awoke and found the sharp razor aimed toward it.

My bloodshot normal eye made eye contact with the other in the mirror. Oh! the horror, how the blood ran cold. I saw the long, hostile shadows of demons—with my acute sight! I averted my gaze from the mirror, that despicable tool, so that I may not be able to see the actual terrors and owners of the shadows behind me through the reflection.

And what should I do? The Eye had figured the mutiny. I, with all my cleverness and quick thinking, made a decision—the Eye had to go. I drove the razor straight into it—pain! fire! Explosions of light! And again—again!—again! the razor went, gouging and slicing and mutilating the last of the torturous eye. Ha! Even though the Eye had punished me for my acts against it with indescribable and unbearable pain, it had gone. Gone! Finally!—free—free—at last!

I had not known I had been screaming—hollering my throat raw, quite like a madman I claim not to be. Whether it had been shrieks of delight and fierce pleasure, or bellows of pain, I do not know—nor do I want to know. With a surreal amount of control, I closed my mouth, shutting off the mad cackles and howls. Dark-red blood ran down my face and onto the hollow tub I set up. Ingenious, yes? My floor did not have to be cleaned later.

My unscathed eye caught movement in the shadows—no, not the tall, cold shadows of the demons, but the ones made from walls and desks. I whipped around, and immediately spotted the intruder.

"Good day," I pleasantly greeted, ignoring the fierce stabs that the Eye sent. The old man who also shared my feelings for the Eye cowered in terror, grasping a long knife. "Perfect morning, isn't it?"

"T-the Eye!" he yelled, standing on trembling legs. "The Eye!" I watched calmly as he scampered out of my house, hollering things about the Eye and the hospital.

A moment later, white-clad doctors rushed into my house. They spotted me, and froze dead in their tracks. I gingerly touched what was left of my eye socket. The doctors seemed to be stirred into action and approached me, staring at the pool of blood in the tub, hands held up.

They treated my eye socket slowly, and I let them. I would be a fool to decline treatment, just when my wounds were throbbing and burning. A few strange-looking men snuck to my side, not unnoticed. They asked me questions, interrogated me about how my face came to be. I answered them truthfully in a calm manner so nobody, not even they, could label me off as crazy. My normal eye was snagged by the words on a man's backside of his shirt: *Asylum for the Deluded*.

Blood boiled like fire through my veins. Suddenly, the shadows of the demons that hunted me for a lifetime appeared, and grew larger—even still larger as my knees weakened, drawing closer and closer like a cat having cornered its helpless prey. I could see the shadows of the fingernails, deadly sharp. The interrogators, facing me, and definitely able to see the monsters behind me, showed no sign of having seen them. Ha! I knew their sneaky little plans! They were on the Eye's side, rooting for all that went against me, its unfortunate owner, or rather, slave. The men were mocking me! Making fun of me! Solely because of my acute senses!

The demons behind me crouched, getting ready to leap at me. I fell to my knees, begging, "Please! No more! I know not why you are haunting me, but I beg of you!

Stop!" I heard the footsteps of even more monsters pounding toward me. "Slay me! Kill me—kill me! So that my troubles may drag me no longer!" I cried, curled up at the foot of the demon. "It was I—me! that gouged out the horrendous Eye! Demons! Monsters! Do not punish me for that!"

The Lost Story

By xdreams2realityx

They told me I would be great. That I would be the savior of the children. They told me that everything I ever wanted, every dream I ever wanted, I would have.

They put too much faith in one simple action.

Neverland. I'm sure you're all familiar with the timeless, old tale. That's the place where kids go to never grow up. The place where magic crosses the lines of reality. Where faith, trust, and a little bit of pixie dust can make anyone believe.

However, Disney is known to shine a nice light on our dark stories.

Disney has drilled it into your brain that Neverland was a happy place, a place where the flowers bloomed and the bunnies hopped and the deer frolicked. And it was like that at one time.

It was called the Light Years. Everything was perfect. There was an abundance of kids believing—almost 90 percent of the population—and there was more Neverlife than ever. The waterfalls were clean and clear, fairies flying around in the billions, pixie dust everywhere. Tink and I would go around and sprinkle pixie dust on nonbelievers, showing them the magic of believing in the sometimes unbelievable.

It was almost 20 years ago when things started going south. Kids began losing faith; we started losing energy. Just like humans survive on food, oxygen, and water, we Pans live off of faith. As more and more kids started to lose faith, Neverland started to lose its magic. The fairies started dying and the mermaids were swimming away. All in all, the island just started dying.

With almost nobody believing in our magic, we resorted to our last hope. Souls. We lured kids out with the prospects of becoming great or rich or whatever they wanted. Then we pounced; we took their young, energetic souls. With the knowledge that souls could energize us more than faith could, it became addicting.

We started going out on raids every night, taking over 1,000 souls with each real-world expedition. As we stockpiled more and more, the island commenced to regrow, but it was different this time.

It got darker, not lighter. The remaining positive energy fueled the negative energy that took over the island. The trees shriveled up, leaving haunting shadows in their wake. The lakes harbored an unknown species of new fish along with gobs of deadly algae. The fairies were on their fast way to an inevitable extinction. The island was coming back alive, but dead. New animals roamed the dangerous nights and strange birds killed in the bright light.

It was just the Pans on the island then. Only around 300 toughened up and made a half-decent life on the island. But tensions were high, and the need for more souls drove everyone crazy. Eventually, Pans started turning on each other, ganging up with their old rivals to swipe even more souls or stealing another Pan's collection. The island started to get chaotic, fights breaking out over souls or territory, the death toll on the rise.

That's when the Pan Wars broke out. Starting in 1995, it lasted over two decades. With four different sides, the Pan race was slowly declining. Dozens of Pans were dying by the week, slowly ruining the once happy atmosphere of Neverland.

The Pan Wars consisted of years of fighting against each other, a multitude of

TWISTED FROM: PETER PAN

different battles, betrayal, and brutal behavior all led by yours truly. I organized a special team of 20 called Panless and, as the Pan Wars were going on, we stole all of the souls from Neverland. We took them back to our secret base and fed off of the energy, becoming stronger and smarter than any Pan. A feat I was, and still am, quite proud of.

When the three opponents realized I had taken their soul collection, things got ugly. They ganged up with Hook, who was an Elder and believed in the old ways, and went after my team and me. However, with the strength of the souls on our side, they stood no chance. We were stronger than they were by miles and had skills they could only dream of having.

In the matter of one battle, we had won. The Battle at Oak Tree ended the war in two days. Two days of constant fighting, strategies, and consuming countless souls had made Panless invincible. We had killed every Pan opposed to us—a solid number of 217 Pans. As for the remaining Pans not on Panless, we gave them the option of joining us or dying. Many converted, but some were not so willing. In the end, only around 45 Pans lived, including the original team.

The Pan Wars were an unfortunate but unavoidable event in our dark lives. Today, around 30 Pans are alive and flying around at night, stealing children's souls for our well-being. If you're awake at night and feel a tingling sensation in your chest, don't worry; we assure you your soul is going to be used for a good cause.

Neverland is nothing like Disney paints it out to be. There was a time of good, but it was quickly taken over by darkness. Light never wins; only the dark prevails. The only thing more powerful than darkness is us. The Pans. There will not be another mistake like the Light Years again in our future, that we are sure of.

"Who is this?" you may ask. "Who was the Pan destined to save children but saved himself instead? Who would be so selfish and greedy with power to discount all of the human kind just to rule Neverland?"

It was me. It *is* me. Now I don't just rule Neverland, I rule your land too. I'll send you a thank-you card later. Who am I?

Peter Pan.

Watch the Queen Conquer
By Jen Lee (AurumArrows)

For years, Wonderland has been engaged with a civil war against rival factions: The Reds and The Whites. Two different ideologies, two different views, two different women fighting for a monopoly on the crown. Both colors symbolize power, but which one will win the struggle?

In the land of topiary and roses, the Queen of Hearts sits and with nearly unmatched skill, commands the chessboard and the cards. The King, the Rook, the Knight, the Bishop, and the Pawn are all at her disposal as well as half the deck. Hearts and Diamonds take up arms against their black counterparts.

In the land of marble and snow is the newly coronated White Queen, otherwise known as the wayward traveler Alice Liddell. She commanded the White Pieces, the Spades, and Clubs. All the people who feared the Queen of Hearts went to her for safety, though in reality, Alice granted haven for people of a certain color.

Well since her coronation, the country was torn apart, quite literally. Roads don't lead to where they were meant to lead. Buildings warped, the green chessboard barren, and the sky, a cacophonous mixture of red and white; only the rising motion of the sun and moon stayed constant. Wonderland was always mad, but this was just ridiculous.

The Queen of Hearts sipped her tea, bit a crumpet, and listened intently to the war board brief. Most of the pieces and aces were there, albeit roughed up. Normally she concerned herself with cards, but ever since Alice captured the Red Queen, the Queen of Hearts assumed her position until she returned. Someone needs to command them, but the Red Pieces were resilient against anyone. Really, the only thing that is keeping this alliance together is Alice and her reign of terror across Wonderland.

"Your Majesty," a man said. It was the Ace of Diamonds, holding a scroll embellished with rhombus designs. The Queen of Hearts couldn't help but wonder how her sister was doing. "I'm afraid that our division in the Mushroom Forest was defeated. We still have a small stronghold, along the western border, but if we don't send reinforcements, then The Whites will most likely take control of the terrain."

Consenting murmurs were heard throughout the table. The Queen of Hearts kept a placid face, but inside, she was extremely exhausted. Her normal energetic personality has faded to weariness. The times of shouting "off with your head" were over and replaced with a halfhearted "send the soldiers here." The latter was more of death sentence than anything else.

She never really beheaded anyone; it was all in good spirit. In the long run, she supposed it was a bad idea since most of her subjects left in fear. On the bright side, now most of those subjects lived in fear under Alice and in an act of quiet defiance, sent her limited but vital information. But what use was the information if you can't handle it right?

The queen had to give Alice some credit for being in charge of a large force at such a young age. But will she be able to handle it, is the true question. She already got her answer, and the answer is no. Although Alice was skillfully commanding an army, she doesn't have any experience. She's young, naïve, and like most people her age, a bit idealistic.

Another person stood up; this time it was the Knight. "I will not allow any more

TWISTED FROM: ALICE IN WONDERLAND

of the Red Queen's people to be decimated. How many Pawns have been lost? How many will lose their lives? The Chess Pieces are all in an uproar. If this alliance shall continue, then we need a victory."

She turned her eyes to him. "I am trying."

The Knight slammed his palms onto the table, causing it to shake and the board members to flinch. "It is not enough! The only substantial win that we had was last month, and that was at the cost of thousands of pieces and cards!"

"Silence!" The queen flared her nostrils and sent a withering look at the Knight. "If I do recall, this is my kingdom. I may be an incapable commander in your eyes, but I am willing to do anything to win this war and bring relative peace back to Wonderland. You know very well that the Chess Pieces cannot function without both a king and a queen. Whether you like it or not, we are allies."

The meeting room fell silent. The Knight stared at the Queen of Hearts, muttered an apology, stiffly bowed, and sat down.

For a moment there, she felt like she was in control, back in the good old days of peacetime when everyone listened to her. Does the same hold true for now? She took a deep breath and stood up, back straight and eyes meeting the faces of everyone at the table. All attention was drawn to her, and she would make it worth their while.

"Well, now that ordeal is over, I propose a change of plans." She took another sip of her tea, for her throat was very dry after scolding the Knight. The queen wasn't the best at strategy, but she knew that this plan was their best chance at winning. "This game has been going on for four years now. Pieces sacrificed, cards discarded, and clearly, just wantonly throwing them at the enemy isn't going to work." She paused. "If it is one advantage we have over The Whites, it is that we have a steady line of supplies.

"Although they do have better-trained warriors, no offense, we live in the warmer parts of Wonderland. Food is available all year-round and we are prepared to fight a war of attrition. I know that fighting this way is, perhaps, not the most exciting but if we are to win this war, then it is the best course." She breathed in deeply. "Any questions?"

She was met with fearful no's and a hint of approval.

The queen clapped her hands. "Wonderful! Now then, let us adjourn and meet again in—you there! What time is it?"

"It is nearly 3, your Majesty."

"—In an hour. I expect no tardiness from anyone."

The room slowly filtered out, leaving the Queen of Hearts to her own devices. Very rarely would she call a meeting in the days before the war. By this time of day, her subjects and she would be outside playing a nice game of croquet with the flamingos.

There seems to be no end to this power struggle. A war of attrition would take months, maybe even years to win. Alice's will was strong, but will it fall to waiting? Only time will tell. The queen remembered the first time she met little Alice, an insolent little girl who managed to worm her way to the royal court. Now, she was still insolent but this time, she was a force to be reckoned with.

Everything associated with the color red was promptly executed by the White Queen's soldiers, by guillotines of all things! In an ironic twist, it was The Whites who were causing so much red to be splattered upon the streets. The event was aptly named the "White Terror" and dropped a dark stain on Wonderland's peaceful history.

For years, the Red and White Kingdoms have peacefully coexisted and it was only now that any sort of major conflict emerged.

This wanton persecution was unlike what the quivering White Queen would do. What exactly was happening? It was only later, when the Queen of Hearts's kingdom was infringed, she knew exactly what was going on. In between the smoke and ash from a burning village, the last person she expected to see was Alice dressed in white regalia holding a sword, a wicked gleam in her eyes, and a diamond tiara situated on her fair hair. The Queen of Hearts was no fool: Alice has dethroned the White Queen.

Both women quickly glanced at one another, condescending blue eyes meeting surprised brown eyes.

"Alice, what are you doing?" the Queen of Hearts fearfully said. "I've never known you well, but this is unlike of what a proper girl should be doing! Please, lay down your sword and let us settle this diplomatically. Why, it was only yesterday when you were in the court and if you're angry about that, then I express my deepest apologies."

Alice looked at the queen with an unreadable expression. "Yesterday? Several years have passed since yesterday. It's no use going back to yesterday, because I was a different person."

The Queen of Hearts grimaced at the memory. A different person indeed. Time works differently in Wonderland: One second here is forever in Alice's world, but yesterday couldn't be the answer. Something changed within Alice, but what was that something, the queen hadn't had the faintest idea.

The queen paused in her thoughts. In retrospect, she too had changed. Films of memories played in her head: yelling at everyone in a fury, executing innocents (she knew her husband pardoned them behind her back, but the orders didn't really mean anything), and abusing her people. She was more of a child than Alice was and if good came out of this war, it was that it taught the queen responsibility. The only thing that stayed the same was her blood-pressure levels. The sun never sets on them.

She looked down at the chessboard. The answer to victory lay in those red and white squares. On the red side, there were two Knights, two Bishops, a Rook, and a handful of Pawns left on the table. The Red King, of course, is safely sheltered away. That was one thing The Reds had going for them; the Red Queen may have been captured, but the game doesn't end until the King is checked.

As for the cards, she still had two aces up her sleeve while Alice only had one. Whether she can use her trump cards correctly is another matter entirely. The queen knew that Alice's alliance with the Spades and the Clubs was tentative as they were of a different color, and she knew that the White Chess Pieces didn't exactly see her as the true leader. It was only a matter of time before Alice's regime collapsed under the strained alliance.

She knew how the game was played. Slowly, deliberately, calculatingly, she moved a Pawn one square up.

Little Red

By Jesse Feemster (minexpert)

Light filtered in through the leaves of great dark trees, making great golden slices through the dense foliage. Birds chirped cheerily and flew through the leaves, echoing around the place. Rabbits hopped back and forth, scurrying around for food. Spring had arrived, and nature was rising to the call admirably. And with nature, came Humans. The liveliness and happiness of the forest transitioned into that of the people who inhabited the forest. One such person was little Red. She was just barely 10 years old but knew her way around this forest adeptly to that of an experienced hiker. Red was nicknamed as such due to the bright red hood she always wore when she went outside. She earned this nickname from her grandmother, who lived in the woods, claiming the air was "good for her lungs." Red's mother often worried about her mother, but being too busy to travel there herself was forced to let Red carry a small (yet heavy) basket over to her grandmother. Red didn't mind this kind act. She would frequent the same path during the weekends, often skipping to her destination, rather than walking as her mother told her to do. However, Red's grandmother was not the only person to live in the woods. There was also a young woodsman, who Red sometimes saw hacking at the trees with an ax that must surely be blunt by now. Even if she didn't see him, she could hear him. The rhythmic thumping of the ax followed by the groaning and cracking of a falling tree would echo through the woods, inescapable. The woodsman wasn't always around the woods, however; Red didn't always see him working in the woods, but just walking around the woods, as if in a daze. He was scary, so Red never wanted to be near him, and whenever he was working near the path, Red would detour off the path slightly, just to avoid him.

One day, Red's mother gave her basket to her and told her that it was time to go visit her grandmother. Red happily agreed and ran to the door to pick up her hood. She put the basket carefully on the ground to reach above her head and retrieve the hood from the hook, lacing it around her neck carefully. She picked up the basket, and, after a kiss good-bye from her mother, she dashed off to the woods. The sun shone brightly as Red dashed through the town next to the woods, happily shouting words of gleeful greetings to the patrons of the town. Red's mother never liked the darkness of the woods, instead preferring to live more closely to the town; the brightness of the lamps at night would hold back her fears of darkness. On the other hand, Red was a brave little girl, taking more after her father and his fearlessness. She didn't mind the cracking and scraping sounds of the animals around the woods. She was almost always keeping her head down as she ran through the woods, always keeping sight of the faint path. She loved the woods, the greeny-golden light filtering through the leaves, the earthy brown leaves on the floor, and the various wood chips stripped from the bark that cracked underneath her shoes. Once she got to her grandmother's house, she would stay the night, and her grandmother would help her up onto the roof, and the trees would part to let them look at the stars. However, Red never wandered around the woods for too long. Once the sun went down, the warm green light would be replaced by a cold gaze of violet light. The path became impossible to see without artificial light, and even then, the darkness presses in on you, causing an increasing sense of claustrophobia. Red had never actually seen the woods at night, but her mother warned her often of its dangers, of the mean animals, of the mean people, and it scared her. So Red made sure to always be arriving at Grandma's before sunset.

Red dashed through the woods quickly, the basket in her hands trailing behind her just slightly. She ran through the woods, playfully jumping on the stripped bark to hear it crack and echo through the woods, giggling for a second before carrying on. She ran through the woods, giggling happily. All of a sudden, she came to a shocked stop, frozen in place. Ahead of her was a great shadow, cast by the furtive leaves. Just like how she would do with the woodsman, she stepped off the path slightly, and walked past the shadow silently, sensibly carrying the basket with both arms straight down, making sure she avoided gazing at the shadow. Her mother had warned her about this, and Red knew exactly what the shadow was. It was a wolf. Her mother had told her all about the stories to do with wolves, the ones used to scare the children away from the woods. About how a wolf's favorite thing to do is to catch little children, and once they caught them, they would eat them slowly, starting with the toes, and savor every bite. Red wasn't scared of the wolf, but she was definitely scared of being eaten, so whenever the wolf was sleeping on the path, she made sure to sneak silently past it. The wolf was never actually awake when she saw it, but she knew it wasn't dead because of its pulsating chest. Red checked behind her as she passed it, making sure it was asleep before she picked up her pace and returning to her usual dash.

As Red started around the curve that led to her grandmother's house, the sun was sinking low on the horizon, filling the forest with a thick mixture of honey yellows and earth browns. Red's hood was the only thing that didn't change its color. Even the sky changed color, becoming a cooler and deeper violet. However, the temperature also dropped dramatically, juxtaposing itself with the warm colors surrounding Red. Red began to shiver slightly. She quickened her pace again, which had slowed to a walk, eager to sit in the basking light of the fireplace. As her cottage came into view, Red broke into a run. As she got close, she slowed down again. The windows were dark, and there wasn't any smoke coming from the chimney. That's awfully strange, as Red's Grandma would always have a fire roaring when she came round, even in summer. She went up to the house and was about to knock on the door, but she hesitated. Something didn't feel right. … Red put the basket down carefully and pushed carefully on the door. It swung open slightly. Red stepped over the door frame and stole down the hallway silently. There were no lights on, so she had to squint slightly as she walked through the hallway, so she didn't trip up. As she traversed the hallway, she became aware of a faint sound. It sounded like a flat smack, like someone was hitting a watermelon with a plank of wood. Red began to get a little scared, but she couldn't stop moving forward, her childish curiosity forcing one foot in front of the other. She followed the sound, moving toward the sitting room. She peeked around the corner slowly, the smacking sound now ringing in her ears. Her eyes widened, and she had to clutch at her mouth to stop herself from screaming.

Grandma was laid across the ground, her blank eyes staring toward Red desperately. Her pearl-white hair was now stained with a thin layer of red. Above her, facing away from Red, was the woodsman, who was raising his ax above his head and bringing it down across Grandmother, over and over. He was mumbling to himself crazily as he did so. Red moved away slowly, then turned and ran. All of a sudden, the carpet that Red so carefully tried not to trip on caught her foot and held on, sending her sprawling to the ground. The loud thump alerted the woodsman, who stepped over Grandmother and started to leave.

"Who's there?!" he yelled in his thick gravelly voice. "I didn't do anything. I set her free from solitude …" He yelled again. Red scrambled to her feet, sprinting for the door. The sun just over it began to set outside the door, casting the trees into the darkness that she was scared of. The woodsman peeked around the doorway, and, spying Red, broke into a chase after her. Red crashed out of the door, kicking her basket aside. The woodsman chased after her, yelling for her to stop running. Raising her hands, she tore through the thin layer of leaves, crashing off of the path quickly. She snapped through twigs and thorns, ripping her hood's cloak in several places. She carried on, tearing through the bracken. She stole a peek over her shoulder, fearfully watching the woodsman break through the branches snatching at his clothing. He blotted out the last of the light from the sun, advancing on Red quickly. She began to scream and tumble through the trees. Suddenly, a branch traitorously snatched her foot from under her. Red rolled forward and landed on her front. She quickly rolled over onto her back. The woodsman jumped onto her, quickly pinning her down. She screamed as loudly as she could, but it wasn't loud enough to alert the town, however, and the woodsman stayed on top of her. He grabbed the knot of her hood, yanking her up into his face. He quickly screamed at her.

"How much did you see?" He screamed at her, saliva flicking through the air. Red, caught defenseless, only began to cry. The woodsman dropped his ax and smacked her around the face. Then he repeated the question, this time into her ear painfully. The shout wasn't too loud, but to Red, it felt as if explosions were detonated next to her. She screamed again, hoping to rouse the nearby town again, to have them come to help her, but there were no sounds of help coming. Red covered her face and screamed into her hands. The woodsman, deciding that he wouldn't be able to elicit a response from her, leaned over and grasped his ax. This girl wasn't going to talk to anyone …, he thought to himself. I won't let her. He raised the ax above his head and steadied himself. He leaned forward slightly, about to pull the ax across Red's chest when he was thrown to the side by a great, grey force. The grey blur knocked the woodsman off of his feet, quickly pouncing on him. Red quickly propped herself up on her elbows and shuffled away slightly. The wolf had come to her rescue and was now straddled across the woodsman, wrestling with him. The woodsman had the ax, and he knew how to use it, but the wolf was atop him, too close to let him use the ax efficiently. The woodsman let out a few strangled yells and tried to throw the wolf off of him, but it was too heavy, and all he managed doing was aggravating it more with his swift kicks to its belly. The wolf quickly began leaning on the handle of the woodsman's ax, using its weight to slowly make him lower it. The wolf began to snap at the woodsman, its jaws snapping shut with every breath the woodsman took. Eventually, the ax dropped enough for the wolf to nick at his nose, and a swift knee connected with the soft spot of the wolf's belly, almost knocking it off. Suddenly, a lunge from the wolf had it clamp its jaws around the woodsman's temples. Blood drizzled down the woodsman's forehead, the man screaming as his skull began to crunch. He flailed about sporadically, no longer trying to push the wolf off, but now just trying to escape. It didn't work. The wolf's jaws clamped tighter and tighter, ignoring the man's screams. Red began to cry silently, tears tracking down her face. The wolf crunched the skull completely, and the screams stopped halfway through, the sound dying in the huntsman's throat.

Red tried to get to her feet, but she fell back flat again with a small cry of pain. Her ankle was swollen slightly, so something must have happened to it. She scrambled away on her elbows, attempting to run away from the wolf. The wolf looked over at Red, a crazed look in its eye. It prowled over to her slowly, looking roughly twice as large. Red shied away as much as she could, pressing into her ripped hood. The beast leaned over her, leaning down slightly. Red, scared out of her mind, shut her eyes. Suddenly, there was something wet pressed to her cheek. She opened them again forcefully. The wolf was licking her cheek, where a bruise was swelling up when the woodsman hit her. Red looked at the wolf as it hopped off of her lightly. She reached out her hands to it, placing trust into it completely. The wolf moved closer to her and leaned down, letting her wrap her hands around the wolf's neck. The wolf stood up fully, pulling Red to her feet. She leaned to the wolf and stumbled out of the bracken with him. The wolf guided Red along the path and eventually, long after night had fallen, Red could see lights in the distance. Despite being in the woods at night, one of Red's biggest fears, she felt an immense feeling of power being with the wolf. She felt as if everything that would've wanted to attack Red was now keeping itself at bay, scared into docility by the wolf. The wolf took Red to the edge of the woods, where it stopped. Its hackles were raised, staring intently at the town. Red wasn't old enough to understand what was wrong completely, but she could tell the wolf was scared. She patted the wolf gently on the ears and whispered a word of encouragement into its ear. The wolf wasn't completely understanding the girl but was comforted by her soft tone. He ambled forward slowly, supporting Red. There were shocked voices from windows, and cries for help but no stones made contact with the wolf. Red's mother came dashing from the crowd, informed of her child's ragged look by the crowd. She scooped up her child, worried, and carried her off quickly. Red whispered something in her ears as she tried to walk away. She stopped and turned around. She set Red onto the ground lightly. Red beckoned the wolf. The wolf stepped forward. Red grasped the wolf's neck in a tight hug and whispered in its ears.

"Thank you."

Twist Fate: Peter Pan

By Ariana Barzinpour (Mnemofysh)

"Papa, Papa, please read me a story!"
The little girl asks her father with glee.
"All right then, just one more, and then to bed.
Now cuddle up close, lay down your head."

Once upon a time lived little Wendy,
Who thought that her life was rather bland.
But, with her imagination and teddy,
She met fairies and saw faraway lands.

Imagine her surprise when she saw that,
Perched on her windowsill, was a young man!
"Who are you?" she asked, to which he tipped his hat—
"I'm the one and only, the great Peter Pan."

He held out his hand, and she knew what to do:
She grabbed it real tight, and away they flew!
Over mountains, forests, and gurgling streams,
Like a compilation of her best dreams!

And at last their journey came to an end
As they landed on a lush little isle.
"Welcome to my humble home, my dear friend,"
Said Peter Pan with a big, friendly smile.

From that day on, Wendy had so much fun:
She sang and played games, picked flowers, and drew,
Bathed in the ocean, pranced under the sun,
No more school, no homework, no chores to do!

But, soon after, she started feeling quite sad;
She wanted to visit her home for a while.
So she asked Peter, but he looked quite mad,
Then he broke into a sinister smile.

At this, Wendy couldn't hold back a shiver.
"You're not going back," Peter Pan said,
"You see, I like nice little girls ... for dinner!"
He laughed, and poor Wendy was filled with dread.

She turned to flee, but he didn't let her,
"Where are you going? You have nowhere to run!"
Wendy cried at the words of her captor,

Peter Pan gloated: He knew he had won.

But all of a sudden, what did they hear?
"Fear not, my child, I am here to save you!"
Peter Pan froze, then turned around in fear;
Because that deep voice was one that he knew.

Truth be told, Wendy found the man scary,
With his pirate's hat and glistening hook.
He looked, in a way, quite extraordinary:
Like a villain from a fantasy book.

"I won't let you take another life, Pan,
Today I defeat you," said Captain Hook.
"Prepare yourself for a shortened life span,
I've waited a long time for this day, crook.

"You see, I've found myself a nice new pet,
Rather large, and of a pretty green hue.
Remember Tick Tock? I believe you've met.
He's had his taste of me—now he wants you."

Pan drew his weapon, but it was in vain,
As from the sea emerged the crocodile.
Jaws open so wide he could swallow a plane,
He ate Pan with an appetite quite virile.

With Pan defeated, at last Wendy was freed,
And Captain Hook's crew cheered for his success.
"How could I repay this wonderful deed?"
"Simple—just stay out of trouble, princess!

"Now, let's get you home," said the kind man,
"Forget all of this and forget Peter Pan,
Just remember, don't judge a book by its cover—
You never know what you might discover."

"And so," said the father, "the story ends:
Wendy safe back home with parents and friends.
But every night she still hoped to see Hook's ship,
Secretly dreaming of another trip.

"I would tell you about another lady,
Who seemed nice, but was really quite shady:
She forced her stepsisters to slave away,
But that's a story for another day."

The Stockings Were Hung by the Chimney with Dread
By Luca Chang (Threshold0)

'Twas the night before Christmas,
When all through the house
not a creature was stirring,
not even a mouse;
the stockings were hung by the chimney with dread,
in hopes that the children would not be found dead.

The children were nestled all snug in their beds,
while visions of Hope had danced in their heads;
and momma in her kerchief, and I in my cap,
had just settled our guns for a restful Christmas nap.

But out on the lawn there arose such a clutter,
that I leapt out of bed and I started to stutter:
"Oh, no, no, no, could it be? I must hope that Saint Nicholas
just came for some tea!"

I charged the stun,
and hoped for no such fun,
and peeked out the window before jumping the gun;
and to my great surprise I saw
Dasher and Dancer, horns and all.

The rider wasted no time,
ringing the door chime;
I could see he was not slowing down.
So I opened the door,
pleading mercy for the poor,
though it seemed to not be enough;
he grabbed the boar,
off a table for four,
and swung it straight at my earmuffs.

Then Dasher, then Dancer, then Prancer and Vixen;
then Comet, then Cupid, then Donner and Blitzen;
they charged the door;
through the boar,
toward my children's wall,
they bashed away,
smashed away, 'twas quite a maul!

The rider looked down with a pitiful glare,
that bore through my soul like an arrow through the air;
though he noticed my crying and wiped my tears up,
with only a hint of the sorrow I cupped.

His muscular body,
cloaked in red,
seemed to pain my heart like my children's small beds;
his entirety seemed to be laughing at me, though alas,
what can I do but accept it wholeheartedly?

He spoke no more,
my weapon on the floor,
he simply walked out of the room;
when he turned away,
all that I could hear,
was perhaps a small little "poof"

But I heard him exclaim,
ere he drove out of sight,
"Merry Christmas to all, and to all a good night!"

Perhaps the night was good for his life,
but not for me,
but not for my wife.

Twist Fate: The Wolf's Tale
By UKEagleclaw

Everyone knows the story of Little Red Riding Hood, the poor young girl, the elderly old woman, and the big bad wolf, but do you not know that history is written by the victor? Bold words inked by deceit and written by liars have been etched across history for long enough. It is time for me to reveal the true story of Little Red Riding Hood. You may doubt my words but remember that I was only one of the victims of man-made devices. We weren't the ones who desecrated pure green forestland and invaded territory; those were invented by mankind. Like a devastating plague you destroy the Earth, spreading black toxic fumes across its expanse. Never caring for the consequences and, well, if my tale teaches you anything, think about how your actions impact us. So, I will begin from the start to allow you to understand the truth. This is my tale: the tale of the wolf …

Born and raised in vast green forestry, I was named Iris. You may think this is a strange name for a wolf, but I was named after the beautiful purple flower, especially since the resilient but fragile flower was native to our once-great forest. My mother taught me the necessities of how to survive in the wild. Besides, it wasn't too difficult; prey was rich and plentiful at the time. There was such an unbelievable amount of prey. Now that I am looking back, it feels like decades ago. Tell me, how could it change so quickly? Perhaps we should have somehow stockpiled it, but it was impossible to foresee the oncoming threat of mankind. Mother also told me and my siblings that it used to snow but that had ceased as the Earth had warmed and because of that some types of prey had died out. Prey had already begun to die out centuries before my time. Yet another consequence of mankind's selfish actions. Before I spew more anger, I shall continue.

Mother and I stayed in the same forest, whilst my siblings ventured into fresh territories. Even then space was running out. However, even without the rest of our family, we lived peacefully and happily in the forest's shelter. With regret, I remember how the forest had been untouched by mankind's poisonous hands. There had been a great oak that towered into the sky, beyond sight. Except now it's toppled along crushed earth, being shredded by metal machines.

Seasons passed and tragically my mother was captured by mankind, taken against her will, in harsh metallic traps. I only just escaped at the urging of my mother, who told me to flee. When I looked back I saw two humans standing over the cage. One young and the other old, exploder sticks strewn over their shoulders. There was a bang, a black pellet whirling past my ear. Whatever it was, it had only just missed. Vines tore my pelt as I ploughed through thick undergrowth. Limping, I eventually reached my leafy nest. Sighing with a mixture of loneliness and relief, I settled down into a deep sleep.

Soon after, I realised the humans had started trampling over the far reaches of the forest, sending dark and vile-smelling fumes deep into the air. A great sweeping clear river once flowed through the forest, but it was soon poisoned; decaying fish began washing up on its shores. Failing to catch me, they seemed content with contaminating the precious water supply. With that, the water transformed into dark grey slime.

Prey began to starve, and into this disastrous and hopeless world my pups were born. I had mated for a short time with a passing wolf, which I soon regretted when he left, worried about the encroaching humans. Perhaps I should have left with him, but I couldn't leave my home that I had grown up in.

But there is a strong side of me that wished we had. We could have left and found new, greener hunting lands, away from mankind's wrath of destruction. I tried and tried but it wasn't enough. The prey was gone. I spent every heartbeat searching but mankind had taken it all. The triumphant and smirking looks of the two humans taunted me in my thoughts and dreams. Soon the earth claimed my pups, and I had nothing to fight for.

Grief stricken, I wandered in random directions, pledging to stop the destruction that had murdered my pups. Mankind had brought chaos to my life; where would their deadly rampage end? They'd murdered my prey, my forest, my mother, and my pups. Deciding that no one else should suffer a similar tragic fate, I searched day and night to find those two humans and bring an end to their evil scheming. It wouldn't bring anything back, but I had to at least try to invoke justice.

Somehow, I stumbled across the younger human at a random forest path. A red hood decorated her small figure. I'd planned to convince one of the humans to leave the forest; what would my pups think of me if I inflicted similar pain on someone else? Even if I had no respect for these vile, careless creatures, I knew that I shouldn't sink to their deceitful levels without good reason. Therefore, I waited for the young human to come closer. Then I stepped out of the bush, blocking her path. Before I go any further, I should tell you that in our lands, humans can understand animals such as myself. This is what made their torture over the forest even worse. I begged her to stop destroying the forest and to think of the animals. To my horror the young human refused, stating that this was their forest now and I better get used to it or else.

I was ready to convince her further, but I leapt back as she pulled her exploder stick on me. Bounding away into the dense forest, my frame was struck by a wild round pellet. A tormenting sting flooded my body; why did I ever think they'd listen? Mankind wasn't to be trusted; surely my life had taught me that by now? At that moment, I had no intention to find the other human, just escape this nightmarish forest. I realised that there was no hope now; the humans were victorious. Nothing could stop their powerful arsenal of weapons.

Despite this, fortune decided otherwise. Not expecting it, I came across a wooden shack in the far edges of the forest. Tree stumps and discarded wood clippings were spread around its borders. It creeped me out, but I was planning to quickly and quietly pass by when the haunting elderly human stepped out, halting me in my tracks. There was a side of me wanting to run and get away from her conquering posture. The other side wanted to find out why they'd destroyed the forest, stomping over the sacredness it once possessed. Muscles tensed, trying to block out the pain of the exploder stick's pellet wound, I prowled up to the entrance. Not wanting to get in a fight, I made sure she spotted me. She instantly stared down at me, and I saw the disdain, clear as the sky, in her eyes.

"Why have you destroyed the forest?" I bellowed, searching for a reason. Anything would have eased my mental and physical wounding.

"Why?" the elderly human mocked. "Because it is mine to take. Pitiful creatures like you don't deserve any right over all this. Soon all the trees will be gone to fuel mankind's industrial productions. This is our Earth, not yours!"

"What makes you think that you can destroy our lives? What have I or any other animal done to you?" I couldn't believe the audacity and disrespect of this human; it was far worse than anything I'd encountered before.

A huge smirk filtered across her face. "Power. You are all weak, unable to defend your territory. I and my strong machines crushed you easily. Now, you've all scattered like the wind. Believe me, it was far too easy."

I shouldn't have, but I snapped, clawing and biting at her until she thumped to the floor. Seeing the ghostly look in her eyes, I was ashamed that I had been like her but also partly relieved that this monster had gotten what it deserved. Possibly others had been saved from her villainous destruction.

Before I had the time to do anything else, a bold black pellet splintered through my body, making me drop. Everything flashed before me; however, I was glad. Soon I would meet everyone I had lost. It would mean seeing my family again. Two dark, tormenting figures stood over me as the light faded from within my temple, leading me to the silvery spirits above.

If you hadn't already guessed, that's from where I tell this tale to you now. I hope that you have been warned to think about your actions and the effects they have on nature. The ice caps are melting and the Earth is warming up against nature's will, and mankind has to take some of the blame. Emissions disrupt the ozone layer and other dangerous gases leak into the air. Don't forget the animals whose habitats you are destroying. If you've listened to my tale so far, remember that you have the power to safeguard the Earth, unlike those pesky poaching mankind. Unfortunately, my time is up, and it's up to you now …

The Princess and the Pea:
A Pea's Point of View

By Sarcasm_is_a_Virtue

Day 14 of utter torment. Another day of abuse. I was released from the freezer to be flicked unceremoniously onto a vast and incredibly comfortable bed. This was fine by me, but the girl in the room? Well, she was something else. In case you're wondering, yes, your derriere does look enormous in that nightdress. Incredibly rude, I thought; letting another stranger in, unannounced. So just as I was beginning to feel quite happy with my huge bed all to myself, an enormous mattress was deposited on top of me, engulfing me in darkness. Several more shakes of the bed followed this first one and I would assume that they were due to more mattresses being loaded above. I sighed resignedly; I already knew that this was going to be another long night to endure.

~~~~~

Well, that was one big woman. I hope you are aware that it isn't just your nightdress making you look that size; you really do have a voluminous rear end. Fortunately, I was returned to my safe haven, so I immersed myself in a cooling ice bath for the remainder of the day to rest in undisturbed peace. That was until the sounds of torrential rain reached my small but sensitive ears. Windows rattled, doors shook and slammed, and my icebox was wrenched uncouthly open. Here we go again. This was different, however. I'd love to say that this girl was as light as a feather and hadn't eaten all the pies but that would be a lie. She was misleadingly slim and of acceptable physique, but boy was she just as heavy as the last 14 hefty women. She sank just as ungraciously onto the now seemingly ridiculously oversized accommodation and settled herself down for her "beauty" sleep. Honey, you need it. Unfortunately, it didn't really make much of a difference in terms of weight; as the night wore on she only succeeded in growing steadily heavier.

The following morning, Colossal Rear End had the audacity to remark on how uncomfortable her night had been. Her night. What about mine? She should try being a pea for once. She didn't have someone with a weight that doubtless broke the scales tossing and turning all night long right above her. But did she see me complaining? No.

The most insulting thing was that they all tried to pin the blame on me. I mean really? Why do I have to be the bad guy? I didn't do anything, I just sat there quietly, not disturbing anyone. Nonetheless, that witch of a woman who condemned me to my bed of Procrustes brought me out as the sole culprit in the matter. Not only this, but in my opinion, I didn't even get a fair trial. We're supposed do the whole speech thing, aren't we? Plead your case? Testify? Well, I didn't even get that. Accusing eyes turned stonily toward me and they regarded me with mixed expressions as I sat there, silent, innocent until proven guilty.

Before I could make my move, the old one lunged toward me, pinched me between her gnarled fingers, and tossed me into the now foreboding freezer along with my silent acquaintances. Time passed quickly and before I knew it we were being scooped up all together. I had to think quickly; there wasn't much time. The pot loomed, ever closer, and without a second thought I rolled away from my comrades and tipped slowly over the edge. Hard, cold stone rushed up at an alarming pace toward me. The momentum was too much; I hit the ground and continued rolling, down the step—bump—through the next room—smack—straight out the door and down three more steps—bang, crash, wallop. Finally, after excruciating pain, after Hell froze over, after the sun crashed down into the Pacific, etc., I came to an ungraceful stop. I checked myself over for breaks; none, thank goodness, except for a small slice on my right—or left depending on which way I thought about it (hard to tell when you're a sphere). Relief was short and sweet, however, as the dulcet tones of an overexcited dog bounded up to meet me as an enormous thing approached. Ah. Right. I guess I should have probably thought things through a little, but I didn't, which was why I was here and why things were rapidly going south.

So that's how I find myself here, with my short life flashing before my eyes. I gulp; this is it: the last stand, the final reckoning, the calm before the storm, the beginning of the end, the—well you get the idea. So you see, not all fairy tales end with happily ever after, at least not if you aren't the prince or the princess or whoever is on the cover of the book, but just think next time what it's like from the bad guy's point of view. From a pea's point of view.

HANSEL AND GRETEL   BY LYRRA ISANBERG (KANILOPE)

Hansel and Gretel
By Lyrra Isanberg (Kanilope)

Hansel and Gretel murder the witch, take her money as well as her house, and, disenchanted with human beings for abandoning them, take up residence in the cottage in the woods to lure in new murder victims.

Also, take a look at the left cage.

Twist Fate: Locked and Loaded
By phantomparley

For hours upon end, the young girl had been traversing the forest in search of food. Alas, she had come to nothing and only had an empty canteen to show for her poor marksmanship. She had earned several images of fleeting animals bounding away into nature's embrace. Everything she came across had escaped such close encounters that she concluded Mother Earth was teasing her pitiable ability, and to make matters worse, any missed shots with her rifle simply alarmed the whole area of her presence and lowered her chances of nabbing anything. The week had been cruel on her, with each day a vicious repeat of the previous.

Feeling defeated, the girl began to walk back home upon the grassy path, dappled with sunlight. The trees all seemed to blur together into a sea of green, making her wonder how much progress she had really made. With the endless onslaught of unattainable prey, she had also lost her sense of time. Perhaps she would become trapped, doomed forever to chase the unachievable. Maybe she would perish of malnutrition, alone.

And thus, she suffered a barrage of her own thoughts, growing increasingly twisted as the day dragged on. Exhausted and famished, she continued walking until she reached a shaded area, and slowly lowered herself onto the ground to rest. When she lay on her back, her eyes spotted a red-brown blur not too far from her current position. She could feel her heart beat faster. Was this her big break? She had never tried to shoot a wolf before, and it would be a messy job, no doubt, but it was right in front of her eyes. The girl gradually rolled over onto her stomach and adjusted her riding hood. The wolf was upwind of her, unable to scent her company.

She could tell it was a young red wolf. It was padding leisurely down the path with a small mammal in its mouth, with its senses overwhelmed by its prey. The girl questioned nothing and didn't think about it, too focused to let her chance escape. She stood her rifle up and began to position it. Shaking, she lowered her head to look through the scope, reminding herself to aim directly at the wolf and not slightly away, like how she had previously. Out of nowhere, there was a sharp click. She had been too impatient with setting up the rifle properly.

The wolf pricked its ears.

She pulled the trigger.

The deafening crack of the shot seemed to echo incessantly, leaving her ears ringing. The birds, formerly concealed by the heavy foliage of the vegetation, left, squawking into the distant blue. When the resonance of the noise finally faded away, she was met with the curious silence of the forest once again ...

TWIST FATE: LOCKED AND LOADED

BY PHANTOMPARLEY

Twist Fate: Mowgli's New Robe
By DragonitaVioleta

What if ... Mowgli became the villain?

Then, he would use Shere Khan's fur to make himself a robe.

The concept just popped out of my head the first time I saw the contest.

I know that this is kind of sick, but thankfully there's no blood involved.

I've spent five to six hours straight on this drawing; that includes the short breaks I had.

Most of the time was spent on Mowgli and Shere Khan, and I made the background quickly since it's straight colors and shading.

TWISTED FROM: THE JUNGLE BOOK

TWIST FATE: MOWGLI'S NEW ROBE

BY DRAGONITAVIOLETA

Twist Fate: Jack and the Beanstalk
By Bethany Powell (Muppy23)

In this version of Jack and the Beanstalk, Jack is overcome by greed (after cutting down the first beanstalk). He picks beans from the rotting beanstalk to revisit the land of the peaceful giants. While there, Jack continuously steals from them and mercilessly slays any who cross his path.

TWIST FATE: JACK AND THE BEANSTALK   BY BETHANY POWELL (MUPPY23)

NEW QUEEN

BY MORYAPANIMA

New Queen
By MoryaPanima

The Red Queen is no longer the ruler of Wonderland. Everyone hates her and her head-chopping routine.

The Old Red Queen is now living the life of a normal girl, slowly learning that the world does not all revolve around her.

But Wonderland still needs a ruler, someone who won't be corrupted by power.

Of course nothing will go wrong with our sweet, pretty, charming, lovable, little Alice as the new queen.

Of course.

Little Red...

... gone mad

LITTLE RED GONE MAD ...   BY CLAWSUNION

Little Red Gone Mad ...
By ClawsUnion

Sculpture of Little Red and the wolf; something is wrong with the little girl ...

Sculpture is made from Super Sculpey(&Firm) over a wire and foil armature, painted with acrylics.

Twist Fate: Snow White
By YumiAkaru

I always wanted to draw a comic like this since I just like to switch hero/villain roles. When I saw the Twist Fate competition, I already had the whole image in my mind and just started to draw.

It's probably not the most creative switch idea, but I still like it since it seems realistic that someone who has always been beautiful starts to freak out once she gets a rival for the first time …

This scene shows the young Snow White walking in a dark room where the mirror is hanging; inside the mirror is a beautiful woman who can answer any question and show you what you desire.

I simply switched the roles.

The young and beautiful Snow White always liked her stepmother but she loved her own beauty more than anything or anyone else, so when the mirror told her that her stepmother became more beautiful, Snow White decided to pay her stepmother a visit and bring her a *"Present."*

TWIST FATE: SNOW WHITE   BY YUMIAKARU

TWIST FATE: UNSPEAKABLE EVIL

BY JESSIE CHIN (ALTJELLIFICATION)

Twist Fate: Unspeakable Evil
By Jessie Chin (ALTjellification)

In this piece, the roles are switched: Samurai Jack is evil while Aku is good. In this world, Jack wants to kill everyone to satisfy his boredom—including the kindhearted Aku.

MAJORA'S MASK

BY AMY JEAN (CHILLY-DOG)

Majora's Mask
By Amy Jean (Chilly-Dog)

An alternate universe where Link is the one who puts on the mask.

TWIST FATE: PIT   BY LIANA CANNON (MANGAZWOLF)

Twist Fate: Pit
By Liana Cannon (mangaZwolf)

NOTE: This is NOT a re-creation of Dark Pit! Dark Pit is an antihero, not a villain! I haven't gotten any flak for this yet, but I'm bracing myself. I was driven to create this because I felt that the idea of the Chaos Kin was largely underexplored. Fights against it were generally underwhelming, so instead of just leaving alone the idea of the little buggy-whatsit puppeting Lady Palutena into a less-than-challenging boss fight, I wanted to give Viridi a REAL reason to have locked the thing up in the Lunar Sanctum. And I think I can safely say she has one now.

SNOW WHITE

BY DERIN KARABULUT (GLAMRA)

Snow White
By Derin Karabulut (Glamra)

"Once upon a time, there was a girl as white as snow, as red as blood, as black as ebony wood with a heart as cold as ice ..."

I was told that I look like Disney's Snow White by my family and friends. So I decided to draw an evil version of Snow White for this contest.

It's my first time drawing an apple.

BELONGING

The Good The Bad The Evil
By Drawing_With_Ink

"The World pushes us without mercy and when some push back, the world points and cries, 'Evil'"—Mewtwo (Pokémon)

~~~~~

Prologue

The snow was cold underfoot. With every step, a paw print the size of a dinner plate was left behind, quickly covered by a fresh bedding of ice. Above, in the trees, the wind howled with an icy cold breath. *It's as if it always has something to say*, he thought at the current moment. *Has it not heard of silence?* He raised his head as another gust caught his dark ebony fur; the fresh scent of tree sap was mixed well with that of oncoming rainfall.

A storm is coming.

Dark clouds tumbled, growing in size and shade. It was at that moment as he watched the sky, he smelled *it*. A scent he had not caught in a long, long time.

Blood.

A snarl erupted from his throat. His lips withdrawing over his fangs. It was close and he knew it, he knew it as the sky knew it, as the wind and trees knew it. The Demon had been alive for a long time, so long he had forgotten his own name, and in its heed had adopted that in which he had been called many times by both mortal and immortal: *Demon*.

His limbs stretched to meet the call his burning throat sang. The steady *thud* his paws made when they hit the snow was in no way silent and deadly as he knew he should be behaving but before he could even start to care for the racket he was making other thoughts had already started to cloud his judgment. *A deer, perhaps a doe or a buck!* For a moment he faltered as the image of a poor starved rabbit caught in a hunter's snare flashed across his mind; a skinny bag of bones would in no way quench the pains in his stomach or the burn in his throat. It wouldn't matter even if it were to be a hare; the Demon was immortal. He didn't need food, at least not as the mortals needed it. He could feel hunger and pain but he wouldn't die without food, but the pain *would* drive him insane. He snarled in disgust. Never.

The scent of blood was stronger than before, hidden from him by a tree. Be it a bag of bones or a flesh feast, he no longer cared; it was *food*.

The soft cry of sobbing was the first thing he heard as he approached his prey.

Surely I have wandered these woods too long. Since when has a hare been able to sob?

Below his claw, a twig that had gone unnoticed snapped and the sobbing ceased.

"Who's," a soft voice hiccupped, "there?"

The Demon froze.

Hare can speak?!

There was no longer a need for stealth, and so in one small step that would surely be nothing less of a leap for a normal wolf, he stepped from behind the old pine. A road that led in two directions with no signs to point to what may lie in either direction came into view. Sitting beside the crossroad was a young human of the female kind with blonde hair pinned in neat waves down her back. Her stockings were torn at the knee where a scarlet scrape was quickly freezing over and turning blue in the wind. A white hood hid her eyes from view.

She gasped when she saw him, the pale pink of her cheeks draining until she, with the aid of her hood, blended perfectly with the snow. She did not scream or run, only stared at the Demon. It was she who broke the silence.

"Excuse me for being so rude," she whispered, "but I have never seen a wolf so large! My name is Red." With a swift sway of her hand, she pushed back her hood, revealing two perfectly blue eyes that sparkled with not fear nor horror but curiosity. The Demon was silent. What a strange creature he had found, to not scream for her mother to save her. "You must be a wise wolf, have you seen my mama?" she asked. The Demon, for a split second, forgot himself and shook his head. The girl's face fell. An angry growl ran from his stomach to his throat, rattling his teeth and shuddering his spine. He took a step forward. It wouldn't be hard; she was small, small enough to fit almost comfortably between his tongue and teeth.

"Mama told me to go deep into the woods and when Papa's money problems go away, I can come home. But I think she's lost, because it's getting late and Mama hates when I stay out late. Maybe if I go to Grandmother's, but I can't remember which way." The Demon stopped; now was his chance. Point her the wrong way, rip her in two, it'd be over in seconds. The girl had been abandoned. The pain in his stomach turned to a ball of twisted knots; without a sound, the Demon turned and walked away. He knew that feeling, the feeling of abandonment. He could not kill the girl, not now. Red called to him but he ignored her and kept walking. When she was out of sight and her sobbing resumed, he stopped. Before long her sobbing was replaced by shivers before finally the small body stopped moving. The wolf left his hiding spot and stood above the girl. He did not know why he stayed. This wasn't his problem; the troubles of a mortal child should not bother him. He nudged the girl with his snout, breathing in the faint scent of roses. Crouching, he pushed and nibbled softly with the tips of his teeth until the girl was lying comfortably between his shoulder blades.

I'm a fool.

He growled. Around him the storm whipped and roared, hail biting his eyes. The smell of sugar roasting on a fire and a gentle voice drifted from the path to the right barely loud enough for even his ears. Softly, so the girl would not fall, he faced the north and step-by-step walked into the storm.

~~~~~

Evil

10 years later …

"Say it!" She laughed and shoved his shoulder weakly. The wolf glared at her but made no noise. "Say it! Please?" Wolf sighed, a heavy deep noise that rumbled through the clearing, then shaped his lips as Red had taught him.

"*Meow,*" he attempted quietly. Red, not for the first time that morning, attempted to laugh, but her weak giggles quickly died off, turning to whimpers as she clutched her side; a jagged wound ran from her ribs to her hip, bleeding violently. Three years ago, Red's mother had returned to retrieve her but Red refused, and a good thing, too. If Red hadn't refused, Wolf would probably have not run into her again that day and he would have never come to rely on her so much. They sat now with Red resting her back against his side as he lay with his neck twisted so his head could rest by her wound.

"I'm going to die, Wolf," Red said quietly. Wolf stiffened. He had found her here, bleeding and crying but, until now, she had not mentioned her wound, or what happened. He turned so he could meet her eyes and whimper worriedly. A breeze caught her hair. The light in her eyes now gone, her doll-like features twisted into an ugly scowl. He had seen her do this before, split moments where her image of innocent perfection was poisoned with hate and disgust. He knew there was darkness inside of her, but he never cared, he saw it and loved it. Every rose has its thorns, and she was the prettiest rose he had ever seen. Against the dark trees and white snow, she was a flash of colour in a black and white world, and she was his.

"They tried to kill me … " she whispered, anger laced with acid in her tone. "Ten years ago my parents counted on me dying in that storm, but I survived and now I'm a constant reminder of what they tried to do. Their guilt has driven them insane; even Grandma hates me now." Her words lost all emotion and passion as she went from talking to the wolf to talking to herself. For a moment they were in the eye of the storm; calm peaceful frozen in time, it would end soon.

"I don't want to die, Wolf." She whispered. Just for a moment he saw the little girl he met on the day of the frost 10 years ago. And then she was gone and the darkness returned, a horror portrait of twisted features and a distorted grin. Her eyes wide, she stopped talking to him and instead turned to inside where her inner demons were surely screeching.

"Horrible pathetic inferior life forms, how dare they try to take my life! They must *die.*" Wolf's eyes widened as he watched her; she was no longer looking at him but at the sky as she released a screeching laugh. Her blood, a dark horrible scarlet, had dyed the left side of her riding hood a bloody red but her wound was long forgotten. "You won't let them hurt me, will you?" Her voice returned to soft as her eyes turned, pleading. "This is the only way, Wolf." Wolf hesitated, his breath fogging the air. It had been a long time since he had killed a human, not since the day he lost his family.

"Don't you see?" A voice within him whispered. *"You remember, don't you? You were empty until you met her.* Alone. *She is all you have left."*

The wolf snarled and stood, his claws ripping the snow. He will not let them hurt her. He will never be alone again. Ever.

She stood, too, and giggled at his anger. "This is the only way." She whispered, running her hand along his fur until she held the sides of his snout. "When you return, just think of the possibilities. We can finally be together, love. You do love me, don't you?" He didn't need to answer; he loved her and she knew it. "I will go and *talk* to my parents." She smiled. To any other, this would seem hopeful, but to the wolf who loved her, he knew this was a lie. She leaned forward and placed a kiss on his forehead before moving so her lips were beside his ear.

"Kill my grandmother, Wolf. She is, after all, the one who gave me this." He looked down at her wound and roared. He turned in a swift movement and lunged forward into the trees away from the meadow, away from *her.*

He did not see her smirk, or how she grinned as she pulled the blood-worn knife from beneath her hood. He did not hear her victorious laugh or the screams of her parents. No, he could only lift his head as he stood on the hill above the old woman's cabin and howled; a cold heartless scream worthy of a *demon* who had fallen in love with a fallen angel.

Ten years earlier, he had left a sad half-dead little girl crumbled on the doorstep and watched from the bushes above as an elderly lady had opened the door. With a look of pure disgust, the elderly woman had pulled the girl onto her feet before hurrying her inside. And, now, as the door fell easily under the wolf's claws, it was this look of disgust that drove him forward. He stalked with hatred into the cabin and took the single room in, almost as if he were sipping it from a cup.

The wind and snow followed him, filling the room with angry howls; every candle within the room flickered and died under the wind's kiss. All around the room, items were thrown and smashed, from plates and plants to chairs and photos. Across the room on a broken chair sat the elderly woman, tears staining her wrinkled cheeks. The woman was frowning at the fireplace where only embers burned. "So, you've returned," she said quietly, her eyes strikingly similar to Red's. When the wolf made no noise to respond, the old lady lifted her eyes, settling them on the wolf. A thousand emotions flickered in her eyes before settling on fear.

And then she screamed.

~~~~~

Wolf ran, with every muscle in his body pushing him forward. The only thing he could think of was her, even with the old lady's blood still pooling on his tongue, slipping from his lips, leaving a trail of scarlet behind him.

Almost there
we will *be happy*
Now she will *love me*
I won't be alone.

It was at that moment, it hit him. The pain started in his shoulder. Four bursts of pain shuddered his body and broke his rhythm. With a sigh, he fell to the earth. A band of shadows surrounded him. Laughing. Bows and arrows, poised to kill. Their leader stepped forward, savagely kicking the wolf's shoulder with his foot.

"Look at it! It's pathetic," the man spat. "*This* is the Big Bad Wolf of the Dark Woods? A God!?" He laughed with his friends. "I've never killed a God before." He joked with sadistic lust. The wolf growled, temporary shock gone. He pushed himself up, ignoring the arrows in his back and lunged at the leader, who sidestepped him easily. The wolf didn't stop and kept running.

Red.
Red will tell them to stop.
Red.

He burst into the field, slowed by the pain, the hunters easily staying close on his heels. In the center of the field stood a lone girl. Her once-white hood now scarlet, a drop of blood against the snow. In her hand, a knife shone sleek red. Arrows tore his skin, attacking him again and again until he broke at Red's feet.

Finally

Red's frantic eyes flashed from his relieved stare to the hunters' accusing glare, seeming to make a decision. She screamed.

"Monster!"

With disgust, Red moved away from Wolf to stand behind the lead hunter. "That … " she said, thrusting her finger at the wolf, "killed my family!" She sobbed into the hunter's side, who grinned. Pain flooded Wolf's body as realisation hit a second too late. He had been betrayed. Only a mortal weapon can kill an immortal and now he would die.

Finally.

Red stepped forward, the knife in her hand. "I want revenge!" She snarled through fake tears. The hunters, amused, stood back to let her through. Leaning down, she pressed the knife to his throat. Wolf closed his eyes, too tired to fight anymore. And then came the whisper only he could hear …

"Love a *demon* … Don't be a *fool.*"

And then there was only Darkness.

He was alone again.

A Second to Madness
By emperatriss

"We're all mad here. I'm mad. You're mad."
"How do you know I'm mad?"
"You must be, or you wouldn't have come here."
Alice in Wonderland—Lewis Carroll

~~~~~

SHE fell through the rabbit hole.

That was a long time ago, a mere fleeting dream that bled into a nightmare. Every once in a while, she pondered, thought, wondered, about the vast *what ifs* stitching her sanity together. What if the verdict had been just? What if the roses had been red? What if the party had been less nonsensical? What if the cake had kept her shrunken? What if the potion had kept her average? What if the white rabbit had stayed a daydream? What if she had been like her sister? And, damn it all, what if she had stayed awake?

But, the queen had wanted her head rolling, the cards had planted white ones instead of red, the tea party had riddled her to mental exhaustion, the cake had multiplied her size, the potion had shrunken her, the white rabbit had distracted her, she had no interest in a book lacking pictures and conversations—and all this, all this dreaming, it had her falling into Wonderland, a figment of her imagination weaved into her reality.

In this world of madness, Alice lost herself.

She never escaped its embrace, no, not even by pinching herself nor by walking into a good old trunk of a sturdy tree. All she ever did after running from the Queen of Hearts's wrath was that. Run. Run on her own, forget about the Cheshire Cat, the White Rabbit, the Mad Hatter—forget them all.

Alas, time prodded her to stop searching for home, to become one with the mad. However, Wonderland got under her skin too late.

Something stirred in her as she hid in the dark, forever waiting for the day she would wake up by the riverbank, surrounded by pieces fitting together unlike the labyrinthine mad lands she trekked upon.

Her bones ached.

Her skin stung.

Every so often, she checked the bottle and the delicacy. As she remained in Wonderland, the liquid tasted bitter in her throat, reminding her of aging grapes, while the delicacy, it changed, growing smaller and smaller, ultimately mirroring the acerbic flavor her drink held.

Shrink. Grow. Shrink. Grow.

All this for the thought of going home.

Alice was dying from all sorts of things.

Dying of waiting, dying of hoping, dying of trying—it fed on her until it drove a hole through her heart.

Everything never resembled their true essence here; she ought to remember that by now, as she trudged toward the towering palace that lay in front of her, its majesty forgotten by the haunting memories that lull her to sleep, only to jolt her back into consciousness in the process. If her imprisonment meant a purpose, a sole hint crossed her mind.

In her initial adventure, she crossed paths with the Cheshire Cat, telling it she had no desire to interact among mad people. The grinning cat, however, assured her, she was as mad as the lot of them, claiming if her state of mind differed from theirs, she would not have come at all.

She would not have come at all.

Maybe what she intended to do would answer her wish.

Alice wanted her home.

A place to call hers, she must have.

The little girl who found herself in the comforts of another realm altogether shattered into such a broken lass who cursed the mad lands.

All because she stopped wondering.

~~~~~

SHE fell through the rabbit hole.

The Queen of Hearts, pleased with the explanation, resumed her game of animal croquet, one of her favorite pastimes aside from beheading all those who had wronged her. All except one. As the thought set in, the satisfaction on the queen's face sizzled into unadulterated rage. Of course, to the ruthless ruler, how the blonde troublemaker stumbled into their world mattered not. Even if she disappeared back into her own world (where she should damn be as Her Majesty berated every single soul in her presence), the queen fumed at the escaped execution.

"OFF WITH YOUR HEADS!"

Bellowing, the cards folded in fear, backing away as Her Majesty threw a fit, waving her scepter-slash-hammer angrily until she decided her army's numbers of thousands had dwindled into mere hundreds. Dismayed, she stalked out of her garden, and into her throne room, leaving both the animals and her card soldiers relieved of worse fates.

Once sitting on her throne, the queen eyed those in her presence with a freezing intensity of rage, making them avert their gaze by faking curt bows. At that note, her blood boiled, egging her on to proclaim an execution order against them. As her lips parted, the doors slammed open, revealing a distressed White Rabbit fumbling with the broken pocket watch in its hands.

"Too late! Too late to save her from hate!" the rabbit uttered, urgency laced in its voice.

"Why have you come uninvited, Rabbit?" Her Majesty demanded irritably, straightening her posture.

"Alice!"

The name brought a rancid taste to her own tongue as she asked, calmly (by a long shot), "What about Alice?"

"She, she, she," the rabbit muttered rapidly, catching its breath when it halts on the steps at her feet. Only then did the explanation leave its mouth. "She has gone mad!"

"How delight—you mean she hasn't left?" the Queen of Hearts questioned, sarcasm lost as her voice rose at the dawning realization. "Alice, that bloody brat hasn't left!" A distinct shrillness accompanied her screeching. Instead of listening any further, she stood up, eyes darting from knight to knight.

"Cards! Go find her, and bring her to me at once!"

"Your Majesty, wait!"

"No need to find me."

An earsplitting sound of metal scratching against the marbled flooring distracted the distraught cards, and earned the queen's prompt attention. As the entrance to her throne room remained welcoming to any visitor, her heart practically stopped beating at the sight, greeting her.

No, that could not be Alice.

That bloodthirsty maniac could not be the little girl Wonderland brought in.

But the resemblance was peculiar.

Her blue dress, tattered at the seams, flowed as if she were a ghost, having its own movement as she sauntered toward the throne, getting nearer and nearer and nearer. If anything, the queen would have thought trouble found her, when she noticed the familiar stain of blood ruining her clothes, her hands, and her face.

The sword she dragged along bathed in it.

It could not be Alice, but it was Alice.

Wisps of hair as dark as the dreadful night the mad lands possessed clung onto the young lady's ashen skin, drained of life, while her eyes as dead as her grace, although one could point out they used to be in the lively shade of blue.

Meaning, she succumbed.

It was better torture than what Her Majesty had in mind.

And she would have reveled in it, if not for the blade pointed at her from the distance.

"What can you do from where you are standing, child?" she chortled, instilling a sense of authority in her presence. Whether or not Alice came here for a sword fight or whatever she had in mind, the Queen of Hearts still ruled Wonderland. "You think you can kill me?"

The queen gestured for her cards to keep their weapons directed at Alice.

"Maybe I can, maybe I will," Alice replied, devoid of any emotion, like her death was not imminent in this place. It ticked the Queen of Hearts.

"Oh, how so?" the queen scoffed, already fumbling with her skirt as she kept staring at the bloodied sword.

Alice lowered her weapon momentarily, a ghost of a smirk gracing her features. "I had problems getting into your palace, Your Majesty. It seemed like the winged creature at the gates wanted to ward me off, but alas!"

She waved the sword in her hands, marveling in her triumphant trespassing as the queen's eyes widened in disbelief.

"It met such a sad fate," Alice concluded.

"You killed my Jabberwocky?" her Majesty echoed, completely out of it.

"Off with your bloody head!"

The cards lunged at the girl—young lady—with their fragile spears and thin shields. Her Majesty watched them clash; pointed blades jabbed at porcelain skin, shields fended sharp blows, cries left the fallen—yet neither of them, neither queen nor rebel, emphasized the silliness of the battle. One side was bound to lose the second the fighting started. Even as the cards grazed Alice, spilled her blood, their numbers decreased by the minute, the loud *clang*ing getting softer and softer until she faced a lone knight while the others lay defeated and torn on the previously pristine floor.

"Good-bye," Alice chirped, taking a step back as she cut up the last of them.

Furious, the Queen of Hearts marched onward, clutching her scepter. Ugh, those damned fools.

"Must I do everything myself?!"

She swung hard at Alice, footsteps heavy with murderous intent. Her opponent dodged idly, twirling like the little girl she used to be. A laugh escaped Alice as she ducked from the reckless attempt of beheading.

It caught her off guard, it seemed; Alice saw it too.

"Too bad," she sighed as she heaved her sword up, disarming the Queen of Hearts completely.

Before the queen planned her next move, Alice twisted her grip, jamming the blunt end of the sword harshly at Her Majesty's forehead. She doubled over, kneeling against her will when Alice kicked her down.

The damn brat circled her as if she were prey. The nerve of her to giggle like a madman in the presence of a queen.

How dare she!

Clang!

Sword dropped beside her, Alice stopped in front of the queen.

"Now, Your Majesty," she spat, voice dripping in acid as she leaned forward to meet the kneeling queen eye-to-eye.

"Off with *your* head."

The Queen of Hearts's blood ran cold as her heart drummed against her chest.

Bluffing would be a lie.

Alice meant every single word.

"How did you turn out like this?"

A foolish question indeed.

The corners of Alice's lips quirked up knowingly, resembling a smirk.

Of course.

She fell through the rabbit hole.

~~~~~

"Where's the queen?" the Cat asked Alice days after her brief confrontation with the Queen of Hearts.

She hid no chortle as she swung her legs over an armrest of the vacated throne. "Let's just say I let her fall through a six-foot-deep rabbit hole."

Wonderland let her ascend, be Madness itself.

The Little Mermaid
By IleanaLewis

Her ways, they were hardly constant. They'd change like the seasons. But 'til the end, she knew what she wanted. Happiness.

But what she wanted was not what was written in her fate.

Her striving toward happiness never ceased, her agenda never flickered. Her definition of Utopia was the only thing that changed, and her approach to making it to her heaven.

But paradise was not what she was destined for.

From being queen to finding love, and then to being free, her wishes changed often. But somewhere, the young mermaid was always fascinated by humans.

And finally, when she turned 15, she was allowed to watch them from the surface. That was when the land of the humans filled her with a desire to be one of them, and find eternity in her very own soul, with them.

And now, while the music played as she danced on the deck, all she could see was the painful image of her hand in Eric's as they faced the city. Eric's soul a part of hers as she pictures immortality, power, and love. Contentment.

She almost had it. Almost.

But, instead of the warmth of Eric's lips on hers in the middle of their wedding ball, all Ariel felt was a shooting pain up her cursed, flimsy legs as she danced against the cold winds on the open deck. She danced to the music from a party that celebrated the wedding of the one she loved the most with someone who hardly deserved it.

And so she danced, hoping that the pain would kill her before her curse.

She could only blame herself for this mess. She promised her soul to Ursula, to be the witch's slave if Eric fell in love with anyone else. She swore to give up her power, her youth, her untainted heart, all of it if anything such as that were to happen. She hardly expected such an outcome. When she swam the darkest, most treacherous areas of the sea in hopes of finding the sea witch who could grant her the ticket to her true love, she was sure that her love for Eric was strong enough to make him reciprocate it.

But clearly, it wasn't, and now Ariel had no other choice but to give up herself to the most malicious witch of her realm.

She feared for her father the most. He would give up his throne to save his daughter— he'd be ousted, for all she knew. He'd be banished, along with her sisters, and the entire kingdom would be underneath the rule of a witch whose sinful powers knew no bounds.

Young Ariel was too pure, too selfless to allow an entire realm to suffer because of her pursuit for love. She wouldn't let that happen.

As a storm began to appear through the North, the princess made her decision.

And so, for the first time, the word came out of her mouth. The word that her father had warned her about. The word that she was urged to use under caution. The word whose power was said to be beyond anything Ariel would ever be able to fathom in her lifetime. The word that could summon greatness; but along with greatness of that magnitude, there came a price, she was told.

But, with a situation like this, she knew that she was ready to pay any price that was required.

"Mother," she called under her breath, scrunching her eyes shut and clenching her fists by her sides.

And as she exhaled, she felt the cold ocean spray on her closed eyes, on her exposed shoulders, running down her arms to her fingertips. The wind blew relentlessly against her, causing her to shiver, due to both fear and frigidity.

"Ariel, my darling," a voice called.

She snapped her innocent eyes open to an overwhelmingly stunning spirit floating before her blue eyes. Blue eyes that looked exactly like the pale, translucent woman before her, who seemed to glow under the darkness of the stormy dusk.

"Oh, my dear daughter," she exhaled, her freezing hand reaching to cup Ariel's cheek, causing Ariel to flinch.

She could barely fathom the fact that this was the woman she'd spent 15 years wondering about.

"I know what you need, love, and you haven't got much time," said the melancholic voice. "Here," she whispered, taking Ariel's hand in her own before placing a beautifully crafted sword in her hand. The piece of metal glistened underneath her mother's pale glow, but what caught Ariel's eye was the Sapphire embedded on the base.

"The sword of Sapphire," Ariel said in silence, marveling at its beauty while wondering in shock.

"Yes, my dear. The sword of Sapphire possesses the form of power that every hound lusts for. Against what belongs to the virtuous, the purest being, it will fill you with goodness. But, against what reeks malice, it will bestow upon them a lifetime of misfortune.

"Ariel. You were the most virtuous across lands until you traded your voice for human feet. Trading your tail showed the discontentedness in you; the greed because of which there is a patch of darkness in your fate. And though it is negligible, it will be the reason you will not have the happy ending you hoped for.

"The least you can do, child, is sacrifice this beautiful hair of yours to Ursula. When lightness of that strength touches her, it will make her kinder. Nothing is strong enough to erase the darkness from her heart, but she still has space for a ray of light. What belongs to a girl who is filled with light like yours can be that ray of light that she needs. She will negotiate, but eventually, you will get your talk back.

"You will never truly be happy, but you will still live with those who love you, Ariel. So take her offer.

"Using magic like this always has its consequences, so be sure that you are willing to bear them."

Those were the last words that Ariel heard before all that was left of her mother was a cloud of cold smoke.

And Ariel stood on the deck, facing the horizon, sinking in her thoughts as the cold metal grazed her skin.

"Consequences," she thought to herself, weighing them. She would only have her family, for she'd never be accepted back by anyone else. Not after she betrayed her own by trading her tail for feet. She'd never long to swim up to the surface for the reminders would be far too painful. She'd never be beautiful or youthful.

But most important, she'd never be happy. She'd never have Eric.

What was a life like that worth?

She looked down at the sword in her hand in that moment; she knew what to do. Her actions would change her forever, but at least, she'd have the happy ending she deserved.

And so, she ran. She ran as fast as those dainty feet of hers would allow. She ran with her gown bunched up in one hand and the sword in the other. She ran because her life depended upon it.

Battling the winds, racing her time, the sparse amount of time she had left, she reached Princess Vanessa's room.

Without a second of hesitation, Ariel flung it open. Before her eyes stood the dazzling figure in white, facing the mirror as she wiped the tiredness off her face.

"I've been waiting to get a moment with you, Ariel. Come in, sit down," she offered, but Ariel stood there defiantly, her grasp around the sword tightening. She held it behind herself, taking not more than three steps inside the room.

"You must be feeling horrible about the fact that Eric fell in love with someone much better than yourself, because I feel terrible for you," she said complacently, perched on the edge of her bed.

"And so, I'd like to give you this." She pulled out a locket from inside the drawer by her mirror.

"A reminder that your fate," she said as she chained the necklace around Ariel's slender neck, "is not in your hands."

A conch for a pendant.

Ariel could feel her heart pounding. This was her moment.

With unprecedented force, Ariel slashed the sword against Vanessa.

In the dim light, all Ariel could see was a dark stain on her wedding dress and a glinting artifact jutting out of the woman.

She couldn't breathe. As the cold sword left her grasp, her senses came back to her. Ariel collapsed to the ground with an overwhelming sense of shock.

The strength in that sword drove her to this. The minute she let go of the cursed metal, she saw her mistake.

Maybe she had far darker intentions than her mother saw.

Before she could take in the situation, Vanessa's body slumped before Ariel with a soft thump.

Instantaneously, Ariel pulled out the sword from her gut and flung it across the room but it was far too late. She was bleeding out.

Ariel desperately pressed the wound, praying that the bleeding would stop as she sobbed.

And that was the moment she realized that what she had her hands on wasn't blood.

She looked to Vanessa's face and it rested with a smile, her eyes open with a grin. The soft skin on her arms slowly began to shed, revealing a rather dreadful, pale, sickening layer—a repulsive excuse for skin. It spread through her hands to her face and the grin only grew.

"You were a fool from the start but this—I barely expected it from you."

Ursula.

"You're far more naïve than I imagined—not that I'm complaining," added the witch.

"You see, Ariel, the thing about being Ursula is that ..." she trailed off, pulling Ariel down, closer to her. "It's that you can't ever die. You can only be killed.

"You see, I inherited a curse from a woman much like myself. Lord knows her story, but she passed on because I killed her and I had to take over, I had to live the treacherous seas for over a few thousand years as a punishment for my folly. A few thousand years with not as much as one visitor. Every generation was warned about 'the evil Ursula,' and I hadn't seen a soul in over 3,000 years.

"Until you, my darling. With a will as strong as yours, it was so easy to get you to agree to my conditions. The moment I saw you, I knew that you were my ticket out of this blazing misery." Her scaly hands reached up to stroke Ariel's frazzled locks but the little girl was far too shaken to react.

"I expected you to beg me for your tail, which I would have gladly given back after having a little negotiation with that father of yours who is willing to do just about anything for you. His kingdom would have made the deal. And then, in this eternal life of mine, there'd at least be something to look forward to.

"But you, my angel, you made this so much sweeter. A blade this powerful can not only end my life, but magnify it.

"And in case you didn't figure it out yourself, you're my dear heir. Because curses like this don't die, they only move on," she cackled, the life fading from her voice.

"Congratulations, Ariel. This is now your life to live," she whispered with a smirk filled with the amount of satisfaction that makes one fear the future.

"Your fate is not in your hands," was the last thing that Ariel heard before Ursula's spiny hands latched themselves onto the necklace hanging on Ariel's neck.

Silence filled the room, along with the electricity that sent sparks along Ariel's skin as the foam that once was Ursula. She looked down at her skin, and to her shock, she could see it hardening.

A scream ripped through Ariel's lungs as she tried desperately to wipe it off.

And underneath her soft fingers, she felt it. The hardened skin.

A look at the mirror was enough to bring Ariel to a blubbering mess.

Ursula was right. Ariel was her heir. And the young princess could only be relieved of this if someone were to kill her.

She needed an Ariel to her Ursula.

~~~~~

Ariel was chained. Trapped. A prisoner in her own nightmare.

Her scaly fingers stroked the polyps that floated around in her castle, occasionally wrenching them because she could.

Ariel represented the wrath of the sea.

Nearly 8,000 years had passed since she last interacted with a living creature—8,000 years since she had spoken to anyone but herself. She was trapped—trapped in her own darkness and vileness.

Eight thousand years and she could not leave her castle without coming face-to-face with her liquidator.

The thought often filled the witch with rage, and often, she'd try to swim outside the boundaries of her prison, only to hit the curse that kept her in.

So, she decided to wait.

She was made to wait for eight millennia before her time came.

One stormy night, Ariel decided to watch the crystal ball that sat before her, showing her the kingdom that could have been hers—as if to mock her—when she saw it.

Princess Esmeralda, the youngest of the five daughters, swam up to the surface to watch the stars. A ship came into the young girl's sight and Esmeralda watched in awe, the beauty of the prince on board.

And Ariel saw it. She saw the same look in her eyes that Ariel had 8,000 years ago.

And Ariel's time was here. She knew she was free.

When dawn broke, she sat on her throne with a smile. It was the first smile that the castle has seen in eons.

"Oh, Ariel," called a timid voice, before a redheaded princess swam in.

"I need your help," she said, shivering.

"I know exactly what you need," replied Ariel. "And I, I know that you will give me exactly what I need in return."

Ariel's eyes shot over to the sword of Sapphire that sat in its scabbard, by the throne.

"You, darling, will give me my happy ending as I will give you yours."

As she spoke, she swam the gates of her castle. Her hands extended to touch the weeds outside her territory.

They were slimy beneath her fingers but they sparked a form of ecstasy that she had never felt before.

Ariel swam over to the princess with a smile, before unhooking the necklace around her very own neck.

"Darling," she whispered, hooking the thin necklace around Esmeralda's neck. "You must remember that your fate is in your hands, no matter what anyone says to you."

The words one heard in a conch were a prediction of the future. And the last word that Ariel heard in the conch was *death.*

The Queer Quill
By Knilesly

"We have officially reached 500,000 readers," a tall woman announced. Jubilance radiated from under her hair, which somewhat resembled a worn-out feather duster.

Gathered in front of the woman was a group of around 20 witches and wizards. Above them, hundreds of owls were flying through the air with multicolored magazines fastened to their claws. The applause from the group along with the clapping of wings cracked like thunder through the large room.

A thin, handsome wizard sporting a long cloak, in vivid swirls of different color, stood in the front of the group. "Marvelous," he exclaimed as he walked up to the woman who had made the announcement and gave her a kiss on both cheeks.

He straightened his back and turned around to face the group. "As you all know, The Queer Quill has fought for the rights of many witches and wizards all over the world for 40 years now. I can still remember the days we rushed about my tiny flat to get our magazines out to our 50-odd readers. I can only thank all of you for your perseverance and hard work that got us to where we are today. Now," he paused and smirked in the direction of a big, pale, dark-haired wizard, "Dolohov, I think this celebration calls for a few pints of butterbeer." Dolohov laughed and raised his fist in agreement. "I'll take out my prized collection, Tom," Dolohov replied joyfully.

Tom Riddle took in the group of people in front of him as they joined in conversation. He could not help but express his feelings of pride. He was the editor-in-chief of The Queer Quill, a weekly magazine that raised awareness of the LGBTQ+ rights of witches and wizards by providing the latest in LGBTQ+ news and happenings. The magazine had something to the likes of every witch or wizard, ranging from Matilda Mantelpiece's weekly motivational article, "A Wand's a Wand," to Pippa Fondleberry's hilariously quirky guide to gay relationships, "What to Do if You Have a Lover in Your Brew," with a useful yet side-splitting tip every week.

For the next hour or so, Tom went around making conversation. He learned that Dolohov had asked his partner's hand in marriage, and, along with everybody else, congratulated him with an off-key rendition of "A Cauldron Full of Hot, Strong Love." Charlie Knaggs recited his trademark joke of two aurors and a goblin—one that he would repeat to anybody unfortunate enough to come across him after he had had a few swigs of firewhiskey, which he hid, to everyone's knowledge, underneath an old Chudley Cannons poster in his top right drawer. Tom nearly gave the floor a fresh coat of butterbeer as he tried to contain his laughter listening to Pippa Fondleberry's unsightly ordeal with a Blast-Ended Skrewt that her nephew had somehow sneaked into the house during their Easter visit. With his eyes tearing from laughter, Tom finished his butterbeer and excused himself from the gathering. He had work to do.

Tom knew that he had to do something special for the following week's issue. The Queer Quill had reached a milestone that would not pass by unheard of. As Tom walked to his office, he brainstormed a few ideas. He would definitely include a special article that he would write himself, and maybe he could even convince Albus Dumbledore to write an article as well. Albus Dumbledore had been one of the first readers of the magazine and was a good friend of Tom's. Tom reached his office and took a seat in his chair—it, of course, sported all the colors of the rainbow. He immediately caught a glimpse of the picture on his desk. A man with an angular face waved back at him, smiling as he posed with a broomstick in hand.

It was his partner, Centennius Burke, the love of his life for 40 years. Centennius was an accomplished businessman—the largest broomstick manufacturer in the whole of Europe. The picture had been taken in front of his then-tiny shop and the broomstick he held was the first one he had made. Love filled Tom's heart and thoughts of the magazine's next issue drifted from his mind and was soon replaced by memories.

Tom relived the day he had met Centennius. *He was back at Hogwarts on his way to one of Professor Slughorn's classes. He was just at the library and had a burning question to ask the Professor.* Tom could not even remember what he wanted to ask him. Horticulture maybe? *He was rushing to get there, so he took a route that he knew to be short, and quiet. He ran up a flight of stairs and down a narrow corridor. He was going at a swift pace as he rounded a corner. He was in such a hurry that he did not notice the figure coming his way. They collided with a thump of heavy books as they hit the floor. Tom shot up and dusted off his cloak as he tried to gather his books. He reached for his copy of Advanced Potion Making—and so did the other person. Their hands met. Tom slowly raised his head. He was met with eyes the color of brilliant green emeralds. The boy in front of him had an angular face with perfectly sculpted cheekbones. His dark hair was cut short on the sides of his head, and the longer hair on top was messy as if he had just got out of bed.*

Tom was not able to keep the wonderful thoughts away. *"You know I love you,"* Centennius whispered. *Tom felt his heartbeat increase. He had only known Centennius for a few weeks, but he knew that he felt the same. "I, I love you too," he whispered back to him. They were in the library. The OWLs were in full swing so the library was packed. Tom thought it a risky move exchanging their declarations of love but did not care much. He loved Centennius and had no interest in what the world had to say.*

The rest of their time in school was magical. Tom and Centennius were inseparable. They spent countless hours on the grounds of Hogwarts together. They were always together at the library. It had turned out that they had both been fond of books, and were still to the day. *They did everything together. They slipped out at nights to be together since Centennius was in Ravenclaw and Tom was in Slytherin. Everyone thought it was weird that a Slytherin and a Ravenclaw could be together and more so that they were both boys. Tom could not have cared less. And Tom knew that Centennius thought the same.*

They were, of course, very fortunate to have Professor Albus Dumbledore on their side. He covered for them during the times that they snuck out, even allowing them a few minutes in his classroom at times when the halls were patrolled more thoroughly. He stood up for them whenever students threw hateful slurs their way. Professor Dumbledore had even jeopardized his post once by standing up to the headmaster after he had told them that they were no longer to see each other.

Tom's favorite memory flooded his mind. Their first kiss. *Tom and Centennius were sitting under a large tree outside. It was sunny and cool. The grass waved effortlessly in the slight breeze. They were on the edge of the castle grounds. Here and there a bug moved. They were comparing their transfiguration homework. Through paging through a heavy textbook, and scribbling down notes, Tom sneaked a few peeks at Centennius. He did the same. They were writing something down from page 2137 when Centennius started closing the space between their faces. At first, Tom thought that he had something on his face, but he soon realized what was going to happen. Centennius's lips were soft and perfect. Tom could not have asked for more.*

Tom snapped out of his thoughts. Contentment crept through his body as he reached for his multicolored quill.

The Good Dementor

By Sophie Wainwright (BisonLover)

Cloaked bodies of obsidian shadow,
Clawed arrows, their dark oddity fallow.
Chillingly equipped, thy soul is at risk,
Fears are ignited with the Dementor's Kiss.

But under one's hood there's a different tale,
Behold! A trifle glow that is free from avail.
A burning credence, destined for glory,
This silhouette is far from enormity.

Watching softly, breathing benign and slow,
The dark Dementor asks not for sorrow.
Instead, he prayed for an ardour so strong;
He only sunk. Oh! Where has yonder light gone?

TWISTED FROM: HARRY POTTER

The Burning Queen

By Jeanna Pittman (ZoeyBlueRose)

It was all running smoothly, just as I knew it would. But many things could still go wrong in the time that would follow. Despite my doubts, I had to go through with this. With the royal family gone, I would be next to power. I wanted to change this kingdom, make it better. All the current ruler wanted was the compliments that being king gave him. I was determined to accomplish my task. They would have to kill me to make me stop trying. And they didn't even know who I really was.

I cautiously looked around the next corner. While I knew all the cameras were unhooked, my doing, of course, the guards were still patrolling the palace.

Slipping the sleeping serum into their food was far too easy. As easy as listening in through the ventilation shafts as the family headed to bed early, thinking that they all must be coming down with something. Lighting the chemically soaked carpet that lined the hall to their sleeping chambers was probably the easiest. Pulling myself away from the beauty of the flames was the hardest. Fire is a beautifully dangerous thing and I admired it enough to consider it my only ally.

I then had turned to run when I heard the scream of the youngest girl. She was about four years old and such a fragile-looking creature. I had never heard her be nasty to anyone and, despite her pampered life, she had never looked down on anyone.

She was the one who I'd had the hardest time killing. I had rationalized by saying it would be painless. She would be asleep. At least this way, I had told myself, she'll never know the cruelties of life.

But now, she was awake and would feel the smoke choke her as she slowly suffocated or the burn of the fire as she was engulfed in flames. I had made sure they would all be sleeping. Perhaps the girl had not eaten enough, or perhaps what she had eaten had had no serum.

Now she would die feeling everything, knowing that she would never see the sun again. My conscience fought against me and I forced myself through the fire. Even as cruel as I knew I was, even I could not live with myself if such an innocent died in such a horrid way.

Running through a blazing fire is excruciating and I felt my flesh burn on my lower body. I pulled the girl up into my arms. My skin was blistering, my eyes tearing, and my throat burning. She wrapped her arms around me tightly and gripped me with all her might. I stepped back through the flames in a way in which she would not be hurt.

I must have forgotten a particular variable, overlooked something crucial because instead of burning away at the world behind us, the fire exploded, forcing us away. I held tightly to the little girl as we were thrown. I felt the fire lick at my skin and heard the girl scream in my ear. My body curled protectively around her just before my head smacked against something hard and everything went dark.

~~~~~

I awoke the same way most fall asleep—very slowly but, then, all at once. All of the noises around me grew in intensity until they all swarmed around my head like busy bees. It was a great challenge to even decipher one noise from another.

It hurt to open my eyes but I really wanted to know where I was. I opened my eyes slowly, letting them adjust. When I could finally focus on the room around me, I realized I knew exactly where I was: a hospital. The blinding-white room and sheets along with beeping machines and a small tube that I had just realized connected to my strangely scarred arm were clear signs.

Suddenly, the door opened with a soft click. My head jerked to face whoever was entering, flaring up the pain in my head. A middle-aged, gentle-looking women stood near the doorway, a clipboard in arms. When she saw me looking at her as well, she smiled.

"Good afternoon, Abigail. It's good to see you awake. You've been asleep for quite awhile," she said.

I looked around. Was she talking to me? That wasn't my name … was it? What was my name? I felt the fear build up inside me as I realized I couldn't even remember my own name. I couldn't remember who I was.

"Who am I?" I asked.

~~~~~

My name was Abigail Lynn Saville. At 23 years old, I have forgotten my entire life before now. But, I have been told, I saved the youngest girl of the royal family, Ciara, from perishing in the fire that had killed the rest of the family. No one knows why I was there that night. They figured I had seen the flames somehow or heard the girl scream. In one month's time, I would be crowned queen of this kingdom. And I will probably never remember who I was before. Or, at least that's what the doctors say.

No one can figure out who started the fire. There was little that could be found out as most of the evidence had been destroyed by the fire. And now neither of us, Ciara nor I, had any remaining family. When they said they were still deciding where to place her until she came of age to care for herself, I blurted out, without thinking at all, that I wished to take the girl in.

I don't know why I said that but I knew that I wanted to. It made sense for the future queen to be raised and mentored by the current queen and so it was decided that I would be her new guardian.

It took a full day and night before they decided I was ready to go home. I was to live in the undamaged half of the palace until the side originally made to house the ruler and his or her family was repaired. I told them to take their time. It wasn't urgent and I wished it to be restored to its original beauty.

I explored the saved part of the palace with Ciara and we decided on two rooms right next to each other. We had quickly bonded and, by the time a month had passed, having had as much information about ruling this kingdom as possible shoved in my head, she was to walk with me during the crowning ceremony. She was excited by the idea and I was glad to make her happy.

The ceremony was extravagant and beautifully put together. The ceremonial crown was placed atop my head. On my finger, a ring was bestowed. I was now married to my country. I could still marry a lover in reality but it was a symbol of how devoted I should be to the well-being of my country. Somehow, I was already aware of what that meant and had no problems accepting it.

After becoming queen, I began to reorganize some of the systems of my kingdom so that we could benefit from the taxes as much as possible. Too much of it was being put toward the beauty of things when it should be put toward the stability of the kingdom. Also, the farmers and the workers were paying far too much in taxes compared to the businessmen. I assisted in developing a new system in which the taxes helped instead of hurt.

We, the council and I, also began to develop systems to help my people. Monetary support for the poor and homeless, as well as more funds for schools and other community necessities, were better managed with our new systems. Everything seemed to be going well and the people began to see me as a truly good queen. But then …

I was sleeping in my room when it happened. I had a vision. I may have been able to do this, to see the future before the fire but, of course, I could not remember. Perhaps it was a side effect of the injury to my brain.

In my vision, I was on a plane and looking out to the wing. And then, the captain announced over the intercom that we had to find our seats and buckle our seat belts as we were about to hit some turbulence.

Everything was fine our first wave. But the second wave was much stronger and, as I looked back out the window, I saw that one of the engines had begun to smoke. I screamed. The captain assured us that since it was only one engine, and we were fairly close to another airport, that we should be fine. That was until another wave hit, knocking out two more engines. People began to talk of terrorists, about how unlikely it was for so many engines to go at once. Many began to weep as we knew that the plane would not make it. We were dropping too fast. And then … we crashed.

My eyes shot open and I sat up in bed with a start. It's just a dream, I told myself. But that didn't seem to help. Somehow, deep inside, I knew it wasn't just a dream. Five days later, I was proven right when a plane filled with passengers crashed in a farmer's field just outside the borders of my kingdom. People spoke of terrorists, just as the people on the plane had. But I knew it was all my fault. I could have stopped the plane, I could have … What could you have done? I asked myself. People would have thought you were crazy. No one wants a crazy queen.

As weeks passed, more and more visions began to fill my head. More and more people were killed under my rule. I did not know what to do. One night, when I could not seem to force myself to sleep, the vision hit me while I was still wide awake. Many buses would be rigged with explosives that would go off mid-rush hour, just in time to catch the people who would be heading home to their families. I had to do something. But what? Even as queen, I felt helpless to do anything.

For a few hours, I roamed the halls of the palace. Only a few security guards were roaming, protecting me and my adopted daughter. None interfered with my business, which I was glad for.

Somehow, I found myself in the damaged part of the palace. I was told that it was too dangerous to be in or near it but I was curious. I saw the progress they were making in reviving the beautiful palace. But I also saw the damage caused by the arsonist.

As I moved through the destruction, I began to feel a pulling at the back of my mind, as if I was desperately trying to remember something. As I examined a particularly strange charred mark in the destroyed wall, my memories came rushing back. I hadn't wanted to remember them, it seems, as they weren't particularly nice.

My mother and father had perished in a fire when I was 17. Because of the "kindness" of the king, I was taken in and allowed to live in the in-law quarters, which were empty due to the absence of both the king's and the queen's parents. As I still had the curious mind-set of a child, I often wandered the palace next door and discovered many secrets about the way the king managed the taxes. I did not like what I found one bit. He used most of it for himself, to feed his many addictions. I had found where he hid the money but had left it alone, knowing that taking his money would not be as effective as ending his corrupt reign altogether.

I became the bad guy in the eyes of the people, planning to overthrow the king who was loved by the ignorant people who had no idea that their beloved ruler was causing much of their suffering. And then, I truly become evil when I no longer wanted to just end the reign of the king, but the life of him and his whole family. I wanted to be queen, with the power to control so many people. I was the villain in this story.

I thought briefly about turning myself in ... but I had too much self-preservation for that. And ... I could make up for it in my own way. I had been the arsonist, the one people speculated was a terrorist. And now a real terrorist is running about, wreaking havoc on people's ways of life. And I could stop it. I knew when, where, and what before anything even happened. I could be the one to save the day instead of the one to ruin it.

As soon as I had brought myself back together, I put together a plan. I didn't think it would work, but I had always been good at persuasion and talking in a way that made people want to trust me. Back then, it had been bad for them, good for me. But now, it would be good for everyone. I didn't feel so helpless anymore.

I ran to what I called my office and used my business phone to call the bus station. Calling the police would result in an investigation against me instead of for me. There was still the risk but I had the hope that they would be grateful, not suspicious.

"Upstreet Bus Network. How can I help you?" a strangely cheerful voice asked.

"This is Queen Abigail. I would like—"

I heard a little gasp and sigh.

"Good morning, your Majesty. To what do we owe the honor?" the woman asked.

"My ... advisers and I have come to believe that the terrorist group that has been striking our country will attack your bus station next. This should happen around rush hour tonight. We advise that you up your security and call in the police force around this time." I tried to sound as professional as possible but my voice wavered slightly. I hoped the woman didn't notice.

"Right away, your Majesty. Thank you, your Majesty. Should I alert the press?" She sounded as if she couldn't think of anything else to say. But what else do you say to a call like this so early in the morning?

"No, no ... that will only cause panic, which is what the terrorists want. They can get their story after everything is under control."

"Of course, your Majesty." She was quiet for a moment. "Should I keep you informed?"

"No, that's all right. I will simply watch the news with everyone else," I said. "Thank you, though."

A soft click was heard as I placed the phone back in its holder.

I sat down on my office chair, leaned back, and closed my eyes, hoping with all my heart that this would work. Maybe I can be the hero instead of the villain …

The Boy of Riddles
By Crystal Lu (flyingwildfyre)

It was half-past 12 when the Riddles decided to venture out into the valley. Little wisps of cirrus clouds danced along the forget-me-not sky, as the sun stood proudly at its peak. Tom Riddle Sr. stood by the old yew tree at the edge of the glen. He had one of his arms wrapped protectively around his wife, Merope, and the other rested gently on the tree's scaly bark. Little Tom Riddle flitted around energetically by the pond.

"I've found it!" he shouted, running back toward his mum and dad. His delicate hands were on top of one another to prevent his discovery from escaping.

"Found what?" asked Tom Sr.

"A toad, of course!"

In his cupped hands was a squat, speckled toad. It was a sparkly shade of emerald green that reminded Little Tom of his mother's eyes. The toad let out a low croak that sounded like a strangled burp. Little Tom giggled, and almost dropped his pet.

"I've named him Croaky," announced Little Tom. Tom Sr. ruffled his son's hair.

"That's mighty original," he said. Tom Sr. couldn't help but smile at his son's youthful innocence.

There was a sudden burst of white light enveloping the spotted creature. Little Tom gasped. He swore he saw something moving inside it. He could no longer feel Croaky sitting on his fingers. As the light faded, Little Tom couldn't believe his eyes. Delicate green wings tickled his palms, as he examined the new creature.

"Dad, look! I've turned the toad into a butterfly!" he shouted, hopping enthusiastically. Tom Sr. glanced at the insect. His eyes widened.

"You've got some strong magic, Junior!" acknowledged Tom Sr. Little Tom grinned, and released the butterfly. It stretched its emerald wings before flying through the air, and into the sky.

"Farewell!" Little Tom waved. Once he was sure that the butterfly had left safely, he turned back toward the small pond, and began searching for another frog.

"I always forget that you're a witch," said Tom Sr.

"Squib," Merope corrected. Tom Sr. smiled.

"Even without magic, you managed to charm me." Merope rolled her eyes, but she couldn't hide her faint smile.

"You only liked me because of the potion."

"Well, I'm mighty glad that wore off. Now, I can truly love you," said Tom Sr., pecking his wife on the cheek. Merope reddened slightly, but quickly regained her composure.

"I'm so lucky," she sighed.

"Don't you mean, *we're* so lucky?" corrected Tom Sr.

"*We're* so lucky," Merope agreed.

~~~~~

"Five more minutes until you turn 11, Junior," said Tom Riddle Sr., capturing Little Tom's bishop. Little Tom's face scrunched up in frustration. He tapped his fingers on the table, scraping his mind for a move that wouldn't put him in a vulnerable position.

"It's not fair," whined Little Tom.

"Don't be a sore loser," Tom Sr. grinned.

"I haven't lost, yet!" As the two argued playfully, Merope gently set down the platter of cupcakes that she baked for Little Tom's birthday. They were his favourite: fairy cakes with purple buttercream frosting.

"One more minute," she said. Tom Sr. feigned tiredness, and yawned. He stretched his arms, and rubbed his eyes.

"Looks like it's time for bed, Junior," he said dramatically. Little Tom shook his head angrily.

"No way! I'm almost 11."

"Well, it's almost 11 o'clock, and that's way past your bedtime," said Tom Sr. Little Tom groaned.

"Aw ... Dad! Could I please stay up just a little longer? Just until I turn 11," Little Tom pleaded. Tom Sr.'s eyes twinkled. He let out a breathy laugh.

"Sure, kiddo." Little Tom cheered, giving his father an enormous hug. His eyes shot toward the antique clock mounted on the wall. His heartbeat raced, as the seconds ticked by.

"Five, four," counted Little Tom.

"Three, two," said Merope.

"One," whispered Little Tom.

"Happy Birthday!" Merope and Tom Sr. shouted in unison, both squishing Little Tom into a hug. He hugged back tightly.

Suddenly, there was a knock at the door. Tom Sr. stiffened, and broke the hug.

"Now, who could it be at this hour?" he asked. Merope shuddered. She knew it couldn't be her father. Marvolo had disowned her after he found out about her marriage with a Muggle. Still ...

Merope shivered, as the door opened, letting in a chilly December night breeze. Merope half expected her father to jump out at her from the shadows, but no such thing happened. Instead, a pale moon-coloured snowy owl flew in. It soared into the humble abode, and dropped a thin brown square into Little Tom's lap.

"Well, what is it?" asked Tom Sr. nervously, latching the door shut. Little Tom stared curiously at the envelope. It was made of a thick, creamy paper, and stamped with a seal that he didn't recognize. He turned it over, revealing a green address:

Mr T. Riddle Jr.
The Second Bedroom
The Other Side of the Valley
Little Hangleton, England

Little Tom meticulously pried off the bright red seal, and pulled out the yellowish letter. He carefully unfolded it, and read:

HOGWARTS SCHOOL OF WITCHCRAFT AND WIZARDRY
Headmaster: Armando Dippet
Dear Mr. Riddle Jr.,

We are pleased to inform you that you have been accepted at Hogwarts School of Witchcraft and Wizardry. Please find enclosed a list of all necessary books and equipment. Term begins on 1 September. We await your owl by no later than 31 July.
Yours sincerely,
Albus Dumbledore
Deputy Headmaster

"A wizarding school, Mum! They've accepted me to go!" shouted Little Tom, handing Merope the letter. Her eyes swiftly scanned the writing; her shoulders relaxed as she read further down the page.

"It's just Hogwarts," explained Merope. "Most wizards are accepted into a school when they turn 11."

"Look, Dad! They've attached a second letter with all of the equipment I need to bring, and it says I can bring a pet! It says 'students may also bring an owl or a cat or a toad.' May I bring Croaky II? You won't miss him too much, right?" Tom Sr. chuckled.

"Do you think we can afford this?" Merope whispered.

"Of course we'll be able to," reassured Tom Sr. He gave her hand a squeeze, and she gave him a hopeful smile in return.

"I don't think the cost is what we should be worrying about. Where in the world will we find all of this? I don't think we'll be able to find a cauldron in town," said Little Tom sadly.

"Diagon Alley, of course," said Merope as a matter-of-fact. "It's even got a wand shop." Little Tom brightened.

"A wand of my very own? Oh, Dad, may we go now? I'm far too excited to go to bed!" Tom Sr. smiled, but shook his head.

"Maybe in a couple days after the new year, Junior. It's late, and you need to be getting to bed."

"Aw ... But you promise to bring me in a couple of days? Please!" pleaded Little Tom.

"I promise," Tom Sr. said solemnly. Little Tom seemed satisfied with the answer, so he proceeded up the stairs in a hurry. Merope carefully climbed up the steps after him.

"I hope a couple of days goes by quickly," Little Tom mumbled, disappearing into his room. Tom Sr. cleaned up some of the toys, and placed the platter of fairy cakes in the fridge. When he was about to head up and retire for the night, he noticed that the chess set was still lying about. Tom Sr. glanced at the pieces, and moved his queen.

"Checkmate."

~~~~~

The Riddles arrived on Diagon Alley early in the morning. There were few customers lingering around, which gave Little Tom the perfect opportunity to explore the vast streets. After the Riddles had traded some Muggle pounds for some galleons, they decided to split up. Tom Sr. headed to Flourish and Blotts to purchase Little Tom's schoolbooks, whereas Merope and Little Tom sauntered off to Madame Malkin's to get him fitted.

The robe shop was bright and clean. Robes of every kind were hung on the racks.

Little Tom eyed the bright yellow one. He wondered if they'd make an exception at Hogwarts, and let him wear that one instead of the plain standard black one. Little Tom hid behind his mum, as a witch dressed in mauve approached him.

"Hogwarts, dear?" she asked politely. Little Tom nodded nervously.

"Well, you're just in luck! The shop is quite empty right now. We can fit you right away," she said, dragging Little Tom to the back of the shop.

He was asked to stand on a footstool, as Madame Malkin draped a large black robe on Little Tom's vertically challenged frame. He shifted anxiously, as she pinned the robe to the correct length. Next to Little Tom was a boy with bright red hair and an abundance of freckles. He was also being fit for a black robe.

"Hullo!" exclaimed the other boy. "Are you going to Hogwarts, too?"

"Yes," replied Little Tom.

"My mum and dad are in Flourish and Blotts buying my books," said the boy enthusiastically.

"So's my dad! My mum's at the front of the shop."

"Blimey, what a coincidence! My name's Septimus. Septimus Weasley," introduced the boy.

"I'm Tom Riddle Jr., but everyone just calls me Little Tom," said Little Tom. Septimus grinned excitedly.

"Brilliant! Do you play Quidditch?" he asked. Little Tom shook his head. "What's Quidditch?"

"It's this totally rad game on broomsticks. I know first years aren't allowed broomsticks, but I might be able to show you once we get to Hogwarts," said Septimus. Little Tom nodded excitedly. Before he could answer, Madame Malkin slipped the robe off Little Tom's small frame, and hung it on a rack.

"You're done, m'boy," she said. Little Tom thanked Madame Malkin, and waved good-bye to Septimus. He scurried to the front of the shop, where his mum waited.

"That wasn't too bad, was it?" asked Merope. Little Tom shook his head. After paying Madame Malkin, Merope and Little Tom headed toward the wand shop, where Tom Sr. was to wait for them. As they entered the shop, they saw Tom Sr. conversing with the man behind the counter.

"Ah, welcome, Little Tom. I've been expecting you," said the man.

"You have?" Little Tom blinked. The man's eyes twinkled.

"Welcome to Ollivanders. Makers of Fine Wands Since 382 BC. I'm expecting that you need a wand then, young Riddle?"

"Yes, please," Little Tom replied. In a fluid motion, Mr. Ollivander pulled out a long tape measure.

"Which is your wand arm?" Little Tom shrugged.

"Well, I'm left-handed," he said, holding out his left arm. The tape measure began measuring Little Tom's arm, his legs, and his head all on its own, before returning to its spot on the counter.

"How peculiar," Little Tom mumbled. Mr. Ollivander swiftly pried the lid off one of the many rectangular boxes, and placed a thin wooden wand in Little Tom's hand.

"Every Ollivander wand has a core of a powerful magical substance. You will never get such good results with another wizard's wand, as no two wands are the same. Now give this one a little wave," said Mr. Ollivander. Little Tom felt a little foolish, but waved the wand anyway. Almost immediately, Mr. Ollivander snatched it out of his hand. Little Tom tried another one, but this one too, was snatched back almost at once by Mr. Ollivander.

"Tricky customer, eh? Not to worry, we'll find the perfect wand for you. Third time's the charm," he said, chuckling at his use of the Muggle phrase. His silvery eyes glowed mysteriously, as he handed Little Tom his third wand. When Little Tom waved it, a stream of energy flowed from the wand, appearing as a shower of gold sparks. He felt a warmness rise in his fingers, as if he was out in the valley on a warm summer day.

"Ah, bravo! Very good! And quite an unusual combination as well. Yew and phoenix feather, 13 and a half inches, nice and supple. You do good things with that wand, young Riddle," counseled Mr. Ollivander. Little Tom nodded at Mr. Ollivander's cryptic words, and paid him seven galleons.

"Well, have a nice day! I sure hope you have a wonderful time at Hogwarts."

~~~~~

Steam billowed from the scarlet Hogwarts Express. It was 10 minutes to 11, and nearly time for departure. Little Tom embraced his mum and dad one more time.

"I'm going to miss you," said Little Tom sadly. Merope and Tom Sr. suppressed their tears, and smiled.

"All young wizards have to start their journeys some day. Today is your day," said Merope.

"You'll write every day, won't you?" asked Little Tom.

"Of course we will," answered Tom Sr. He ruffled Little Tom's curls one last time. Merope wiped a tear from her eye.

"Now, have you got your ticket? Your schoolbooks? Croaky II?"

"Yes, Mum," said Little Tom. He knew that his schoolbooks were in his trunk, but he checked his shirt pocket one more time. His ticket was still there. Croaky II let out a happy burp from his spot in Little Tom's pants pocket. When the train whistled, Little Tom waved good-bye to his parents. He wheeled his luggage onto the train, and entered a compartment. Little Tom continued to wave by the window, only this time, he was accompanied by a boy with red hair.

"Stay safe!" shouted Merope.

"Don't get into too much trouble!" yelled Tom Sr.

"I won't!" Little Tom replied. "I love you!"

As the train left the station, Merope and Tom Sr.'s hearts shattered a little when the boy with the dark curls disappeared. They held one another, trying to comfort each other.

"He'll be okay, won't he?" asked Merope. Tom Sr. nodded.

"Little Tom's smart. He may not become the best wizard of all time, but he has good judgment. He'll be a fine wizard. Good, responsible, and always there in times of need."

Beyond the Grave
By Estelle Bookwalter (Estelliot)

Kylo was disgusted.

With his father. His room. The melted mask that usually brought solace.

Mostly with himself.

He glanced at his lightsaber, hoping the memories it held would chase the light away.

The red light tore through the man before him with no remorse or hesitation, unlike the man wielding the weapon. Han Solo didn't even look surprised, only reaching up and laying a hand on his face ...

Why? Why was it that all he could see was that last act? The clear act of forgiveness that was the last thing Han Solo—the man Kylo hated and still hates—ever did.

Even after literally being stabbed through by his son.

Kylo's stomach gave a terrible lurch, and he tore his gaze from the weapon.

Why had he been forgiven? He didn't need ... He didn't deserve ...

His eyes found Darth Vader's mask, and quickly averted.

He looked down at his hands, because elsewise he would see the accusing eyes of the twisted mask or the lightsaber he hadn't been able to even hold properly since its—his—last act of murder.

More important, he asked himself to divert his attention from that last moment, why hasn't it worked?

Killing Han Solo was supposed to kill the light as well. Darkness should have finally accepted him; the light should have given up.

But it didn't.

The pull of the light was stronger than ever. He felt ... Guilt. Remorse. More sharply than he had ever felt either before.

He also felt duty. Power. Fear. The ever-present fear that Snoke would sense his light, his weakness, and realize that Hux was right, that he had always been right, about Kylo's weakness and about his moral qualms.

The two opposing, and now equally strong, sides were tearing him apart.

Kylo beat his injured side with his fist. Pain, Snoke had always taught, made the dark side stronger.

Only, this time, it wasn't working.

He stopped and instead grabbed his side, squeezing. There just needed to be more. More pain. More suffering. More power.

~~~~~

Han Solo was disoriented.

He couldn't remember anything after landing on the Starkiller.

Looking around in a disoriented daze, he took in the room he was apparently in—it was dark. Everything was in shades of grey, some dark enough to be black. There seemed to be nothing personal at all in the place, save for the lightsaber.

At the sight of the weapon, the memories came rushing back.

The shields lowering, the fighters doing little damage, sneaking in with Finn, Rey, and Chewie.

Seeing his son.

Then the bridge ...

Han looked down at himself, confused. How had he survived? Why was he in this room instead of a hospital bed?

... Was he glowing?

Han cast his eyes around for a mirror and, upon spotting one, stopped cold.

Wow, he was looking good.

You know, besides being transparent and blue.

He was dead. But the whole looking-30-years-younger thing was totally worth it.

Funny, though, that he didn't remember actually dying. He had been alive when he fell off the bridge, he knew that much, but sometime between then and hitting the ground everything had just ... stopped.

He must be one of those force projections Luke had always talked about. Though he didn't know how that was possible seeing as he didn't have the force ...

Han was pulled out of his musings by a choked sob and, for the first time, he noticed someone else in the room. For a moment, it was too dark to see him properly, and the black he was wearing didn't make that easier. But then the man turned slightly, and despite the shadows and his screwed-shut eyes, Han knew him immediately.

Ben. His son. His murderer.

What was he supposed to do?

Han had no delusions about his parenting skills. Any he had previously were crushed years ago. So what's a father to do when he sees the son who just murdered him suffering?

A question for the ages, no doubt. Han was fairly certain that no other father had been faced with this particular problem, and he definitely wasn't the one to solve it.

He'd always been a walk-it-off kind of guy, but thought that probably wasn't the right answer in this case.

"Ben?" he asked hesitantly, taking a cautious step forward.

"Don't call me that!" The man snapped, jumping up from the bed and facing the intruder while simultaneously calling his lightsaber to his hand. The weapon felt wrong, and he didn't activate it like he would have even just the day before for fear of seeing his father's forgiveness again. The forgiveness that cut deeper than any scathing remarks, hateful glares, or accusing stares ever could.

The demand was more of a reflex than anything, overriding the first logical question: Who are you?

"Why not? It's your name, isn't it?" Han shot back immediately, momentarily forgetting that he had started this conversation to comfort the kid.

"... Who are you?" Kylo had seen the pictures, mostly mug shots and "wanted" posters, of his younger father. He had heard stories with descriptions of how he looked. But Kylo knew only Jedi had force projections, and his father was no Jedi. Kylo had to believe that it wasn't his father. If it really was Han Solo ... It just ... It couldn't be.

"What, you don't recognize your own dad?" Han asked, raising an eyebrow snippily. He knew Kylo was smart enough to know who he was.

Kylo felt a torrent of conflicting emotions. Fear, first and foremost, but wasn't it always? Then dread, and anger.

The one he hated most, the one he tried desperately to suppress, was relief.

Happiness, maybe? That his father didn't hate him, that Han was here and yet not within Snoke's grasp.

Disgusting. He was Kylo Ren, second only to Snoke in power, disciple of the dark side and leader of the Knights of Ren. He shouldn't feel things like relief—not in response to something as sentimental as forgiveness.

Han saw the many emotions rage through his son's eyes, saw the still-dormant lightsaber droop as the hand holding it relaxed before suddenly grasping it harder than before.

He allowed a grin; he'd never really been good at poker faces unless in a life-or-death situation (which, he supposed, would never be the case again). Kylo was conflicted. That meant killing him didn't work; Ben was still in there somewhere, perhaps even closer to the surface now.

"So you've made some bad decisions, kid. You know what Luke's dad was like; he was misled, just like you, and when he finally found the right path he was accepted right away." Han really, really hoped that this was the right thing to say. Seeing the steel behind his son's eyes falter once more, Han decided to push just a bit more. "Your mother and I still love you."

Kylo nearly crumpled to the floor at those words. His mother.

The pain he'd been seeking earlier hit like a wall, but it wasn't physical. This time, it was emotional. And this time, it did strengthen the force.

But not the right side of the force.

The dark receded and the light shined brighter than it had since he was a child.

Kylo ground his teeth together, one hand grasping the lightsaber as if he thought he actually had the willpower to activate it while the other once again tried to chase away the light with physical pain.

That was stopped by an image of his mother flashing through his mind, accompanied by a sob tearing out of his throat.

"I don't deserve ...," he forced out, trying to keep the tears at bay. Kylo caught himself when he saw his ghostly father begin to reach for him, hand tightening around his lightsaber once more. "I don't need your forgiveness!" he spat, trying to slap Han's hand away.

The ex-con gave his son a wholly unimpressed look as the flailing appendage passed right through him.

"Look, kid, you aren't getting rid of me that easily."

~~~~~

When his father had said he wouldn't leave that easily, Kylo had hoped he was bluffing. He'd hoped that the dead man would get fed up with his constant anger and refusal to listen and eventually either just fade away or maybe leave to see Leia instead.

But he didn't.

He wouldn't just stay in the room, either. Han would follow him everywhere—the jerk claimed he had nothing better to do since he didn't even have to eat or sleep anymore. And he wasn't well behaved.

Han would make derisive comments about Snoke ("What, you've only seen this hologram thing? This guy could be a Gungan for all you know!") during important meetings. He would make fun of Hux's failed clone problem at the most inopportune moments, which was a rather large problem because Kylo actually found those comments vindictively funny. It was his tendency to go behind anyone who happened to be talking and distract Kylo in any way he could think of, including, but not limited to, break dancing, looming, pretending to force-choke the speaker, pretending to be force-choked, and attempting to move physical objects (which Kylo, though he was mortified by the feeling, thought was actually amusing on occasion). The real problem, though, was that Han was growing on him. Yes, the man was still irritating. He was obnoxious and insolent. But, occasionally, he was also insightful and even fatherly.

When Kylo's eyes would seek the twisted mask of Darth Vader for reinforcement of his beliefs, they would instead catch on the glowing blue man reclined sloppily on the floor beside it. Every time that happened, Han would smile at him. As if he had planned it that way. As if he had strategically placed himself, literally a beacon of light, between his son and the well of darkness.

Kylo could feel the light inside him. It would swell and ebb just as before; it was still unstable. But now, with a constant reminder of what the light could produce stalking him everywhere, it was getting undeniably stronger.

And that, like nearly everything else, scared him.

What scared him even more, though, was when he caught himself wondering how the rebels would react if he did change sides. Would they accept him, as Han insisted? Would they possibly shoot first and ask questions later? Would he go only for the darkness to return, and then have to chase away the feelings that would come from betraying them? ... Could his mother really still love him after all he had done?

No. No. Maybe they would, maybe he could. But he wouldn't. He had pledged his allegiance to Snoke. He would not leave.

His loyalty to Snoke was not borne out of positive feeling such as love or friendship, as Han had taken to pointing out. He was loyal because he was terrified.

Terrified of what Snoke would do to him if he weren't loyal. Terrified of losing his power. Terrified of facing the world without his power. Terrified of what people, of what she, his mother, would think of him if he were to step down from his self-made pedestal and face them as if he were their equal. Because if he were their equal, then their thoughts would matter. So he simply wasn't.

~~~~~

Han regarded his sleeping son with conflicted emotions.

The kid was wavering, that much was clear. But he was also incredibly stubborn. A trait that Han wished hadn't been passed down from both himself and Leia while also being strangely proud of Ben for being able to hold his ground.

How was he supposed to act now? He thought he'd been doing a pretty good job of not being as flippant as usual, but was acting so ... well, Leia called it childish, but it apparently got her to like him, so it couldn't be that bad. Was it the right choice?

Ben tried to get him to believe the snarky comments and obnoxious actions only made him angry and annoyed, but Han sometimes caught what seemed to be an aborted laugh or even a slight upturn of the lip that might have been a suppressed smile.

Ben started grumbling as he awoke (Han rolled his eyes; the kid was even irritable when he was asleep), and his eyes slowly slid open.

Still half asleep, the first thing Ben Solo saw was his father's blue and transparent form as he had been when Ben was a child.

Thinking he was still asleep, he smiled.

Han nearly died of shock.

The dumbfounded expression switched almost immediately into a face-splitting grin, even when Ben's eyes widened almost comically and he sat up explosively.

"What are you smiling about?" he snapped, trying to cover up his slip. It wasn't nearly as biting as he wanted it to be.

Han didn't stop grinning even as his son made a special effort to glare even harder than usual as he got ready for the day, but decided not to comment on it just yet. He followed silently, spring in his step as his son led the way to the main meeting room and was confronted by Hux.

Han's grin grew even more, if possible, as he quickly positioned himself behind the redhead.

One of these days, he was going to make Ben laugh.

Rumpelstiltskin and His Husband

By Eva Nemirovsky (Bek516)

Once upon a time, two men lived in a cottage in the woods that had space for a child. These two men were Fisil Rumpelstiltskin and his husband, Markus Roak. They wanted a child desperately, but they didn't know what to do.

They sat around their kitchen table, mugs of tea in hand, and racked their brains for a solution to their problem.

"What if we went to the local orphanage?" suggested Markus at first.

"No, they would never let us adopt a child; we're a 'bad influence' on children because of our relationship, remember?" Fisil scowled.

"All right, well what do you suggest we do?" Markus's cold, calculating blue eyes revealed a hidden passion behind them, one only ever revealed to Fisil and, even then, rarely.

It was as if a light clicked on in the small ginger's head. "I can't believe I forgot about this! My childhood friend, the miller's daughter, owes me a favor; more than that, she promised me her firstborn child if she were to marry the king, which she did. I can go to her," Fisil said, beaming up at his mountain of a husband.

Markus nodded, thoughtfully. "All right, I don't see why not."

"Great! I'll leave tomorrow, then!"

The following morning found Fisil approaching the palace; he stood awestruck and dumbfounded in front of the magnificent gates. The queen was delighted to see her friend, and quickly led him into her private study so that they could speak as equals.

She placed her crown down on the desk and offered him tea from her private stock, but he refused. She looked into his green eyes quizzically. "Is something the matter, Fisil?" She laid her soft hand on his.

"No, nothing is the matter; I've simply come to collect the debt you owe me for saving your life." Fisil pulled his hand away from hers and rested his chin on his knuckles.

"Collect what?"

"Your firstborn child," he said blatantly.

"What?! Why?" The queen placed a hand over her abdomen, sheltering the life that grew there.

"Because! Because I'm gay and I'm married. I cannot have a biological child from my union with my husband so I've come to take what you've promised me." Recognition flashed in the queen's eye; that was all the prompting that he needed. "You'll barely miss it. I'm sure you'll have plenty of children, and it's not as if we would starve the poor thing; both of us would care for it as if it were truly born of our union."

Clarissa looked down at where her hand rested and then back up at his face, "No, Fisil. I can't." Her voice cracked, "Please don't ask this of me. Just, please, leave." She pushed him out the door and slammed it shut behind him before sliding down the door shakily.

Fisil stood there in shock. He fumed and turned, punching the wall beside him; his knuckles bled but he didn't care, he would try again tomorrow. He would continue to try until she gave in.

He came again the next morning and repeated his request, again the queen refused, and once more the door shut in his face, but Fisil would not back away. He kept coming back, again and again, and the cycle just kept repeating over and over until, finally, the queen realized that Fisil would not stop coming, and she reluctantly agreed.

As each month came and went and the date of the birth grew closer, both Fisil and the queen grew increasingly anxious: one with excitement, the other with dread.

On the day the royal birth was announced, Fisil came for the child, holding his arms out expectantly.

The queen refused. "No, you cannot take my son for he is too clever."

"But you promised me your firstborn!" Fisil shouted.

"I know, I know. I promise I'll give you the next one." The queen appeased the small fuming man and Fisil had to settle with another one of her fickle promises.

Another nine anxious months passed and soon Fisil stood again before the queen, demanding for her second child to be passed into his care.

Again the queen refused. "No, you cannot take my son for he is too strong." He asked for her next child, and the queen agreed. Again, they waited anxiously and again Fisil asked for her child to be given to him.

The queen refused again. "No, you cannot take my son for he is too handsome." Fisil did not ask for her next child as his heart could no longer take this cold rejection. He ran back to his little cottage in the woods, sobbing.

Fisil felt his husband's arms engulf him in a comforting hug and Fisil took the comfort gratefully. Markus brewed tea for his husband and cooed to him; he whispered soft comforts into Fisil's ears. After a long time in this cocoon of comfort, Fisil had calmed down enough to explain just why he was so upset.

"Markus, it was horrible. Clarissa broke her promise to me three times over. It is true her sons are what she said they are: clever, strong, and handsome, but she broke her promise and she broke my faith in our friendship. Markus, I just want to be able to raise a child with you; is that really so much to ask?" Fisil's voice shook and his green eyes shone with leftover tears.

"No, no, of course it's not too much to ask, Fisil. What if I go to ask for the next child?"

"No!" He shouted desperately. "She'll just break her promise like she did with me. I don't want to see you hurt." He pouted, looking up at Markus.

"Fisil," he said softly, taking his partner's small hands in his own, "it already pains me to see you cry. Please let me at least try." Markus would not budge; he was as stubborn as a rock. Fisil knew this, and the next morning Markus set out toward the castle.

He crept past the guards and easily gained entrance to the castle proper. He knocked on the study door of the queen and waited for a reply.

A servant stepped out of the room and looked up at Markus's looming presence; the small girl squeaked and, in a small voice, said, "Who are you and what do you want of the queen?"

"I request an audience with her. My name is Markus Roak, the husband of the queen's friend, Fisil. I've come in his stead." The girl disappeared inside the room and came back out to escort the big man inside.

"Come in," said the small girl, leading him inside. She bowed at the queen and took her place far behind the queen.

"Your Majesty, I am Markus and I've come—"

The queen cut him off. "I know why you've come, Markus Roak. I will give you my next child, as I promised to Fisil. That is the end of the matter; anything else before I have you escorted out?"

"Nothing at all, you've hit the nail on the head." Markus stood wordlessly and left the chamber without a bow and without an escort.

The time passed quickly and soon on a cold winter night, the queen gave birth to a baby girl. Markus was there, ready to accept the small child, for the babe was late and Markus had been hanging around the castle for a few days. He was prepared for rejection but he held out his arms for the babe regardless.

"Might I have the child now, my Queen?"

The queen looked down at the girl and recoiled, nearly shoving the child into his arms. "Here, you take the girl. I have no need for an ugly, dark-haired babe."

Markus didn't care about the child's appearance; actually, he found her quite stunning. He took the babe swaddled in red cloth, bowed, and left the room. The infant slept as they traveled back to the small cottage in the woods.

Fisil was sleeping by the time Markus stepped inside their home. Markus laid the girl down in her crib, and went to wake Fisil.

Markus shook his shoulder, saying, "Fisil, get up!" Fisil woke quickly, afraid something terrible had happened but it was, in fact, quite the opposite. A miracle had occurred. In the room next to theirs, the infant slept swaddled in her red cloth and wrapped in blankets.

Fisil was in tears as he beheld the radiant beauty of their daughter. They slept well that night and the next morning, they named the girl Raven, for her dark curly locks.

The family of three lived happily and did not hear from the queen, until a year later, when a notice was sent out throughout the kingdom stating that the queen had passed away during the birth of her fifth child.

Fisil, Markus, and Raven never worried that the queen could come after them. The three of them lived in peace in their cottage in the woods for the rest of their days.

Unless—But It Never Happened
By NutsAndBees

With the seed in hand, the young boy finally returned to his synthetic hometown of Thneedville.

His heart was racing at an unbelievably fast pace, his breathing got heavy, and multiple scenarios and questions clouded his mind and his vision. When did he even get to town, though? He hardly noticed that anymore. He should be relieved that he even got back alive and unscathed, considering the condition the valley he came from was in, but that didn't matter now. His focus was completely centered on the very last seed that he now held in his hand.

Imagine! The last truffula seed ... It could do just so much for this town and its people. A new, better way of life. Everyone would be happier and healthier, and everything would be less ... artificial. Nature would spring up again, and so many new possibilities would arise.

He scanned his surroundings, eyeing all the fake trees and plants that completely covered the town. By the sidewalk, there parked the O'Hare Air Delivery Service, bringing in a tank of fresh air to a warm and welcoming household.

If I plant this seed ... it will change everything ... people don't have to pay for air anymore ...

Ted took in a deep breath, clutching the seed tight in his hand and started heading toward his home.

He passed by town square, where numerous "trees" lined the way, and people went on with their daily lives without a single care. As he passed on farther, he saw families and groups of friends, all laughing and talking and just idling by, enjoying their lives and what this town had to offer.

Blissful ignorance, that's what. A thought occurred to his head, as he vividly recalled the grey, gloomy skies beyond town. The air was so terrible; it was smoky, toxic even, and it was very hard to breathe as it felt like your throat was burning with every breath you took.

Nothing in those fields would grow anymore except tall, dry, dirty grass. It never rained, and it never shined, and to think one old man still decided to live all the way out there. It was all his fault, he had said; he decided to accept what he had done.

That seemed to have stirred up a certain emotion inside the young boy. To think that all these people were living such blissful lives, hiding themselves behind a literal wall, that without it, they would be forced to live under such same conditions. But it is always easier to just sweep the dirt under the rug, isn't it?

His grip on the seed grew tighter, and he decided to just keep moving on.

If I plant this seed ... things will get better ... everything will change for the better ... But they all chose this lifestyle, didn't they?

Ted decided to observe his surroundings again. He was by the mall this time, passing by a bunch of stores putting up new models of their so-called trees and inflatable topiaries and flower beds and the like by their display window. And there were a number of happy customers walking in and out to buy them.

They would lose their jobs, their business, they would reject the idea of bringing REAL trees back.

But that would just be a minor setback, wouldn't it? If he were to plant this seed ...

"Mom!! Can we get that new shinier tree like what John has at his house? It's so cool! It can play music, easy to clean up, easy to put away ..."

Ted frowned at what he heard. He was sure real trees couldn't ever do that. Could a plain old tree ever compete with what they already had? The townspeople's concept of a tree had already been so corrupted for dozens of years. What would they think of such a simple tree?

If I plant ... this seed ...

...

The young boy arrived in his neighborhood now. He overheard another child asking a parent what it was like past the wall.

"Oh, it's nothing, honey; it just serves as our town's border, kind of like a fence!"

Ted started biting his lower lip.

"It's nothing to worry about; we have everything we need here in town after all."

Ted zoomed straight for his house, unable to take anymore of what he was hearing. When he arrived home, his mother was busy in the kitchen, and his grandmother was nowhere in sight, so he quickly made a break for his room, shutting the door behind him.

Finally.

Some silence.

He was leaning against his door, and he held out the seed on the palm of his hand.

He picked it up with his other hand and examined it further. It was a dark wooden brown in colour, and had a nicely distinct spiral pattern on it that looked as though it was just carved onto it. It was so small; to think it would sprout to become a tall, marvelous tree one day.

He had always thought about giving this to the girl of his dreams; that was his main reason for even seeking out this seed in the first place, but after everything ... It seemed as though a much bigger picture came into view. It wasn't just about Audrey anymore, it concerned the whole town now, too. And whether or not they would take lightly to such a new, and now foreign thing such as a real tree ...

"*Then, make them care!*" he recalled the Once-ler telling him.

But how could he?

Everyone ... they all looked so content with their way of living. Having real trees and real nature again ... it would be such a huge thing to adjust to. And, as for what happened to the valley, they were all at fault too. Whether they'd admit it or not. The valley was stripped and desolated because of their constant wants, their never-satisfied hunger for those thneeds and progress. They were all a part of the reason why the trees no longer existed. But what did they do? They chose to ignore it. And even found another way to survive without them.

Ted became more aggravated as his thoughts continued. Mental images of the cheery town and the gloomy valley flashed in his mind all at once.

He stared at the seed again; by now he had mindlessly walked toward his desk, where there lay on top a blue tumbler with some water still left in it, and just below to the side of his table was the trash bin.

He felt uneasiness in his stomach.

"If I plant this seed ..."

Would they be even worth it?

His hands were trembling slightly as his free hand slowly reached for the water bottle.

"It could change things for the better ..."

Would they even CARE?

He remembered the conversations he heard, the people he saw and heard laughing and going on with their lives, not even caring about what lay beyond the barrier.

"If ..."

Do they DESERVE a second chance?

Just as he was about to grab hold of the water bottle ...

He stopped.

"..."

The young boy then felt a void, empty feeling filled his chest. And all the anxiety, fear, and nervousness he felt before had now disappeared, and his thoughts finally grew quiet.

His now steady hand moved away from the water bottle. His eyes darkened as he hovered his open palm, the one containing the seed, over the waste basket, flipping his hand over as his fingers loosely held onto the seed ...

"No."

"They don't."

And then he let go.

Have You Ever Wondered ...
By Maja Czerniachowska (Segraece)

I always wanted to make my world. I didn't mean to hurt anyone, make them feel bad.

I just wanted to show them the beauty. The calm.

This endless quiet. I was sure that I could make a perfect place, full of love, beauty, and joy.

My intentions were pure, but somebody understood them in the wrong way.

Now, my world is collapsing—the stars are fading, the never-ending night is becoming the day. My poor children, they don't know the light. Single light rays can make them scared, or even blind. I want to hide them in my shadow, but my body isn't big enough.

Those, over my head, they think that they're heroes, the chosen ones. But the one who's suffering the most is me. I want to tell them that I didn't mean to.

But, unfortunately, we're on completely opposite sides—the day and night. Please, don't.

PaintTool SAI
Time: Too much. Definitely too much.

HAVE YOU EVER WONDERED ...   BY MAJA CZERNIACHOWSKA (SEGRAECE)

Twist Fate: The Prodigy
By pikooroo

"Had I not used them in such a manner, would my parents still have loved me?"
"Could I have been a hero like that stupid, stupid flabby panda"
"What a late time to think it all"

This is something I felt Shen could've thought when Po gave him the hero speech. Shen was a great villain; sure, he was typical villain material, but at the same time interesting.

Loved his parents, was terribly bitter, felt betrayed, and too smart for his own good.

When Shen closed his eyes before he died, the scene felt a lot different from most villains screaming as they're defeated.

His demise was always a scene that struck me as particularly intriguing.

I thought that it wouldn't have taken much for him to have used those very same weapons to have saved China rather than destroy had he not misstepped.

Oh, wait. He was born with the red eyes of doom, deeming his fate a villain.

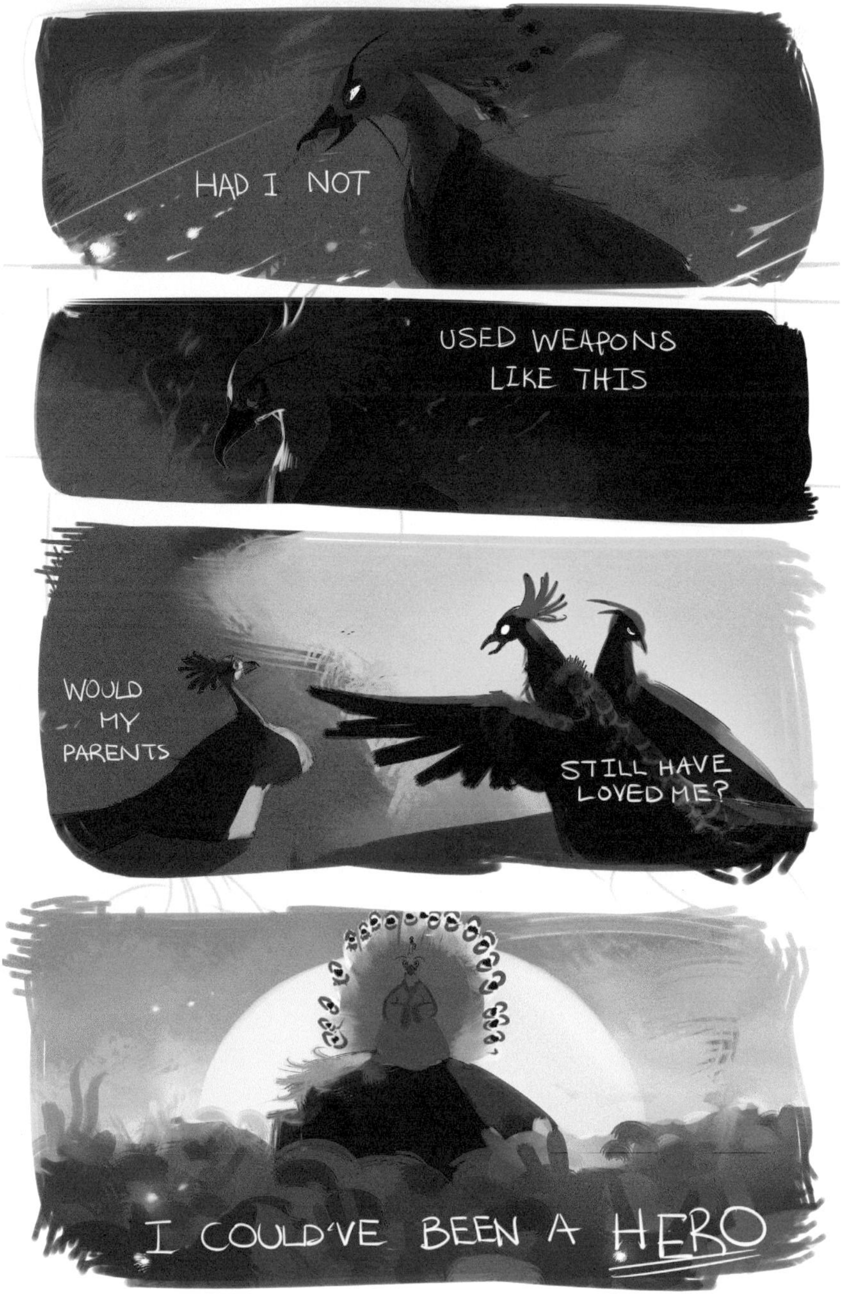
HAD I NOT
USED WEAPONS LIKE THIS
WOULD MY PARENTS
STILL HAVE LOVED ME?
I COULD'VE BEEN A HERO

TWIST FATE: THE PRODIGY

BY PIKOOROO

Sleeping Beauty
By UnityUniverse

In this picture, I took a twist on the story of Sleeping Beauty. I always loved Maleficent as a character, in the Disney film, Kingdom Hearts games, and in her new-ish film, so I wanted to create a picture based on her. But the issue was that the two films had explored her as a villain and hero so I was wondering, "What could I do?" So I decided, what would be better than to put her in dragon form as the prince? And what would be a better situation than to put the dragon with her in the kiss scene!

So, I made her in dragon form ... less evil? And mixed the room styles from the original film and the new film, but Aurora is styled off the original film.

In this timeline, beautiful Aurora was born and had blessings granted by the fairies. The prince's family wanted to have Aurora marry their son when she turned 16. Aurora's parents did not agree and the prince's family vowed they would get their way. The king, scared for Aurora's safety and kidnapping, sent her away with the fairies. There, she explored the forest and discovered the kingdom of the monsters and found a beautiful dragon that she became good friends with. Time passed and she attended her 16th birthday party, where the prince found her and proposed. Logically, she turned down this stranger. The prince, in anger, took out his sword and struck her before taking the king and queen captive. The kingdom fell into misery over her supposed death and under the harsh rule of the prince. The dragon, seeing the kingdom in sadness, went to see what was wrong. The prince fought the dragon, but the dragon overpowered the prince, pinning him to the wall. Searching the castle, the dragon discovered Aurora, in a deep sleep—possibly death, I haven't decided. Cue dragon kiss and lots of tears. The princess's wounds healed from the tears and she woke from her sleep/death? They lived happy ever after, hugs and credits.

SLEEPING BEAUTY

BY UNITYUNIVERSE

Queen of Hearts
By Elise Ngo (lapicureuil)

What if ... the Queen of Hearts was actually what she sounds like? Kind, loving, and gentle ... And what if her younger sister, the White Queen, was evil?

Everyone in Wonderland would know the story of how the Queen of Hearts put an end to the White Queen's reign and saved the kingdom ...

Long ago, Wonderland was ruled by a king and his queen. They had two daughters. The eldest, with red hair, was kind and made friends with everyone she met, while the youngest, with white hair, kept to herself. For whatever reason, the king and the queen always favored their youngest daughter, and although this left the elder sister feeling neglected, she still loved her sister very much. Eventually, the time came when the king and queen were old and frail. Before they passed away, they gave the crown to the younger sister, who became the White Queen. The eldest was devastated at the loss of her parents, and confused as to why her sister had received the throne instead of her, but she decided that she would make the best of the situation and support her sister however she could.

However, the White Queen quickly revealed herself to be a cruel and violent ruler, and the land turned from a place of wonder to a place of fear. The eldest realized what needed to be done. She took back the land that had been rightfully hers in the first place, and saved the kingdom from the White Queen's reign of terror. Although it pained her do it, she also banished her sister from the kingdom. The eldest sister brought back peace to the land. Today, she is known as the Queen of Hearts in all the land, because never before in Wonderland has there been a ruler so kind and understanding.

This Queen of Hearts doesn't chop off the heads of everyone she meets, or use animals as inanimate objects. Everyone in Wonderland adores her!

I had a lot of difficulty choosing which hero/villain to illustrate. Designing the dress for the Queen of Hearts was lots of fun.

QUEEN OF HEARTS

BY ELISE NGO (LAPICUREUIL)

Twist Fate: Hunted
By Graciel Manaig (BrokenPencil13)

"Legends say that her hood was once white ... before she went insane."
This seems a bit cliché, but I've always been a sucker for stories where innocent children become the total opposite of themselves (Lord of the Flies by William Golding is one of my favorite books). I had this idea of the wolf being a human child and Red Riding Hood as a savage.

I was listening to Annabel by Goldfrapp when I was painting this. Listen to it for the full effect.

Alternate title: Little Gray Wolf Cloak

TWISTED FROM: RED RIDING HOOD

TWIST FATE: HUNTED   BY GRACIEL MANAIG (BROKENPENCIL13)

Sherlock, You Are in My Game
By Gosiuska

What if Sherlock used his mind in a bad way?

I was wondering which character to draw, and then that idea popped to my head. [What if Sherlock used his mind in a bad way?] It's obvious. If Sherlock was bad, he would be a very, VERY big problem for the authorities.

It took me some time, but I'm pleased with the end result.

I decided to draw the TV series version because it's closer to me. Everything started to take form in my head with great help from my friends.

SHERLOCK, YOU ARE IN MY GAME

BY GOSIUSKA

Attack on Human

By Gabriela Knihs da Luz & Mariana (Nightmare)
(Laylakl & DarkHeart-Nightmare)

DarkHeart-Nightmare and I made a collab.

I made the line art, while DarkHeart-Nightmare made this incredible colouring!

This is a fanart of "Attack on Titan!"

The drawing is about the humans (in this case only Eren) being the "evil giants," while the Titans are being the "good guys."

ATTACK ON HUMAN

BY GABRIELA KNIHS DA LUZ & MARIANA (NIGHTMARE)
(LAYLAKL & DARKHEART-NIGHTMARE)

Robbing Rapunzel
By Anna Peintner (Makessami)

"Oh, I had a dream once, too ... Since I was a little girl, I wanted to see the lanterns rising into the evening sky on my birthday. *sigh* Mother forbid it. On my 20th birthday, I ran away and looked at them on my own. From close up they were even more beautiful ... But when dawn came, I found myself without a dream, without a plan, and without the desire to go home. On the way back through the woods, I found this charming little tavern, and, suddenly, there were so many opportunities, it was hard to decide. In the end, I decided to be a common bandit; plunderers have to carry too much, and you still have to sell the stuff you steal as a thief ... "

The text above is just the general idea I had when I started painting this. I hope you like it. This is a criminal Rapunzel from Disney's Tangled.

ROBBING RAPUNZEL   BY ANNA PEINTNER (MAKESSAMI)

LET'S GO!

BY VIVIANA B. (PURPLEMANGAPOWERS)

Let's Go!
By Viviana B. (PurpleMangaPowers)

Undertale fanart. As you can see, Chara is a good guy now and is leading Frisk through the underground. Oh, and there's Flowey, too. It was Flowey's job at first to lead Frisk but NO MORE; Chara is stealing the spotlight! He's confused as to what Frisk is looking at ... by the way, he can't see Chara.

I guess it's just my version of that Undertale AU. I can't remember ... the one where everyone is evil? Yeah, that one// (Oh, wait, it's underfell ... I think!)

DALEKS LOVE CATS

TWISTED FROM: DR. WHO

Daleks Love Cats
By Emily Jones (186lilly)

LITTLE RED RIDING WOLF!   BY JULIA SIECZAK (PREDATORY DUCK)

Little Red Riding Wolf!
By Julia Sieczak (Predatory Duck)

GANGSTERS OF ZOOTOPIA

BY AMBERLINA-CHAN

Gangsters of Zootopia
By Amberlina-Chan

I really like the movie, where Judy the police officer rabbit and Nick the con artist fox are very cute together.

The Boy Who Lived

By Selin Ogut (demenian)

This Harry was placed in the house of Slytherin, and became influenced with the house's dark history. Also, with a part of Voldemort inside him, he had temptations about the dark sides of magic. Eventually, he became a valuable assistant to the dark lord. He was blind to anything besides the dark arts with the help (pretty much brainwashing) of the dark lord.

I did the whole drawing with prismacolor colored pencils, and it took me a really long time.

TWISTED FROM: HARRY POTTER

THE BOY WHO LIVED

BY SELIN OGUT (DEMENIAN)

ROBIN

BY QOSTINE

TWISTED FROM: ROBIN HOOD

Robin
By Qostine

When Robin got tired of being a hero, he decided to betray his friends. Now, he just robs the poor to feed the rich.

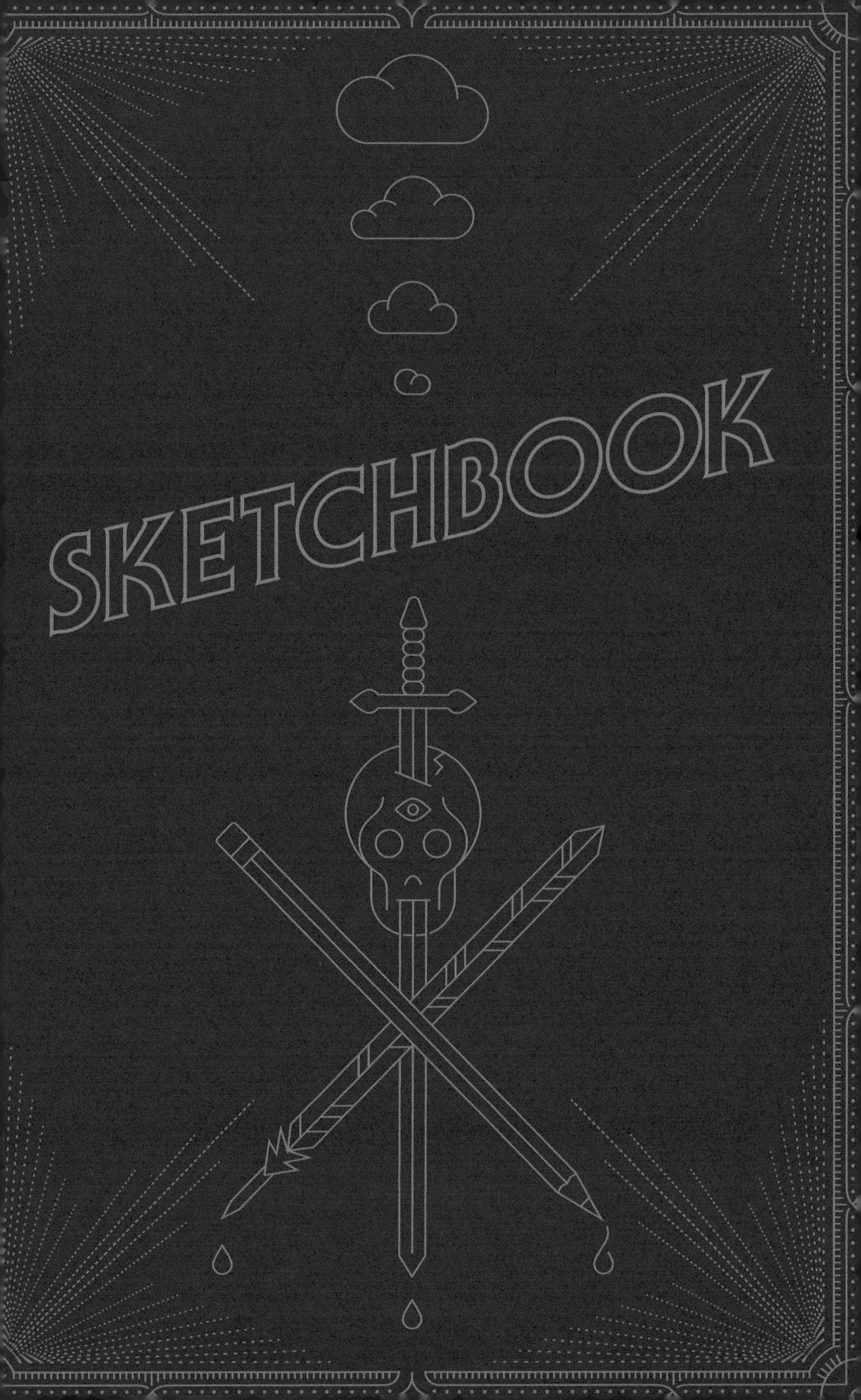
SKETCHBOOK

TWIST FATE

SKETCHBOOK

Contributors

DeviantArt

Alissa "Alichee" Ren
Amberlina-Chan
Amy Jean (Chilly-Dog)
Anna Peintner (Makessami)
Ariana Barzinpour (Mnemofysh)
Asha DaHyeon Choi (Laonasa)
Bethany Powell (Muppy23)
blogybo
calamityneko
ClawsUnion
Crystal Lu (flyingwildfyre)
Derin Karabulut (Glamra)
DragonitaVioleta
Dragoreon
Elise Ngo (lapicureuil)
Elizabeth Ellister (TheCroissantThief)
Emily Jones (186lilly)
Estelle Bookwalter (Estelliot)
Eva Nemirovsky (Bek516)
Felysia Chew Shin Yin (ufo-galz)
Gabriela Knihs da Luz & Mariana (Nightmare)
	(Laylakl & DarkHeart-Nightmare)
Gosiuska
Graciel Manaig (BrokenPencil13)
Heliocathus
Iotzu
Jeanna Pittman (ZoeyBlueRose)
Jen Lee (AurumArrows)
Jesse Feemster (minexpert)
Jessica Sunderland (To-Yo)
Jessie Chin (ALTjellification)
Julia Sieczak (Predatory Duck)
Juliana "Jensonator" Henson
Julianna Teoh (PrincessAutumnArcher)
Largoyzniaar
Liana Cannon (mangaZwolf)
Luca Chang (Threshold0)
Lyrra Isanberg (Kanilope)
Maja Czerniachowska (Segraece)
Maja Rogocka (Mayo) (Majkarogo)
Melissa Wang & Tiffany Wang (Mint-Glass)
MoryaPanima

Contributors

DeviantArt

Nick Wong (Nocluse)
Olivia Bordeleau (tootalu)
phantomparley
pikooroo
Qostine
Ramon Elias D. Lopez & John Aldrin D. Bernardo
    (Lorcan Tiberius & The-Jed-The-1-0nly)
Saige Baker (Saige199)
Sanjana Raveendran (CMYKidd)
Sarah Hulton (ActuallySarahART)
Selin Ogut (demenian)
Shelby Eagleton (umshelby)
Sophie Wainwright (BisonLover)
UKEagleclaw
UnityUniverse
Viviana B. (PurpleMangaPowers)
YumiAkaru

Contributors

Wattpad

acrdbty
AfterSangster
ahsoka228
aiessei
ArcticKaturn
beginwithanend
BrainNemesis
Drawing_With_Ink
emperatriss
Ghoulish Tendencies
girlwho_lovestowrite
IleanaLewis
inanidealworld
JaneApricity
Knilesly
Lupinehowl
MochaLiterati
myth_iz_amaze
NitroStation
NothingRonWithMe
NutsAndBees
NyLovesBooks
rain_rebellion
Sarcasm_is_a_Virtue
ShadowApple567
_Slyytherin
sowhatsitabout
StephMikaelson
ThatOneFangirl108
thefluffmuffin
uponthenightsky
Words-Of-Fate
xdreams2realityx
-X-X-Scomiche-X-X-
zuko_42